Natural Law in Jurisprudence and Politics

In *Natural Law in Jurisprudence and Politics*, Mark C. Murphy argues that the central thesis of natural law jurisprudence – that law is backed by decisive reasons for compliance – sets the agenda for natural law political philosophy, which demonstrates how law gains its binding force by way of the common good of the political community.

Murphy's presentation in this book ranges over the central questions of natural law jurisprudence and political philosophy, including the formulation and defense of the natural law jurisprudential thesis, the nature of the common good, the connection between the promotion of the common good and requirement of obedience to law, and the justification of punishment.

Mark C. Murphy is Professor of Philosophy at Georgetown University. He is the author of *Natural Law and Practical Rationality, An Essay on Divine Authority*, and *Philosophy of Law* and is editor of *Alasdair MacIntyre*.

T0372684

Cambridge Studies in Philosophy and Law

Some other books in the series:

Larry Alexander (ed.): *Constitutionalism*
Peter Benson (ed.): *The Theory of Contract Law: New Essays*
Steven J. Burton: *Judging in Good Faith*
Steven J. Burton (ed.): *"The Path of the Law" and Its Influence: The Legacy of Oliver Wendell Holmes, Jr.*
Jules Coleman: *Risks and Wrongs*
Jules Coleman and Allan Buchanan (eds.): *In Harm's Way: Essays in Honor of Joel Feinberg*
R. A. Duff (ed.): *Philosophy and the Criminal Law*
William Edmundson: *Three Anarchical Fallacies: An Essay on Political Authority*
John Fischer and Mark Ravizza: *Responsibility and Control*
R. G. Frey and Christopher W. Morris (eds.): *Liability and Responsibility: Essays in Law and Morals*
Steven A. Hetcher: *Norms in a Wired World*
Heidi M. Hurd: *Moral Combat*
Jody S. Kraus and Steven D. Walt (eds.): *The Jurisprudential Foundations of Corporate and Commercial Law*
Christopher Kutz: *Complicity: Ethics and Law for a Collective Age*
Timothy Machlem: *Beyond Comparison: Sex and Discrimination*
Larry May: *Crimes Against Humanity: A Normative Account*
Stephen R. Munzer: *A Theory of Property*
David Reiff: *Punishment, Compensation, and Law*
Arthur Ripstein: *Equality, Responsibility, and the Law*
Robert F. Schopp: *Automatism, Insanity, and the Psychology of Criminal Responsibility*
Robert F. Schopp: *Justification Defenses and Just Convictions*
Warren F. Schwartz (ed.): *Justice in Immigration*
Anthony Sebok: *Legal Postivism in American Jurisprudence*
Philip Soper: *The Ethics of Deference*
Suzanne Uniacke: *Permissible Killing: The Self-Defense Justification of Homicide*

Natural Law in Jurisprudence and Politics

Mark C. Murphy

Georgetown University

CAMBRIDGE UNIVERSITY PRESS
Cambridge, New York, Melbourne, Madrid, Cape Town, Singapore, São Paulo, Delhi

Cambridge University Press
32 Avenue of the Americas, New York, NY 10013-2473, USA

www.cambridge.org
Information on this title: www.cambridge.org/9780521108089

First published 2006
Reprinted 2007
This digitally printed version 2009

A catalog record for this publication is available from the British Library

Library of Congress Cataloging in Publication data
Murphy, Mark C.
Natural law in jurisprudence and politics / Mark C. Murphy.
p. cm. – (Cambridge studies in philosophy and law)
Includes bibliographical references and index.
ISBN 0-521-85930-1 (hardback)
1. Natural law. 2. Natural law – Political aspects. I. Title. II. Series.
K460.M87   2006
340'.112–dc22   2005015277

ISBN 978-0-521-85930-1 hardback
ISBN 978-0-521-10808-9 paperback

for Cormac Alasdair

Contents

Acknowledgments

I placed myself in the debt of a number of good and generous people while writing this book. Henry Richardson, Brian Bix, and two referees at Cambridge University Press offered helpful criticism of the manuscript as a whole. I also received comments on various portions of the argument from Nick Aroney, Terence Cuneo, David Dyzenhaus, Bill Edmundson, John Hare, Chris Kaczor, Pat Kain, Matthew Kramer, Brian Leiter, Larry May, Bob Roberts, David Schmidtz, and Paul Weithman.

I am grateful for invitations from the Social Philosophy and Policy Center at Bowling Green State University, the University of Toronto Law School, the University of Texas Law and Philosophy Program, and the University of Virginia philosophy department, all of which gave me the opportunity to present and get feedback on some of the material that appears here.

The arguments of Chapter 3 and Chapter 6 were developed during two summers spent in Grand Rapids at Calvin College Summer Seminars in Christian Scholarship, one of which was led by Nick Wolterstorff, the other by Jay Budziszewski. I am grateful to Nick, Jay, and my fellow seminar participants for their help, and to Calvin College, the Pew Charitable Trusts, and Fieldstead and Company for supporting these seminars.

I began work on this book in 1998, when I had the good fortune to be in residence as an Erasmus Fellow at the University of Notre Dame. The book that I promised to work on at the Erasmus Institute – a book on natural law theory in the theory of practical rationality, political philosophy, and theistic ethics – expanded in the usual fashion and had to be split into three books (*Natural Law and Practical Rationality* (2001), *An Essay on Divine Authority* (2002), and this one); I am grateful to Erasmus for its support for a year of research to think more carefully about what shape natural law accounts of politics and theistic ethics should take. I finished this book in 2005 at my home institution, Georgetown University, which generously supported my research with a senior faculty fellowship and several summer grants.

I thank the following parties for permission to use previously published material. Cambridge University Press gave me permission to use material from "Natural Law, Consent, and Political Obligation," *Social Philosophy and Policy* 18 (2001), pp. 70–92, and "Natural Law Jurisprudence," *Legal Theory* 9 (2003), pp. 241–267. I owe thanks to Blackwell Publishers for permission to use some of the text of "Natural Law Theory," which first appeared in William Edmundson and Martin Golding, eds., *Blackwell Guide to the Philosophy of Law and Legal Theory* (copyright © Blackwell, 2004). Finally, the *Review of Metaphysics* kindly granted permission for me to use material from the article "The Common Good," which appeared in the *Review of Metaphysics* 59 (copyright © 2005), pp. 143–177.

I am grateful to Ronald Cohen for the great care with which he edited the manuscript and for making many valuable suggestions. I thank him for his work.

The final debt I must record is to my wife, Jeanette. I cannot state adequately how much I owe to her. It will have to suffice to say that in everything I do I am sustained by her love and friendship.

Natural Law in Jurisprudence and Politics

Introduction
Natural Law Jurisprudence and Natural Law Political Philosophy

0.1 The Central Claims of Natural Law Jurisprudence and Natural Law Political Philosophy

The central claim of natural law jurisprudence is that there is a positive internal connection between law and decisive reasons for action: law is backed by decisive reasons for action. (For there to be a decisive reason to ϕ is for ϕ-ing to be a reasonable act for one to perform and not ϕ-ing an unreasonable act for one to perform, and so for a law to be backed by decisive reasons is for there to be decisive reasons to perform any act required by that law.) The central claim of natural law political philosophy is that law has this reason-giving force through the common good of the political community. Natural law jurisprudence most fundamentally asserts that it is of the essence of law to bind in reason; natural law political philosophy most fundamentally asserts that what makes law bind is its role with respect to the common good of the political community.

Why should we take the view that these are the central theses of natural law jurisprudence and political philosophy to be anything more than stipulation? As the term 'natural law theory' is now used, Aquinas is the paradigmatic natural law theorist. If one would like evidence for Aquinas's status as the paradigm, one can look at any anthology of moral, political, or legal philosophy that includes a section on natural law theory: any such anthology contains a selection from Aquinas or about Aquinas. His thinking in moral, political, and legal matters is the reference point by which later natural law theories (for example, Hobbes's, Locke's) are classified as such, and his thinking on these matters is the reference point by which earlier writers (for example, Aristotle, the Stoics) are assessed as proto-natural law philosophers. So we have reason to take Aquinas as the paradigmatic natural law theorist, and we thus have reason to hold that the theses that are central to Aquinas's natural law jurisprudence and politics – that is, those theses that structure and organize his thought on those topics – are the central theses of natural law jurisprudence and politics. What are those theses?

The first argumentative move in the section of Aquinas's *Summa Theologiae* that later commentators labeled the 'Treatise on Law' is the claim that law is "something pertaining to reason": as a law is something that rules and measures conduct, and rational beings' conduct is ruled and measured only by dictates with which there is reason to conform, law must be something with which agents have reason to conform (IaIIae 90, 1). Following on the heels of that article is an argument that this connection between law and reasons is realized through the common good: as the good is that by which individuals regulate their conduct, the common good is that by which members of a community regulate their conduct, and so the reasons for conformity with law arise from its relation to the common good (IaIIae 90, 2). These theses hold good of all law, divine and human alike (IaIIae 91, 1–4), and when Aquinas turns to the task of drawing more detailed conclusions concerning the range, scope, and source of the authority of human law (IaIIae 95–97), it is in terms of these theses that he makes his case. (For further discussion of the structure of Aquinas's arguments for natural law jurisprudence, see Murphy 2004.) So the fundamental theses of natural law jurisprudence and political philosophy that Aquinas affirms are that concerning the internal connection between law and reasons for action and that concerning the central role of the common good in the provision of law's reason-giving force. And since Aquinas is generally acknowledged as the paradigmatic natural law theorist, it is not at all arbitrary to frame the natural law view here in terms of these theses as well.

These theses, while clearly incompatible with a number of widely held polit-ical and jurisprudential views, are nevertheless rather vague, and the would-be defender of a politics and jurisprudence of natural law must make them more precise. But even in their present form, it is clear what sorts of questions the defender of this view would have to answer. We need to know more about why there exists such a connection between law and decisive reasons for action. We need some account of the nature of the common good, of its character and normative force, and how the law inherits its normative force from the common good thus conceived. We need to know what we should say about those enact-ments that we pretheoretically label 'law' but which seem not to be backed by adequate, let alone decisive, reasons for compliance.

The argument of this book attempts to meet these needs. In Chapter 1, we consider the natural law legal theorist's claim about the internal connection between law and reasons for action. Here I will consider three readings of the natural law thesis: the *strong* reading, on which a norm's legal validity is in part constituted by its being backed by decisive reasons for compliance; the *weak* reading, on which a norm's legal non-defectiveness is in part constituted by its being backed by decisive reasons for compliance; and the *moral* reading, on which a norm's moral authoritativeness is in part constituted by its being backed by decisive reasons for compliance. While I will reject the moral reading as a formulation of the natural law jurisprudential thesis because of its extreme lack of interest, I will show that the strong reading can deflect the objections commonly leveled against it, and that the objections commonly raised against natural law jurisprudence do not raise even *prima facie* suspicions against the weak reading.

In Chapter 2, I defend the weak reading of the natural law thesis. I begin by considering John Finnis's 'legal point of view' argument for the natural law jurisprudential thesis. While I reject that argument, I think that there are two more promising arguments – an argument from the function of law, and an argument from the status of legal norms as illocutionary acts – that establish the truth of the weak reading. But these arguments not only give reason to believe the weak natural law jurisprudential thesis; they give reason to reject the strong reading. So the natural law legal theorist should affirm the weak reading. This thesis – that law that is not backed by decisive reasons for action is defective as law – sets the agenda for natural law political philosophy, which is to describe the conditions under which non-defective law is in place.

In Chapter 3, we consider the natural law political philosopher's central political concept – that of the *common good*. The concept of the common good has this central place in virtue of its carrying out the agenda set by natural law jurisprudence: the common good is supposed to underwrite law's reason-giving force, so that a law that is non-defective with respect to its reason-giving force has that virtue through its connection to the common good. The aim of this chapter is to clarify the understanding of the common good to which the natural law view should appeal. In this chapter, I defend an aggregative conception of the common good, on which the common good consists in the state of affairs in which every individual in that community is fully flourishing, on the basis that it is able to fill the reason-giving role that the common good must fill and that other extant conceptions gain their plausibility only by way of the aggregative conception.

In Chapters 4 and 5, I consider how the common good should be held to underwrite the reason-giving force of law on a natural law conception. In Chapter 4, I consider whether the natural law theorist needs to appeal to consent to explain how the common good provides the law with normative force. Natural law theorists, like most contemporary political philosophers, have been deeply suspicious of consent theories: they have argued not only that such theories are generally philosophically objectionable, but also that consent theories are at odds with the basic thrust of the natural law position, and at any rate are not needed by the natural law theorist to explain how the common good provides law with its normative force. I show in this chapter that, although the criticisms of standard consent theory are extremely damaging, contemporary natural law theorists have drastically underestimated the extent to which they need help from something like a consent view. In Chapter 5, I give the details of a non-standard consent account that offers the help that the natural law theorist needs in explaining how the common good provides the law with its reason-giving force while evading (most of) the difficulties that have been pressed against more typical consent views.

Natural law jurisprudence and political philosophy have traditionally treated punishment as a secondary question: it is no part of the definition of law that law involve threat of sanctions, and there could be an authoritative legal order that did not make use of punishment. But it would be a mistake to think that legal punishment is not to be justified in terms of the common good and its demands: for, as I argue in Chapter 6, legal punishment is to be understood first and foremost in terms of its authoritative character, and since the natural law view holds that all authoritative dictates are to be justified in terms of the demands of the common good, the justification of punishment must be in terms of the common good as well. Rejecting both the quasi-utilitarianism and appeals to equal distributions of benefits and burdens that have characterized much natural law thought on punishment, I defend a view of punishment that is both retributivist and expressivist.

In Chapter 7, I consider the limits of natural law political philosophy. The most pressing challenge that the natural law view – indeed, *any* view of the authority of law – faces concerns the accommodation of superpolitical and subpolitical concerns. I discuss these challenges, and the natural law view's inability to respond fully to them, in this chapter.

0.2 Natural Law and Practical Rationality

'Natural law theory' names not only theories of political philosophy and jurisprudence; it also is a name for a theory of morality, or, better, a theory of practical rationality. According to the natural law account of practical rationality, the fundamental reasons for action are certain basic goods, whose status as goods is grounded in human nature, and, further, there are correct principles of practical reasonableness that govern how one ought to pursue these goods, which principles have their warrant from the features exhibited by the basic goods. (See Murphy 2001a, pp. 2–3, and Murphy 2002b.)

Stated in their abstract forms, the central theses of natural law political philosophy and jurisprudence are independent of the central theses of the natural law account of practical rationality. For while the central theses of natural law political philosophy and jurisprudence make claims about the connections between law and reasons, and law and the common good, they make no claims about the specific character of those reasons or the common good; but it is the business of the natural law account of practical rationality to make specific claims about the nature of the good and of reasons for action. So one could affirm a natural law jurisprudence or a natural law political philosophy while rejecting a natural law account of practical rationality.[1]

---

[1] One might wonder why this jurisprudential thesis about the connection between law and reasons for action has been labeled 'natural law theory.' The reason is, as far as I can see,

So even if one thinks, as I do (Murphy 2001a), that the natural law theory of practical rationality is the best theory of practical rationality on offer, it may well be possible for one to offer a defense of natural law jurisprudence and political philosophy without appealing to any premises from a natural law account of practical rationality. Indeed, Chapters 1 and 2 rely on no such premises, and the argument of these chapters for an internal connection between law and decisive reasons for action is compatible with a variety of theories of practical rationality. But the chapters that follow, chapters that are more political philosophy than jurisprudence, employ several key theses of the natural law account of practical rationality that I endorse, though (as is obvious) these claims are by no means unique to the natural law account. The claims that I employ are as follows.

First, that there is a correct, formally objectivist notion of an individual's good. By 'an individual's good' I mean that individual's overall well-being, what makes him or her well off. It is the fundamental concept of the theory of prudential value. To say that there is a correct formally objectivist notion of an individual's good is to claim that those states of affairs that make an agent well-off do not have their status as such in virtue of that agent's desires, preferences, pro-attitudes, and so on, whether actual or in some way improved by idealized information. (This is not to say that those states of affairs that make an agent well-off might not include states of affairs that involve that agent's subjective states.)

That a formally objectivist account of well-being is correct is a controversial thesis, but it is not one that is held only by those that are classified as natural law theorists. Aristotle held such a view, as do a number of neo-Aristotelians, but Aristotelians are not as such natural law theorists. Griffin, a utilitarian of sorts, affirms this view (1996), as does Scanlon, a Kantian (1998). Nor are the particular goods that tend to be recognized by defenders of such a view distinctive of the natural law position. All of these views tend to recognize physical integrity, knowledge, friendship, rational agency, accomplishment, play, and aesthetic experience as human goods. There are some disagreements – for example, whether pleasure, or religion, should be included in the list – but in appealing to goods as examples I will stick to those that are by and large uncontroversial among those who affirm objectivist conceptions of well-being.

Second, that the content of this formally objectivist notion of an individual's good is knowable, at least in broad outline, by mature adults. This is simply

simply historical. The jurisprudential thesis bears this label because its most historically important defender is Aquinas, and Aquinas identified the principles of rational conduct for human beings as the principles of the natural law. Thus, given Aquinas's particular theory of reasons for action, the fundamental thesis of natural law jurisprudence can be equivalently formulated as asserting a connection between human law and natural law. A danger with this label, of course, is that one might confuse theses of Aquinas's theory of practical rationality with theses of his theory of law, and take objections to one of these theories to constitute objections to the other.

the view that the contours of well-being are not the province of philosophers alone – or, indeed, any class of experts – but is available to the rational reflection of adult humans generally. Again, this is not at all a view distinctive of a natural law position, but one that is widely held.

Third, that any two distinct individuals' goods are incommensurable with each other, and, indeed, the value of the goods of any two disjoint classes of persons are incommensurable with each other. These are strong claims. The idea is that if one is asked to assess the intrinsic value of the goods of any disjoint classes of persons, one should deny that the value of one is greater than, lesser than, or equal to the other. In making this claim, I do not mean to equate 'A's being more valuable than B' with 'there being sufficient or even decisive reason to prefer A over B.' The value of the states of affairs is here understood as part of what supports claims about what there is reason, or most reason, to do or want. So if it is true that there is sufficient or even decisive reason to save five trapped miners by going left rather than to save one trapped miner by going right, what the incommensurability thesis that I affirm rules out is that the *basis* for holding that there is sufficient or decisive reason to go left is that the good of the five miners to the left is *simply more valuable* than the good of the one miner to the right.

The argument for incommensurability is as follows. Imagine a choice in which one has a source that can be used to promote A's good or B's good. This choice is always *practically significant*: one cannot realize all of the value through one choice as one does through the other, and vice versa. Evidence for this is that one can recognize the sense of regret in not having taken the other option in any such case; no matter what one chooses, one will have missed out on some value that could have been realized in the choice. But for one option to be more valuable than another is for one option to include all of the value that the other includes, and more as well; for two options to be of equal value is for each to include all of the good that the other includes. Since neither of these is the case in practically significant choice, all distinct individuals' goods are incommensurable (Grisez 1978; also Murphy 2001a, pp. 182–187).[2]

---

[2] To repeat: the claim of the incommensurability of distinct individuals' goods does not entail that there cannot be decisive reason to promote one individual's good over another: that would follow only if we add the further premise that we never have decisive reason to promote one individual's good over another's except when one individual's good is more valuable than another's. That is false, on my view. For one thing, if one could promote A's good by giving A a dollar and B's good only by cutting the throat of the innocent C, then one has decisive reason to promote A's good over B's. One way to choose between options to promote incommensurable goods, then, is to rule out one of those options on independent grounds. Another way to choose between such options is by employing norms of impartiality, for example, original position type of thinking: if I did not know whether I was A or B, which would I prefer to have helped – A or B? For more on rational choice in the face of incommensurability, see Murphy 2001a, pp. 198–209 as well as 3.5 of this book; see also Chappell 2005.

Fourth, that there are a number of modes of reasonable response to the good. Here the important contrast is with straightforwardly consequentialist understandings of practical rationality. All such views are *promotionist*: they understand the only rational response to the good to be that of promoting it, of bringing it into being (cf. Murphy 2001a, pp. 147–156). But there appear to be other modes of rational response to the good. One can respect it, or honor it, and the reasonableness of respecting or honoring the good cannot be plausibly captured in terms of promoting it. (I will make further arguments for this view in 6.6.)

None of the argument of the first two chapters of this book relies on these four natural law premises, and most of the argument of the remaining chapters of the book could be carried out without appeal to them. But at important points, the argument would have to proceed at such a level of abstraction that it would be both difficult to follow and evaluate, and nearly incapable of holding anyone's interest. With them in place, though, I can proceed to a somewhat more substantive account of political matters, and the increase in interest is I think sufficient to justify my taking on argumentative promissory notes that have to be satisfied elsewhere (for example, in Murphy 2001a).

1

Natural Law Jurisprudence Formulated

1.1 The Fundamental Claim of Natural Law Jurisprudence

Natural law political philosophy takes its lead from natural law jurisprudence. For natural law jurisprudence most fundamentally claims that law is backed by decisive[1] reasons for compliance, whereas natural law political philosophy attempts to describe the conditions in which law, in this sense, is present.

The immediate challenge faced by defenders of the thesis that law is backed by decisive reasons for compliance is that it seems open to obvious and devastating objection by counterexample. For that thesis appears to entail that if one does not have decisive reason to comply with a dictate, then that dictate is not law. But it seems that we readily acknowledge as law dictates for which we do not, or would not have had, decisive reasons for compliance. The Fugitive Slave Act of 1850 required citizens not to hinder, and even to aid, federal marshals who sought to return runaway slaves to bondage. This act was passed in order to enforce a Constitutional provision and was enacted in due form by the federal legislature. It was socially acknowledged and judicially enforced. It seems that, as a matter of social practice, the Fugitive Slave Act *was* law – regardless of the fact that those under it did not have decisive reason to comply with it. It thus serves nothing but obfuscation to deny that the Fugitive Slave Act was law. And if we refuse to deny that the Fugitive Slave Act was law, are we not, therefore, refusing to affirm the fundamental thesis of natural law jurisprudence?

Here is another way of putting the point. However we properly understand law, we should recognize that the referent of 'law' is fixed by social practice. Regardless of whether we think that some people (for example, judges) count as privileged with respect to the way that their use of 'law' fixes its referent, we should allow that there are cases in which there is general agreement that a deeply immoral rule is a law. With respect to the fixing of the reference of 'law,'

---

[1] Recall from 0.1 that a reason (or set of reasons) to ϕ is decisive if and only if that reason (or set of reasons) renders ϕ-ing reasonable and failure to ϕ unreasonable.

social practice is bedrock, and so any analysis of 'law' that entails that there is error on a matter with respect to which the social practice seems to speak with one voice must be in error. As Bix writes,

The basic point is that the concept of 'legal validity' is closely tied to what is recognized as binding in a given society and what the state enforces, and it seems fairly clear that there are plenty of societies where immoral laws are recognized as binding and enforced. Someone might answer that these immoral laws are not *really* legally valid, and the officials are making a mistake when they treat the rules as if they were legally valid. However, this is just to play games with words, and confusing games at that. 'Legal validity' is the term we use to refer to *whatever* is conventionally recognized as binding; to say that all the officials could be wrong about what is legally valid is close to nonsense. (Bix 2002, pp. 72–73)

Marmor offers a similar basis for rejecting the natural law thesis:

Take a certain legal system, say Roman law in the first century AD; let us presume that a certain norm, P, was recognized by the Roman lawyers at the time as part and parcel of their legal system. Does it make sense to say that this community of lawyers has made a mistake, since according to the 'real nature' of law, P did not lie within the extension of their legal system even then, despite their inability to recognize this?

I presume that a negative answer to this question is almost self-evident; such an extensive misidentification in law would be profoundly mysterious.

(Marmor 1992, pp. 9 6–97)

A recent response to this perennial criticism of natural law jurisprudence is that natural law theory has really never been concerned to deny the obvious fact that there can be deeply immoral laws, laws with which those subject to them lack adequate, let alone decisive, reason to comply (cf. Soper 1983, p. 1181, George 1996c, p. viii, and Bix 2002, p. 63). According to one line of response along these lines – what I will call the 'moral' reading of the natural law thesis – all that the natural law theorist wants to do in affirming a connection between law and reasons is to issue a dramatic reminder that adherence to some laws would constitute such a departure from reasonableness that there could not be adequate reason to obey them; the only law that merits our obedience is law that meets a certain minimum standard of reasonableness. Thus Robert George writes that "what is being asserted by natural law theorists [is] . . . that the moral obligatoriness which may attach to positive law is *conditional* in nature" (George 1996c, p. viii).

There are two reasons to reject George's suggested reading of the natural law thesis. The first is that this reading transforms that thesis from a claim belonging to analytical jurisprudence into a claim belonging to moral philosophy. The natural law view is, so understood, not at all about the defining conditions of law, but only about how agents ought to respond to the law's demands. That the natural law theorist is concerned to make not a claim about the nature of law but only a claim about the morality of obedience to law is implausible in itself – remember that the paradigmatic natural law theorist is Aquinas, and that in presenting this natural law thesis he does so in the context of a discussion of the nature of law generally, much of which is irrelevant to practical concerns (0.1) – and, further, requires us to believe that centuries of debate between natural law jurists and their rivals have involved into no more than a misunderstanding, both by the natural law theorists and by their opponents, about what the natural law theorist affirms.[2] The second reason to reject George's suggestion is that the natural law claim, understood as a moral thesis, is excruciatingly uninteresting, a claim that almost everyone in the history of moral and political philosophy has accepted, and thus is not much worth discussing.

What we are looking for is an understanding of the natural law thesis that preserves its status as a contentious claim of analytical jurisprudence while pointing toward the resources to answer the obvious objection – reasons to think either that the natural law thesis does not imply that the Fugitive Slave Act was not a law or that, while the natural law thesis does imply that the Fugitive Slave Act was not a law, we can nevertheless see why that implication is not so deeply counterintuitive that natural law theory can be dismissed out of hand.

Consider the following two jurisprudential readings of the natural law thesis, which I will call simply the *stronger* and the *weaker* natural law theses. According to the stronger reading, *law is backed by decisive reasons for compliance* is the same sort of proposition as *triangles have three sides*. There is a class of propositions of the form 'S's are P' or 'The S is P' from which we may deduce, in conjunction with the premise of the form 'x is not P,' a conclusion of the form 'x is not an S.' *Triangles have three sides* belongs to this class: from *triangles have three sides* and *this figure does not have three sides*, we may deduce *this figure is not a triangle*. According to the stronger reading of the natural law thesis, from *law is backed by decisive reasons for compliance* and *this dictate is not backed by decisive reasons for compliance* we may deduce *this dictate is not a law*. It is this stronger reading of the natural law thesis that underwrites the common natural law dictum, '*lex iniusta non est lex.*' Given the plausible further premise that a law that requires the doing of injustice is a law that one cannot have decisive reason to comply with, the strong natural law thesis entails that an unjust law is no law at all.

By contrast, according to the weaker reading, *law is backed by decisive reasons for compliance* is not the same sort of proposition as *triangles have three sides*. Rather, on this reading, *law is backed by decisive reasons for compliance* is a proposition like *the duck is a skillful swimmer*. There is a class of

---

[2] I am, of course, willing to allow that sometimes arguments are at cross-purposes, and that this can remain unrecognized over lengthy stretches of time. But it defies imagination to hold that such a debate could persist between one party forwarding an exclusively ethical thesis and another person forwarding a strictly jurisprudential one.

propositions of the form 'The S is P' or 'S's are P' from which, in conjunction with a premise of the form 'this x is not P' we cannot conclude that 'this x is not an S'; rather, we can conclude (and can conclude no more than) 'this x either is not an S or is a defective S' (cf. Thompson 1995 and Foot 2001, p. 30). So if we come across an animal that is not a skillful swimmer, we cannot conclude that the animal is not a duck; we can conclude no more than that it either is not a duck or is a defective duck. According to this weaker reading of the fundamental thesis of natural law jurisprudence, then, it does not follow from a dictate's not being backed by decisive reasons for compliance that it is not a law. It follows only that it is not a law *or* that it is defective precisely as law.[3]

Each of these readings of the natural law thesis succeeds in remaining jurisprudential, a claim about the nature of law, rather than moral. But for each of these theses there is an immediate difficulty that needs to be dealt with. The immediate difficulty for the weaker reading is not that it falls prey to the Fugitive Slave Act objection. For the weaker reading does not imply that the Fugitive Slave Act was not a law; it implies only that it either was not a law or that it was defective. But this way of describing how the weaker reading avoids the Fugitive Slave Act objection may leave it open to the opposite objection, that it succumbs to the same charge of triviality that I leveled against George's moral reading of the natural law thesis. According to the moral reading, laws that there are not good reasons to comply with ought not to be obeyed. According to the weaker jurisprudential reading, laws that there are not good reasons to comply with are, at least, defective. Why isn't the weaker jurisprudential reading even *less* interesting than the moral reading, less interesting because the moral reading at least identifies the defect in question – that is, that of being unworthy of obedience – whereas the weaker jurisprudential reading says only that there is a defect somewhere in the vicinity of the dictate? Thus Bix, who puzzles a bit over why anyone would think that the moral reading of the natural law thesis is anything but "banal," immediately identifies the moral reading with the view that immoral law is a perversion of law, or defective as law (Bix 2000, p. 1620, n. 34; also Bix 1999, p. 30).

The objection has purchase only if one confuses the specific notion of *defectiveness* with the more general notion of *objectionableness*. If the weaker reading were simply that law with which there is not decisive reason for compliance is in *some* way objectionable, then it would be true that this reading would not hold a great deal of interest. But the concept of *being defective* is not to be identified with the concept of *being objectionable*: a thing may exhibit a feature that is in some way objectionable without that feature's in any way constituting

---

[3] Robert Alexy labels the distinction between criteria that establish the legality of a norm and criteria that establish the legal nondefectiveness of a norm as a distinction between "classificatory" and "qualificatory"; see Alexy 1998, p. 214 and Alexy 1999, pp. 24–25.

a defect in that thing. It could be that a certain pattern of feathers on a duck is very ugly indeed. There is a clear sense in which one would find a duck with that pattern of feathering objectionable. But the presence of that pattern would not, as such, make the duck *defective as a duck*. Again: it could be that, due to there being too many ducks about for human comfort, we rightly find duck reproduction objectionable. But two ducks' managing to reproduce would not thereby constitute deficiencies in them. The standards for duck defectiveness are, we might say, *internal* to the life of the duck: what counts as a defect in a duck is not just anything that is objectionable or unpleasant or unprofitable about the duck, but only what falls short in a duck with respect to the form of life of its species. The notion of defect is kind-specific – that is, is always to be understood in terms of the kind of thing at issue. As Thompson remarks, "A true judgment of natural defect supplies an 'immanent critique' of its subject" (Thompson 1995, p. 296).

A failure to mark explicitly this distinction between *being defective* and simply *being in some way objectionable* also generates problems for Kretzmann's otherwise plausible weak rendering of the natural law '*lex iniusta non est lex*' thesis. Kretzmann defends that slogan by noting that it is a common phenomenon for one term to have two sets of conditions of application, one of which is non-evaluative, the other of which is evaluative (Kretzmann 1988, pp. 102–107). So one might claim that this doctor is no doctor at all; or that one's son is no son at all. In each of these cases, the correct application of the former term depends entirely on non-evaluative conditions (having the socially recognized credentials of physicians for the former example, and perhaps being one's male biological offspring, or being legally recognized as a male dependent of a certain sort, for the latter example), while the correct application of the latter term depends at least in part on evaluative conditions (having a proper care and competence with respect to furthering health, or showing the proper sort of care and deference to one's parents). As Russell has noted (2000), Kretzmann does not elaborate sufficiently on the nature of the relationship between the evaluative and non-evaluative conditions of application, thus leaving Kretzmann's view open to the charge that the sense in which the *lex iniusta* claim is true may be a sense that everyone, including the most hardboiled positivists, can accept. Russell's claim, in essentials, is that Kretzmann has not shown that the *lex iniusta* thesis is more like the (interesting) weak natural law reading rather than the (uninteresting) moral reading. To avoid Russell's criticism, Kretzmann would have needed to show that the evaluative conditions the failure to satisfy which lead the natural law theorist to call a rule 'no law at all' are conditions that are internal to law and so genuinely count as a natural defect in it.

The weaker understanding of the natural law thesis is, then, an interesting and contentious view. For the claim that the defender of the weaker jurisprudential reading affirms is that there is some standard internal to legality, to being law, such that a law that is not backed by decisive reasons for compliance fails to measure up and thus is defective precisely as law. Whatever the demerits of the weak understanding of the natural law thesis, triviality is not among them.

Obviously, triviality is not a problem for the stronger reading either. The difficulty with the stronger reading is that, as the Fugitive Slave Act objection suggests, it fails to countenance as laws rules that are, as a matter of social fact, designated as laws. Thus the stronger reading seems vulnerable simply to objection by counterexample. And, further, even those sympathetic to natural law theory have taken the strong view to be not just mistaken but incoherent. Finnis, for example, has argued that the natural law motto that an unjust law is no law at all is, construed literally, "pure nonsense, flatly self-contradictory" (Finnis 1980, p. 364); Soper has written that "The very obviousness of this contradiction" shows that no one could ever have meant to affirm the strong natural law thesis (Soper 1983, p. 1181); and George has remarked that the fact that Aquinas was perfectly willing to talk about unjust laws shows that the paradigmatic natural law position does not affirm the *lex iniusta* thesis (George 2000, p. 1641). So the stronger reading is subject not only to the criticism that there are clear counterexamples to its thesis about the features that laws necessarily exhibit but also to the criticism that its very thesis is incoherent.

The defender of the strong reading should begin the reply to the charges that his or her thesis is really a non-starter by responding to the claim of incoherence. First, and obviously, it is not at all necessary for the defender of the strong reading to formulate his or her position in terms of the common natural law dictum that an unjust law is not a law. Given the generic formulation of the natural law thesis as the claim that law is backed by decisive reasons for compliance, one might well reject this natural law slogan, phrasing its negative implication as the thesis that no dictate (or command, or rule (etc.)) that one lacks decisive reason to comply with is law. This entirely lacks the appearance of self-contradiction that appears in the natural law slogan. But, second, even if one were to stick with the natural law slogan, the charge of self-contradiction can be deflected. For it is not always self-contradictory to make assertions of the form 'a——X is not an X.' David Lyons has noted that 'counterfeit dollars are no dollars at all' is simply true (Lyons 1984, p. 62); 'fake diamonds are not diamonds' is also simply true. Generally, 'a——X is not an X' is not self-contradictory if the blank is filled by an *alienans*, a certain sort of attributive adjective. 'Fake' is always an *alienans*, and so 'fake diamonds are not diamonds' is not self-contradictory: 'fake diamonds are not diamonds' is not properly analyzed as 'nothing that is both fake and a diamond is a diamond.' But there are adjectives that only in certain contexts – that is, as applied to certain nouns – count as instances of the *alienans*. 'Glass' is not generally an *alienans* (a glass slipper is a slipper), but it can be (a glass diamond is not a diamond). 'Rubber' is not generally an *alienans* (a rubber band is a band), but it can be (a rubber duck is not a duck). A natural law theorist who takes the strong view could hold that in the claim "*lex iniusta non est lex*," *iniusta* is, as applied to *lex*, an *alienans*. Or, to return to the formulation of natural law jurisprudence that I have employed, a strong natural law theorist could hold that 'unbacked by decisive reasons for compliance' is, when applied to law, an *alienans*. Either way, the strong natural law view escapes Finnis's charge that the position is flatly self-contradictory. (For a brief discussion of the *alienans* and its status as an attributive adjective, see Geach 1956, pp. 33–34.)

Indeed, reflecting on the aptness of the slogan "*lex iniusta non est lex*" for expressing the thought of the fundamental natural law thesis can help us to see why it is not so obvious that the strong reading of the natural law thesis succumbs so easily to the Fugitive Slave Act objection. 'Law unbacked by decisive reasons for compliance,' on this view, is like 'glass diamond.' What makes it appropriate to use the expression 'glass diamond' to describe something that is no diamond at all is the fact that some of its features are such as to cause people to treat it as if it were a diamond: it looks like a diamond, generates some of the interest that a diamond generates, and so forth. Indeed, it has those diamondlike features *in order to* cause people to treat it, in some ways, like a diamond. Similarly, a law unbacked by reasons, while on the strong reading really no law at all, may well have some of the features of genuine law, most notably the proper pedigree. These features may cause those under it to treat it as a dictate with which they have decisive reason to comply. Indeed, a legal rule may have these features *in order to* cause people to treat it as something with which they genuinely have weighty reasons to comply.

How, then, should the strong natural law theorist respond to Bix's claim that to deny legal validity to dictates conventionally recognized and enforced as law is to court incoherence? We should grant, of course, that if it were a criterion for success in any account of law that it designate as 'law' all those things that are designated 'law' by citizens, or perhaps by officials, then the strong natural law view would be doomed, for it undoubtedly does deny the designation 'law' to some of those items. But the question to be raised is whether this general agreement is to be treated as infallible. Consider, as an instructive analogy, van Inwagen's story of the 'bligers':

When the first settlers arrived in the hitherto unpopulated land of Pluralia, they observed (always from a fair distance) what appeared to be black tigers, and they coined the name 'bliger' for them. . . . A few centuries after the settlement of Pluralia, however, a foreign zoological expedition discovered that, in a way, there were no bligers. "A bliger (*Quasi-Tigris Multiplex Pluralianus*)," their report read, "is really six animals. Its 'legs' are four monkey-like creatures, its 'trunk' a sort of sloth, and its 'head' a species of owl. Any six animals of the proper species can combine temporarily to form a bliger. (Combinations lasting for several hours have been observed telescopically.) The illusion is amazing. Even a trained zoologist observing a bliger from a distance of ten meters would swear he was observing a single, unified animal. While the purpose of this combination is doubtless to protect its members from predators by producing the illusion of the presence of a large, dangerous carnivore, we can only guess as to the evolutionary history of this marvelous symbiosis.   (van Inwagen 1990, p. 104)

Now, it is not perfectly clear what moral to draw from this story. Van Inwagen draws the moral that Pluralians nonetheless spoke truly when they said "there is a bliger in the back field!" and the like; in saying "There is a bliger in the back field!" the Pluralians did not express a view on whether the various objects arranged bligerwise composed an object, a bliger. If I understand Merricks (2001) correctly, he would hold that the Pluralians spoke falsely when they said "There is a bliger in the back field!": though what they said is nearly as good as true, and good enough for normal practical purposes, what they said was nevertheless simply false. Whichever way one goes in reading this fable, it seems to me that there is room for one to make the sensible claim – as van Inwagen does – that, really, there are no bligers. By van Inwagen's lights, what needs to be done to give his assertion sense, and to distinguish it from the Pluralian folk's way of speaking, is to provide a gloss on his claim. By Merricks's lights, the assertion really – if we were uncorrupted – requires no gloss; what requires explanation is why the Pluralians are less confused in saying "there is a bliger in the back field" than in saying "there is a unicorn in the back field." On either view, one can make sense, in the context of van Inwagen's story, of eliminativism about bligers.

What the strong natural law theorist should claim is that laws unbacked by decisive reasons occupy the role that bligers occupy in van Inwagen's story. Rules unbacked by decisive reasons have been recognized as law by citizens and officials, have been treated as binding as a matter of social practice. But that fact does not make citizens and officials infallible with respect to the philosophical problem of whether these rules ungrounded in reasons are really laws. As with the case of the bligers, the strong natural law theorist can go one of two ways here. The strong natural law theorist can claim that while folks are perfectly right to say that some unjust laws are laws, there is an important sense in which they are not laws. The central task for this sort of strong natural law theorist is that of explaining what that sense is, and showing that this sense is sufficiently interesting. (The sense in which unjust law is not law cannot be merely 'what merits obedience,' on pain of asserting only the dull moral reading of the natural law thesis.) On the other hand, the strong natural law theorist can claim that in the ordinary sense of law, law that it is not reasonable to comply with is no law at all. The task here is, I take it, that of showing that there are presuppositions of the social practice of designating certain rules as laws that could be brought to light by closer analysis and that could nevertheless turn out to be false. Closer inspection yielded the result that a bliger is not one animal but six; and given the centrality to the practice of bliger-talk that a bliger is one animal, the most straightforward inference to draw is that there are not really any bligers. Closer inspection may yield the result that laws unbacked by decisive reasons for action lack some feature whose assumed presence is central to the practice of law. And if it turned out that this were the case, the most straightforward inference to draw is that there are not really any laws unbacked by decisive reasons for action.

Now, one might respond: even if it is not incoherent for the strong natural law theorist to claim that laws unbacked by decisive reasons for compliance are no laws at all, there is a key disanalogy between the case of the bligers and the case of laws unbacked by decisive reasons. We see the situation with the bligers and we recognize that something is amiss, recognize that there is at least potential tension between the Pluralians' bliger-talk and what is the case with bligers. But we see the strong natural law theorist's purported claim about law – that it is necessarily backed by decisive reasons for action – and we are yet unmoved. Officials go on applying unjust laws (or recognizing that they are laws, yet refusing to apply them), citizens go on obeying or reforming them, and no tension is felt. Does this not show that even if there is conceptual room for the sort of claim that the strong natural law theorist wants to make, there must be in fact no basis for the view that law must be backed by such reasons?

No. First, the claim that the strong natural law theorist wants to make does not immediately imply that folks – ordinary folk, or legal officials – cannot go on using the term 'law' very much as they did before. This much is clear from (at least seemingly) revisionary metaphysical theories that do not of themselves include recommendations for changes in ordinary linguistic practice. Second, the fact that folks have remained unmoved by the claims of strong natural law theory does not show that the claims of strong natural law theory are false. Ordinary users of the language do not enjoy a final authority on the correctness of analyses of the terms they employ, nor on the presuppositions of the practices that they are engaged in. Again, think of the bligers. Suppose that a Pluralian is shown the facts about bligers, yet continues to think that there are bligers. A philosopher might note that there are features of bliger-talk that show pretty clearly that it was essential to the designation of that mass in the back field, and others like it, as bligers that they be individual enduring objects rather than temporary animal collectives. Yet that Pluralian just might not see it. While how the Pluralians use the term 'bliger' fixes its reference, they do not enjoy some sort of infallibility, either individually or collectively, on how their use fixes its reference and whether on any given occasion they are applying that term correctly. The same holds of law. The starting point for marking out a set of phenomena as law is the practices of human agents, but that does not make those agents infallible about whether they are correct in thinking that any particular instance is a case of law. I acknowledge, of course, that Bix's point places a weighty burden on the strong natural law theorist. But this burden is no greater than that which falls on any philosopher when his or her view runs contrary to common opinion. The strong natural law theorist bears the burden of showing that it is central to law that it be backed by decisive reasons, and this burden is made weighty by the fact that this view commits him or her to the thesis that a number of socially sanctioned rules called by consensus 'laws' are not really laws at all. But we knew this already. It is no criticism of a philosophical position that the defender of that position needs an argument for it.

One might grant much of my argument in the case of bligers while denying the force of the analogy between the zoological expedition's debunking of the existence of bligers and the strong natural law theorist's debunking of the existence of laws unbacked by decisive reasons. Leiter, in commenting on recent accounts of the standards of success in analytical jurisprudence, has usefully distinguished between treating the concept of law as a natural kind concept ("a concept whose extension is fixed solely by whatever well-confirmed scientific (lawful) generalizations employ the concept") and treating law as a hermeneutic concept ("any concept which satisfies two conditions: (i) it plays a hermeneutic role – that is, it figures in how humans make themselves and their practices intelligible to themselves – and (ii) its extension is fixed by this hermeneutic role") (Leiter 2003, p. 40). The concept of a bliger is a natural kind concept in Pluralian discourse. But the treatment of law as a hermeneutic concept is now deeply entrenched. One might think that this difference between the concept of a bliger and the concept of law might translate into a difference in the extent to which users of the concept could be in widespread error about the objects to which that concept applies. It is, however, far from clear why we would accept any view that requires exclusivity in natural-kind or hermeneutic approaches to the concept of law, and it is far from clear that, even if we did accept it, it would translate into a rejection of the sort of fallibility that the strong natural law theorist must affirm.

First: any concept that has a deep hold on persons' self-understanding and that is practical (that is, concerned with the guidance of conduct) is bound to make itself manifest in the behavioral tendencies of those who understand themselves in terms of it. *Law* is just such a concept. So *law* will have to be understood in a way that is both adequate to its role in self-understanding and can have a place in adequate folk or social-scientific generalizations about the behavior of persons with respect to legal institutions. To put it another way: if we aim to give an adequate account of law as a hermeneutic concept, we will know that we have failed if that concept cannot also be put into service in the generalizations of social science. If this is correct, then the concept of law, like the concept of bliger, serves a natural kind role, and so there is not the hard distinction between them that might lead one to doubt whether the possibility of massive error in the identification of objects as bligers also suggests the possibility of massive error in the identification of objects as laws.

Second: even focusing entirely on law as a hermeneutic concept, it is not at all apparent why a hermeneutic concept would not admit of widespread fallibility in application by the concept-users. If there are any concepts central to the self-understanding of us language-using beings, the concepts of speech-acts such as asserting, questioning, commanding, deeming, and so on are among them. But it seems very clear that large classes of persons could err about the application of these concepts in certain types of cases. It is safe to say that the large majority of users of moral or religious concepts would take a large chunk of their usage of those concepts to be assertive, whether positively or negatively (*giving to Oxfam is/is not right*; *God exists/does not exist*). But when the logical positivists claimed that these uses of moral and religious concepts (or pseudo-concepts) were not assertive at all (for example, Ayer 1946 [1936], pp. 102–120), surely they were not making an incoherent claim, regardless of its ultimate plausibility. Even if the users of the language, the speakers and listeners, were convinced that assertions were being made and responded to, the response is available that these users are confused about what items were genuinely assertions, and the basis for this critique would have appealed to the constitutive features of assertions that are not, on the logical positivists' views, actually present in the case of moral and religious utterances.

One way, then, to attack Bix's dismissal of the claims of strong natural law jurisprudence is to show that it is based on too low an estimate of the extent to which concept-users are fallible in their application of those concepts. Here is another way to respond to Bix's charge of incoherence: show that the charge applies with similar force even to widely held jurisprudential views that define themselves in opposition to natural law theory. If Bix were right, then it would be a condition on the eligibility of a jurisprudential theory that, necessarily, if all of the legal officials in some society hold that x is law in that society, then the theory implies that x is law in that society. But no extant jurisprudential theory, including both crude Austinian and sophisticated Hartian positivisms, satisfies this constraint. So Bix's argument fails through proving too much.

I will content myself here with showing that both Austinian and Hartian positivisms fail to satisfy the constraint. With respect to Austin's view: on Austin's general jurisprudence, every law is a command, issued by a sovereign and backed by a sanction (Austin 1995 [1832], Lecture I, p. 21). A sanction is a credible threat of harm to a subject attendant on a violation of the order (Austin 1995 [1832], Lecture I, p. 22). It follows from Austin's view that there is no law that is not backed by a sanction. But, possibly, all of the legal officials in some society might hold that some particular norm, a norm unbacked by a sanction, is law. If Austin's view is true, law without sanction is no law at all. Thus Austinian positivism violates Bix's constraint.[4]

---

[4] Bix rightly notes that Austin's argument against Blackstone's natural law view rests on a confusion. Here is Austin: "To say that human laws which conflict with the Divine law are not binding, that is to say, are not laws, is to talk stark nonsense. The most pernicious laws, and therefore those which are most opposed to the will of God, have been and are continually enforced as laws by judicial tribunals. Suppose an act ... be prohibited by the sovereign under the penalty of death; if I commit this act, and I object to the sentence, that it is contrary to the law of God ... the court of justice will demonstrate the inconclusiveness of my reasoning, by hanging me up, in pursuance of the law of which I have impugned the validity" (Austin 1995 [1832], Lecture V, p. 158). As Bix points out, Austin's argument proves too much: it would generalize to exclude the possibility of any legal mistake by officials, a position that would be affirmed only by the crudest of legal realisms (Bix 1993, p. 86).

With respect to Hart's view: on Hart's position, whether something is law in a given society depends on whether it is recognized as such by the rule of recognition, the usually tremendously complex rule that guides legal officials in making, identifying, and applying law (Hart 1994 [1961], pp. 94–95). It follows from Hart's view that there is no law that is not acknowledged as such by the rule of recognition. But, possibly, all of the legal officials in some society might hold that some particular norm, a norm not acknowledged by the rule of recognition, is law. (The rule of recognition might hold that if norm N were part of the originally adopted constitution, then it is law; but they might all hold a false view about whether norm N was part of the originally adopted constitution.) If Hart's view is true, law unacknowledged by the rule of recognition is no law at all. Thus Hartian positivism violates Bix's constraint.

One might object at this point, claiming that while all of the legal officials could be confused about what is acknowledged as law by the rule of recognition, they could not all be confused about what the rule of recognition is. But while we should of course grant that the practice of legal officials is what makes the rule of recognition what it is, because the rule of recognition is not something that legal officials need to be able to make explicit, it is possible for all legal officials to be deeply confused about what the rule of recognition is. All that is really justified by the doctrine of the rule of recognition is that there is *something* about the actual practice of legal officials that fixes the content of the rule of recognition. But it is consistent with this position to hold that there is a necessary truth about whatever activities that we would be willing to call the 'actual practices of legal officials' that would commit us to affirming the view that the rule of recognition cannot confer legal validity on any rule that is insufficiently backed by reasons for action. It may be *false* that there is any such necessary truth. But it is by no means *incoherent* to hold this.

Indeed, it would suffice to show that Hartian positivism runs afoul of Bix's constraint that the Hartian doctrine of the rule of recognition implies *either* that all legal officials could be wrong about what the rule of recognition is *or* that all legal officials could be wrong about whether a particular instance is a law. Again, imagine a society in which all legal officials seem to be guided by the rule that if norm N were part of the originally adopted constitution, then it is law; all of them explicitly accept the rule 'if norm N is part of the originally adopted constitution, then it is law'; but all of them falsely believe that some instance, n, is part of the originally adopted constitution; thus all of them believe that n is law, and all of them would, were they to learn that n was not in fact part of the originally adopted constitution, cease to say that n is law. (Assume that n is not recognized as law by any other element of the rule of recognition.) We have to say one of the following: either all of the legal officials are confused when they say that 'if norm N is part of the originally adopted constitution, then it is law' is part of the rule of recognition, or all of the legal officials are wrong when they say that n is law. Both of these seem to run afoul of the constraint that, according to Bix, rules out the strong natural law thesis.

One final remark on the basic thesis of natural law jurisprudence. It is sometimes put forward as a criticism of natural law jurisprudence that it confuses law as it is with law as it ought to be. Now, if this were true, then it would count as a serious criticism. Excepting theories about God, any theory that identifies x's as they are with x's as they ought to be is false. But it is obvious that natural law jurisprudence is not open to the criticism as stated. First, as the weak natural law thesis allows that there may be laws that are defective, surely the weak view does not identify laws as they are with laws as they ought to be. So the only version of natural law jurisprudence that needs to take this criticism at all seriously would be the strong version. But, second, the objection does not apply to the strong version either. For it may be that there ought to be a law on some matter but there is not: the legislature might have neglected its responsibilities, and failed to pass the requisite law. Perhaps, then, the objection in its slogan form is not to be taken seriously: perhaps it is better read as the objection that, according to the natural law theorist, what ought not to be law is a subset of what is not law; if a measure ought not to be law, then the strong natural law view denies it that status. But this chastened objection misses the mark as well. For there may be norms that satisfy the strong natural law criteria and thus count as law, but nevertheless ought not to be law. It could be that there is a norm that is a slight deviation from justice, either in its content or in its manner of adoption, but with which nevertheless there is now decisive reason for compliance. (Imagine a tax law that gave slightly more to the worse-off than was their due.)

The objection is groundless. The natural law theorist, whether of the strong or the weak variety, is interested in asserting a connection between the law's existence and the law's prescriptive force. The objection assumes that the natural law theorist is interested in asserting a connection between the law's existence and the desirability of its existence. The connections between a would-be rule's prescriptive force and the desirability of its existence are contingent. There is no way to transform the objection so that it applies to a recognizable version of the natural law view.

We have not yet seen any reason to believe the stronger or the weaker readings of the natural law thesis. But we have seen that both of them emerge from the stock criticisms as live possibilities.

1.2 Natural Law Theory and Legal Positivism

There have recently been moves to create some sort of rapprochement between natural law jurisprudence and legal positivism. This is, in a way, surprising, for if there is anything that has defined legal positivism as a movement, it has been its rejection of natural law theory. The idea behind this rapprochement seems to be that the legal positivists have misunderstood what is central to the natural law position, so that what the positivists have been concerned to reject is in fact not essential to the natural law view and that what they have been concerned to affirm is compatible with, or even part of, the natural law view. We have already seen one such attempt at rapprochement – that is, the moral reading of the natural law theorist's thesis (1.1). If all there were to the natural law theorist's thesis were the opinion that some laws are so bad that they ought not to be obeyed, then it would be obvious that the positivist would have little to which to object. For legal positivism is a thesis about the existence of law, about when law is present, not a thesis about when obedience to law is due; and it has continuously been a theme in the writings of legal positivists to emphasize the fact that there could be bad law, law worthy of massive reform or even of disobedience (cf. Hart 1983c [1958]). But we have rejected the moral reading of the natural law thesis, insisting that the natural law thesis is jurisprudential rather than moral. To what extent are the jurisprudential readings of the natural law thesis that we have considered – the stronger and weaker theses – compatible with legal positivism?

There are as confusing a variety of statements of the fundamental claims of legal positivism as there are of the fundamental claims of natural law theory. But all of these views affirm something like what Coleman has called the "separation thesis," the claim that

> there exists at least one conceivable rule of recognition (and therefore one possible legal system) that does not specify truth as a moral principle among the truth conditions for any proposition of law. (Coleman 1982, p. 141)

A rule of recognition is, among other things, that rule by which other norms receive their status as law (Hart 1994 [1961], p. 100; for an account of the various functions of the rule of recognition, see Coleman 1996). So, according to the separation thesis as formulated by Coleman, there is a possible rule of recognition that confers the status of law on some norms irrespective of whether those norms are true moral principles.

While the separation thesis as formulated by Coleman surely would be affirmed by all legal positivists,[5] it can be made less narrow, and thus more informative, while not losing any positivist support. The first way in which

---

[5] See also, for example, Austin 1995 [1832], Lecture V, p. 157; Hart 1983c [1958], p. 55; Raz 1979a, pp. 39–40; and Gardner 2001, p. 201. I do not include Hobbes in this list, though he is characteristically described as a positivist (see, for example, Gardner 2001, p. 200). For one thing, Hobbes places content restrictions – restrictions that have their source in the natural law – on what can count as civil law (see Murphy 1995); for another thing, Hobbes's account of law includes that it proceed from the sovereign, where (unlike on Austin's view) a sovereign is defined in *moral* terms as the party to whom the members of the commonwealth have ceded their rights by way of a valid covenant. Thus Hobbes places constraints of merit on both the source of law and its content; this is a deeply non-positivist thing to do.

Coleman's formulation of the separation thesis is too narrow is by the exclusive focus on "moral principle": for, after all, positivists have been concerned not only to rule out the necessary connection of law and the domain of moral value specifically, but of law and the domain of practical reasonableness generally. The second way in which the formulation is too narrow is by appeal to the notion of "*truth* as a moral principle": as stated, the separation thesis is compatible with the claim that there is no conceivable rule of recognition that does not specify *consistency* with true moral principles among the truth conditions for any proposition of law. The separation thesis as the common thesis affirmed by positivists is thus better expressed as the view that there exists at least one possible rule of recognition (and therefore one possible legal system) that does not specify compatibility with true practical principles among the truth conditions for any proposition of law.

Clearly the strong reading of the natural law jurisprudence is incompatible with legal positivism's separation thesis. For, according to the strong reading, it is part of the truth conditions for the existence of law that law be backed by decisive reasons for action. Any alleged rule of recognition that confers the status of law on a norm that is not thus backed by reasons must therefore be impossible. There are, of course, some things that the defender of the strong reading can say to the positivist as a matter of concession. He or she can allow, for example, that there is a technical sense of legal validity that can be employed by citizens and is the stock in trade of lawyers and judges, the standards for which do not or may not include any appeal to practical principles; and he or she can allow that there are good reasons to have this limited, technical sense of legal validity available as a *lingua franca* for those otherwise inclined to disagree on questions of practical reasonableness. But the defender of the strong reading can go no further than this: the defender of that view must reject the separation thesis outright.

The weak reading of the natural law thesis is, however, entirely compatible with at least the letter of legal positivism. For it is compatible with the weak reading that departures from conformity with true practical principles do not necessarily preclude norms from attaining the status of law; such departures may, given the weak reading's view, do no more than to make those norms defective as law. It is consistent with the weak natural law thesis that there be rules of recognition that recognize as law norms that are quite deficient as rational directives. And the compatibility of legal positivism with this sort of natural law view has been remarked upon by positivists. Here is Neil MacCormick who, while affirming the weak reading, calls himself a positivist:

Of course there may be legislation properly enacted by competent authorities which falls far short of or cuts against the demands of justice. The validity of the relevant statutory norms as members of the given system of law is not as such put into doubt by their injustice. The legal duties they impose, or the legal rights they grant, do not stop being genuinely legal duties or legal rights in virtue of the moral wrongfulness of their imposition or conferment. *They are, however, defective or substandard or corrupt instances of what they genuinely are – laws, legal duties, legal rights.*

(MacCormick 1992, p. 108, emphasis added)

And while there are, no doubt, those positivists who have explicitly claimed that views such as the weak natural law thesis ought to be rejected (cf. Kramer 1999), they have recognized the need for further argument in order to do so: the weak natural law thesis is not ruled out by any formulation of legal positivism that is itself uncontroversial among positivists. So there is no reason to think *ab initio* that the affirmation of the weak natural law thesis must involve the rejection of legal positivism.

One might, however, claim that although affirmation of the weak natural law thesis is compatible with the *letter* of legal positivism, it is somehow contrary to the *spirit* of positivism. For if the weak natural law thesis is true, it follows that one cannot have a complete descriptive theory of law without having a complete understanding of the requirements of practical reasonableness. For one cannot have a complete descriptive theory of law without an exhaustive account of the ways that law can be defective, and one cannot have an exhaustive account of the ways that law can be defective without having a complete understanding of the requirements of practical reasonableness. And surely it is contrary to positivist theoretical aims, even if not to the explicit formulations of positivist theses, to hold that a complete understanding of the requirements of practical reasonableness is necessary for a complete description of law.

That one cannot have an exhaustive account of the ways that law can be defective without having a complete understanding of the requirements of practical reasonableness is a pretty straightforward inference from the weak natural law thesis. But what is the warrant for claiming that there cannot be a complete descriptive theory of law without an exhaustive account of the ways that law can be defective? The first point to note is that in any of those cases that are not here at issue, we would find very peculiar a theory of x's that claimed to be a complete descriptive theory of x's but did not offer an exhaustive account of the ways that x's can be defective. Suppose, for example, that I claimed to have an exhaustive descriptive theory of automobiles, but freely acknowledged that I did not have an exhaustive account of when automobiles are defective and when they are not. Or suppose that I claimed to have an exhaustive theory of the kidney, but freely acknowledged that I did not have an exhaustive account of when kidneys are defective and when they are not.[6] It seems perfectly obvious in

---

[6] One has not said nearly enough in providing a theory of automobiles if one has not provided an account of their function. But to commit oneself to a view of automobile function is to commit oneself to a view of automobile defectiveness. And so if one is to give a complete descriptive account of automobiles, it must include a complete account of the automobile's function, and to provide a complete account of the automobile's function, one

these cases that a complete descriptive theory of the automobile or kidney would include a correspondingly complete theory of automobile or kidney defect. The burden of proof, then, seems to be on one who would hold that one can have a complete descriptive theory of law without a complete account of when and how law can be defective. But I have not the slightest idea how one would meet this burden.

Insofar, then, as positivism has presupposed a methodology that allows one to proceed further in jurisprudence without commitment to a particular conception of how agents ought individually and collectively to act, defenders of the weak natural law thesis must reject positivist methodology; no rapprochement is possible on this issue. As I noted at the beginning of this book (0.2), the natural law jurisprudential thesis can be formulated and initially defended without appeal to the particulars of a moral or political theory. But the weak natural law thesis, once defended, implies that a rich jurisprudence – even one that aims to be just descriptively adequate – cannot forego moral and political theory (cf. Finnis 1980, pp. 15–19).

---

must include a complete account of the automobile's defectiveness conditions. The same argument obviously applies *mutatis mutandis* to kidneys. (One might, of course, deny that the notion of defect strictly and literally applies to natural objects like kidneys. But that is not what is at issue here. What is at issue is, given that the notion of defect non-vacuously applies to kidneys, whether a complete descriptive theory of kidneys could fail to provide a proper account of kidney defect.)

2

Natural Law Jurisprudence Defended

2.1 Three Routes to the Weak Natural Law Thesis

The strong natural law thesis holds that law unbacked by decisive reasons for compliance is no law at all. The weak natural law thesis holds that law unbacked by decisive reasons for compliance is defective precisely as law. I have two central aims in this chapter – first, to defend the truth of the weak natural law thesis; second, to show that the success of this defense of the weak natural law thesis is not merely a way station to the defense of the strong natural law thesis but provides the premises to call the strong natural law thesis into question. So while the standard criticisms of natural law jurisprudence (1.1) fall short of providing serious reasons to reject the strong natural law thesis, reasons to reject the strong thesis emerge in prosecuting the task of defending the natural law view.

I will consider three initially plausible routes to the weak natural law thesis. What makes each of these an initially plausible route to that thesis is that each exhibits on its face a technique for distinguishing between law's existence conditions and its non-defectiveness conditions, and provides some clue to identifying what law's non-defectiveness conditions are. One route, the 'legal point of view' route endorsed by Finnis, appeals to the notion that there is a distinctively legal point of view, and it is law as characterized from this point of view that is paradigmatically law (2.2). Another route, the 'law as functional kind' argument described, but not quite endorsed, by Moore, appeals to the notion that law has a function, and fails to perform that function if not backed by decisive reasons for compliance (2.3). A third route, the 'law as illocutionary act' argument, likens or identifies law with speech-acts of a certain sort, and notes that the non-defectiveness conditions of these speech-acts obtain only if law is backed by decisive reasons for compliance (2.4).[1] I will not endorse the

---

[1] One might be surprised that I fail to consider Dworkin's views here, since Dworkin expresses at least a limited willingness to describe himself as an advocate of natural law theory

first of these arguments: it seems to me that the legal point of view argument generates theses of normative rather than descriptive jurisprudence. But the second and third of these argumentative strategies succeed; and that they both succeed is not merely a (suspicious) coincidence (2.5).

2.2 The Legal Point of View and the Weak Natural Law Thesis

Finnis writes that we should not hope to provide an account of the necessary and sufficient conditions for law, such that some legal systems and individual norms and decisions in cases will count as law through exemplifying these conditions, whereas the remainder will not. Rather, we should hope for an account that provides us with the central, paradigmatic instances of law and legality. With this account, we will be able to classify some social systems and social norms as clearly law, some as entirely extralegal, and some as simply falling short of or distinct from the central case in one or another specific way (Finnis 1980, pp. 9–11).

Finnis's argument for the natural law thesis is that the natural law thesis thus drops out of Hart's and Raz's jurisprudential method, a method that in Finnis's view has shown itself to be fundamentally sound. Finnis writes in praise of Hartian and Razian jurisprudence that Hart's and Raz's views were able to advance so far beyond earlier positivist views by their more-or-less self-conscious employment of three methodological features: attention to the practical point of legal systems, use of a focal meaning approach to definition, and adoption of the viewpoint of those who take an insider's point of view. It is the third of these that serves as the basis for Finnis's argument for the natural law thesis. Hart had argued against earlier positivist views that such views had failed to take into account the point of view of the person who takes the internal point of view with respect to a legal system, treating it as a standard by which he or she guides his or her conduct. So Hart's view privileges the internal point of view, and it is the point of view of one who treats the law as a standard for conduct. Hart is insistent that no further differentiation of the internal point of view is called for. People who treat the law as a basis for their conduct out of a calculation of long-term advantage, on a whim, out of altruistic concerns, out of the demands of morality, to please their parents, to conform to time-honored tradition, and so on are all taking the internal point of view, and Hart is not interested in taking their different motives as shaping his theory of law (Hart 1994 [1961], p. 203).

(Dworkin 1982, p. 165). But it is hard to square the notion of Dworkin as natural law theorist with Dworkin's limited theoretical ambitions – that is, to provide an account simply of *our* practice of law: "General theories of law, for us, are general interpretations of our own legal practice" (Dworkin 1986, p. 410). A parochial natural law theory is no natural law theory at all.

Finnis's argument for the natural law thesis is to take Hart's starting point – that analytical jurisprudence must adequately take into account this insider's point of view – and to try to show that its characterization of the internal point of view is too undifferentiated, that it fails to take into account that some of these insiders' points of view are more paradigmatically insiders' points of view than others. By Finnis's lights, there is a clearly *most central* internal point of view with respect to the law:

If there is a point of view in which legal obligation is treated as at least presumptively a moral obligation . . . , a viewpoint in which the establishment and maintenance of a legal as distinct from discretionary or statically customary order is regarded as a moral ideal if not a compelling demand of justice, then such a viewpoint will constitute the central case of the legal viewpoint.   (Finnis 1980, pp. 14–15)

But even within this central legal viewpoint, we should note the following distinction:

Among those who, from a practical viewpoint, treat law as an aspect of practical reason-ableness, there will be some whose views about what practical reasonableness actually requires in this domain are, in detail, more reasonable than others. Thus the central case viewpoint itself is the viewpoint of those who not only appeal to practical reasonableness but also are practically reasonable.   (Finnis 1980, p. 15)

Law that fails to be morally obligatory will be seen, from this central legal viewpoint, as defective, deficient, falling short. And since the central legal viewpoint is the proper vantage point from which to do analytical jurisprudence, we have a basis for holding that law that fails to serve as a mandatory requirement of practical reasonableness is defective precisely as law.

This strategy is meant only to establish the weak natural law thesis, and it is obvious that it can establish no more than that: its appeal to the central, paradigmatic notion of law is not meant to preclude the presence of a limited, technical sense of legal validity. But it is hard to see why we would follow Finnis in his extension of Hart's methodology on the basis of this argument. Hart has good reason for taking the burden of proof to be on those who wish to make some particular version of the internal point of view more privileged: while his arguments against the legal realists show that legal theory must account for the datum that people can take the internal point of view with respect to a system of legal norms (Hart 1994 [1961], pp. 88–91), this datum just is that people treat the existence of legal rules as reasons or constituent parts of reasons for action; it does not naturally extend further to the *basis* on which they so treat those norms. Far from the internal point of view's just being an "amalgam" of different viewpoints, Hart's undifferentiated take has a clear rationale, and so is not unstable; it is up to Finnis to destabilize it. But nothing he says in the crucial stretch of argument discussed above succeeds in destabilizing it. The law tends not to care for the motivations that one has for complying with it; and while

Finnis appeals to the greater efficacy of some points of view in generating a legal system, one might rightly retort not only that the tasks of explaining how a legal system comes into being and explaining what it is for a legal system to be in place are, while interestingly related, different questions, but also that there are some points of view that may have greater efficacy in generating and sustaining a legal system than that of the person of full practical reasonableness – for example, that of the person who holds a false tribal or nationalistic morality.

By so closely identifying the task of characterizing law with the task of saying what a fully practical reasonable person should be interested in when dealing with the law, Finnis's view seems to become simply applied ethics – he is asking what features of the law the fully reasonable citizen, or the fully reasonable judge, should be interested in responding to, and in particular what features of the law are such that, when present, the fully reasonable citizen or judge may treat the law as authoritative. But this seems to make Finnis's view too much like the uninteresting moral reading, leaving his critics to wonder what all the fuss was about natural law theory (1.1). This massive privileging of the internal perspective carries Finnis beyond the descriptive jurisprudence that he takes himself, along with Hart and Raz, to be practicing, and into a more straightforwardly normative jurisprudence. (One might wonder whether Finnis did take himself to be doing descriptive jurisprudence. That he did seems to me very clear – see Finnis 1980, p. 21 – though for a contrary view, see Leiter 2003, pp. 33–37.)

It seems, then, that Finnis's argument here for the centrality of the point of view of the party who treats the law as presumptively obligatory is, to say the least, not self-sufficient. Hart repeatedly compares legal rules to rules of games, and it is useful here as well. In understanding the rules of cricket, one needs to understand them not just from a third-person perspective, but from the perspective of a participant in the game: one needs to understand how the rules of cricket function in the decision-making of players and officials in a cricket match. But it is not relevant *why* the cricketer takes the rules of cricket as a guide to his conduct. All the descriptive theorist need do is provide an account of those rules that shows how it is possible for one to take such a stance with respect to its rules. Now, law is not cricket, and so it might be that there is reason to privilege the view of one who treats the law as morally obligatory, while there is not reason to privilege the view of one who treats the rules of cricket as governing his conduct for some particular reasons. But the explanation will have to be driven by something other than remarks about point of view; it will instead have to be driven by some features of law that distinguish its rules from the rules of cricket. Perhaps these will be further facts about the *function* of law, in contrast to the function of cricket; or perhaps these will be further facts about the *claims* made by legal officials, those in a privileged position to speak on behalf of the law, that contrast with claims made by cricket officials. And both of these do seem to be fruitful points of departure for defenses of the natural law thesis.

2.3 Law's Function and the Weak Natural Law Thesis

A promising line of argument for the weak natural law thesis takes as its starting point the common notion of *function*. We can, according to this line of argument, see that some legal systems or individual legal norms have non-defectiveness conditions that include the presence of reasons for action by getting clear on the functions of those systems or of those norms. One might worry that this sort of argument for the natural law thesis is doomed to triviality: what could be easier, one might ask, than to assign a morally charged function to law and then, on the basis of such an ascription, hold that law that does not perform this function, or perform it satisfactorily, is either no law at all or law only defectively? It is obvious that no interesting argument for the natural law thesis that proceeds from the idea that the law has a function can follow this pattern. But the ascription of a function to an object is a much more constrained matter than such an argument would suggest. I cannot simply assign the function 'keeping New Haven populated' to law professors, and then declare that law school faculty who do not reside in New Haven are no law professors at all, or are law professors only defectively. What *are* the conditions that must be met to ascribe a function to some object or institution, and how can these be brought to bear to show that one or another formulation of the natural law thesis is correct?

Roughly (and not at all originally, and not entirely uncontroversially), we can say that for an x to have the function of ϕ-ing, the following conditions must be satisfied:

(*characteristic activity*) x is the kind of thing that ϕs
(*goal productivity*) x's ϕ-ing tends to bring about some end-state S
(*teleology*) x ϕs because x's ϕ-ing tends to bring about some end-state S
(*value*) S exhibits some relevant variety of goodness

There is reason to think that each of these conditions is individually necessary; and there is reason to think that they are jointly sufficient. The heart has a characteristic activity: it pumps. Its pumping tends to bring about the circulation of the blood, and indeed the heart pumps because its pumping contributes to the circulation of the blood. (This is so in two ways: in animals with hearts, there is a feedback loop such that the circulation of the blood is in part what causes the heart to be able to continue pumping; and the very structure and activity of the heart was selected because of efficiency in causing the circulation of the blood.) Some would take these first three conditions to be jointly sufficient, but it seems to me that it is also important that the circulation of the blood is beneficial for the animal. As Mark Bedau has noted, a stick pinned against a rock in a stream by the backwash that that very stick has created may exhibit the first three features: it is pinned against a rock, its being pinned against a rock causes the backwash, and it is pinned against the rock because its being pinned against the rock causes the backwash. But no one would be tempted by the view that it is the stick's function to be pinned against the rock (Bedau 1992a, p. 786). One way to accommodate such cases is to emphasize that functions are ascribed when there is, in some sense, a good realized through the activity: either an end sought out by the designer of the object, or the self-maintenance of the thing in question, or the like (see also Bedau 1992b and Murphy 2001a, pp. 26–28).

To show, then, that the natural law thesis is true in virtue of the law's function (or one of the law's functions), one needs to show that these various conditions are satisfied, and that a particular legal system or law fails to perform its function when it fails to serve as a rational standard for conduct. An instance of this strategy is the argument offered by Moore. Moore has suggested that the most promising route to the natural law jurisprudential thesis is through an argument concerning the function of law. When characterizing the nature of law, writers have often thought that law is to be defined in terms of some set of distinctive structures. But Moore wants to say that it is far more likely that law is to be defined in terms of its *function*, by its serving some end. In order for this to be the case, Moore claims, we would have to find some *distinctive* goal that law serves – otherwise, we would not be able to define law in terms of the function of serving that goal. If it turns out that there is such an end, then if it can be shown that law must be moral-obligation-imposing in order to promote this goal, then we have a basis to say that there is a necessary dependence of law on moral obligation: law must be morally obligatory, and any norm that cannot be morally obligatory cannot be law. Indeed, Moore thinks that if the premises of this argument can be established, the conclusion would be the strong natural law thesis (Moore 1992 and Moore 2001).

As Moore notes, there are all sorts of difficulties involved in making out a plausible argument that fits this schema. His constraint on definition by functional-kind-membership generates, on his view, a dilemma for the natural law theorist: either the attempt to define law in terms of its serving some end will fail, or the attempt to show that the law must be moral-obligation-imposing in order for it to serve this end will fail. The problem is this. In order for law to be defined by its serving some end, that end must be distinctive – it must be an end that is served *only* through or by law. So the goal that law serves cannot simply be 'everything that is worth pursuing and promoting.' But, Moore wonders, how can anything short of 'everything that is worth pursuing and promoting' be the source of the moral obligation that is, on the natural law theorist's view, essential to human law?[2]

---

[2] Moore suggests a tentative response to this dilemma: that the end that law serves, while not identical to "all the values there are," is so connected to their realization that moral obligation can result. Moore takes Finnis's understanding of the common good, which is the sum total of those conditions that individuals can draw upon in order to realize their own choiceworthy conceptions of the good (Finnis 1980, p. 154; for discussion, see 3.3), to be potentially such an end (Moore 1992, p. 223).

As the argument is laid out, the second horn of the dilemma strikes me as unproblematic. For as Moore sets out the argument, it is not necessary that the source of the moral obligation to obey the law be identical with the goal that law serves. So one might hold that while there is some distinctive goal S that law serves, it is not the law's serving S that is alone sufficient to make law morally obligatory. It might be, however, that for S to be served, or to be served properly, people must be under a moral obligation to obey the law, and this moral obligation might arise from various sources – consent, fairness with respect to the promotion of S, gratitude to the law for helping us to promote S, and so forth. If there is a genuine difficulty to which Moore's formulation of the second horn of the dilemma points, it is that of finding some end of law that can be promoted *only through* obligatory norms, regardless of the source of that obligation. Suppose, for example, that serving the Finnisian common good (3.3) were the function of law. It is obvious that this can be served other than through means that impose obligations. Moore mentions that a regime of sanctions might do the trick (Moore 1992, p. 225). Or a set of common standards that did not impose obligations might be sufficient in a community where citizens were extremely public-minded and extremely conformist. Their public-spiritedness and conformism could be sufficient to lead them to act on a common standard.

More troubling still is the difficulty that it just seems obvious that there is no good 'distinctively served by law' in Moore's sense. There is no good that is served *only* by institutions that could by any stretch of the imagination be thought of as legal systems. The Finnisian common good, Dworkinian integrity (Dworkin 1986, pp. 95–96) – these can be served by institutions that are obviously pretheoretically extralegal. Moore sees the problem and thinks that, if this is true, then the upshot is that law cannot be a purely functional kind (Moore 1992, p. 223).

While I agree there is a real concern in the vicinity, part of the fault must lie with Moore's overly strict understanding of what makes something a functional kind. There is, so far as I can see, no reason to think that for something to be a functional kind it must be adequately marked off simply in terms of its serving some goal. As we have seen, functional kinds are typically marked off by the serving of some goal *through some characteristic activity*. Thus, functional ascriptions involve both ends and means: to say that x is a member of functional kind F is to say, in part, that its characteristic activity of ϕ-ing tends toward the realization of some particular end-state S. Not every x whose characteristic activity tends toward the realization of the same end-state S belongs to the same functional kind, for their characteristic activities may be of such different sorts that they could not be placed in the same kind. Moore is obviously right that *heart* is a functional kind, that there could be hearts of various structures and made of various materials. But while the end of the heart is to circulate the blood, it is clear that only objects whose characteristic activity is that of *pumping* can be classified as hearts.

What causes unnecessary trouble for Moore's argument is his spartan understanding of functional kinds in which such kinds are individuated entirely by
the ends they serve. Given an understanding of functional kinds in which such
kinds are individuated also by the characteristic activities of the members of
that kind, it could be that it is law's characteristic activity for the sake of its end
that provides the needed support for the natural law thesis. So, one might say
that while legal systems might promote various ends, all of these involve the
imposition of order; but one might say that it is the characteristic activity of law
to realize this end through the provision of rules with which agents have decisive reason to comply. This would give us reason to say that the (or a) function
of law is to impose order by laying down rules with which agents have decisive
reasons to comply. And thus the natural law thesis would take its warrant not
from the end that law serves (as in Moore's view) but from the characteristic
activity of law in serving this end.

It is clear that there is nothing incoherent about holding that it is some
object's function to provide dictates backed by decisive reasons for action, and
thus that that object would be defective if its dictates were to fail to be backed
by such reasons. Suppose, for example, that I attempt to build a 'reason-backed
rule' machine. When a person pulls the handle of the machine, the machine
is supposed to display on its screen a rule, in the handle-puller's language,
with which the handle-puller has decisive reason to comply. It is an accurate
description of the machine to say that its function is to exhibit rules with which
its operators have decisive reason to comply. If one is going to provide a fuller
account of when the machine is functioning as it is designed to function and
when it is not, one would have to draw on one's views, theorized or not, about
what agents have reason to do: if, for example, you were to pull the handle on
the machine and it were to display "You should give one-third of your income
to Oxfam," you would not be able to say whether the machine is functioning as
designed unless you could say whether one in circumstances such as yours has
reasons to make sacrifices of this sort. So normative conditions enter into the
account of the machine's function, and normative argument would be needed
to establish when the machine is defective and when it is not. But there is
no doubt that the ascription of this function to the machine is a descriptive
matter: we are describing what the machine's function is, not imposing such
a function or recommending that we conceive of the machine as having that
function.

Now, in the case of this reason-backed rule machine, it is easy to see why
the giving of dictates backed by decisive reasons for action is its characteristic
activity: we have an authoritative statement from the designer of the artifact that
this activity is what the machine is meant to do. How, then, would one show that
this is the law's characteristic activity? Since we lack an authoritative statement
from the designer of the institution of law, we might be suspicious of the claim

that we could come up with a defensible account of law's characteristic activity, or suspicious of the claim that any such account would include 'provide rules backed by decisive reasons for action' among law's characteristic activities. But we need not be suspicious of the possibility of providing an account of the law's function; and once we see how this can be done, it turns out that the ascription of the function 'provides rules backed by decisive reasons for action' is plausible after all.

Consider, first, how you would show that the reason-backed dictates machine has the function of providing dictates backed by decisive reasons for action in the absence of an authoritative statement from the machine's designer. All you have at your disposal is your observations of what people do to the machine, of the machine's outputs, the inner workings of the machine, and the environments in which the machine operates. Suppose that you have the following evidence. The machine's handle is often pulled by rational beings. Usually the machine's output is a dictate with which the handle-puller has decisive reason to comply. That the machine's output is a dictate with which the handle-puller has decisive reason to comply is explicable by appeal to the inner workings of the machine: its parts are, most of the time, structured so that the machine's output is a dictate backed by decisive reasons. When there appear several dictates that are not backed by decisive reasons for action, this is explainable by some change in the inner workings or environment of the machine, and people appear and begin to tinker with the inner workings of the machine or move the machine to a different environment or try to alter the present environment, and they do this until the machine again begins to produce a series of dictates backed by decisive reasons for action. This is the sort of evidence you would need to ascribe the function of providing dictates backed by decisive reasons for action to the machine: its activity is to provide such dictates, and it seems to be constructed and adjusted to enable it to continue to carry out that activity.

The way to show that it is law's function to provide dictates backed by decisive reasons for action is, then, as Moore suggests: look at the various ways that systems pre-theoretically designated as 'legal' operate, and see whether their activities tend to be explicable in terms of, and regulated by, the giving of dictates backed by decisive reasons. One might note the features of legal systems to which Raz has drawn our attention – that they claim to be authoritative (see Raz 1979b, p. 30) and that, characteristically, their dictates go with the flow of normative reasons rather than against them (Raz 1985 and Raz 1986, pp. 53–69). One might note the way that law characteristically ties sanctions to certain activities, which sanctions give agents further reason to abstain from them. One might also take notice of Fuller's eight ways to fail to make law: on his view, putative legal rules can fail to achieve legality when they are *ad hoc*, inadequately promulgated, retroactive, incomprehensible, contradictory, requiring conduct adherence to which is beyond the powers of subjects, ephemeral, or insincere (see Fuller 1964, p. 39). For our purposes, what is relevant about Fuller's eight ways is that each of them indicates in some way in which law can fail to serve as a reason for action for those living under it. On the basis of such considerations, one might well come to the conclusion that it is part of law's characteristic activity to lay down norms with which agents will have decisive reason to comply. Even, then, if the end that law's characteristic activity serves is itself not an obviously obligatory end – if it is, to follow Hart and Fuller, something like that of realizing social order, or social control – the natural law thesis could be sustained if law's characteristic activity is to provide dictates that are rational standards for conduct and that it provides these dictates as a means to, and because they are a means to, realizing social order.

Now, one might retort: it can hardly be the case that it is law's characteristic activity to provide dictates that are rational standards for conduct, when it is clear that so many dictates of law are no such thing. To take the low road, we can appeal to cases as dramatic as the Fugitive Slave Law or as banal as parking ordinances. To take the high road, we can appeal to the growing literature in support of the claim that the law lacks authority, that its dictates do not in fact typically constitute decisive reasons for agents to comply with them.[3]

The initial response here is just that to say that ϕ-ing is x's characteristic activity is not to say that all x's always ϕ. It is to say that x's are *the kind of thing that ϕ*, and this is compatible with there being instances – even perhaps in the majority of cases – where x's fail to ϕ. But the retort does raise an important question: how do we know that these cases in which law fails to provide dictates that are backed by decisive reasons for action count not as counterexamples to the claim that this is law's characteristic activity but rather as cases in which law is failing to perform its characteristic activity?

With artifacts, often the answer is easy: our source of information about what kind an object belongs to, and what is the characteristic activity of that kind, is usually determined at least in large part by the maker's intentions. But with law, as with other large-scale social institutions, we have something that is not the product of some thinker's intentions. Here the more apt analogies are the systems of organisms. We know that a heart's characteristic activity is to pump blood, and that this is its function; and we can know this without appeal a designer's intentions. We can know this in spite of the fact that animals can have heart attacks. We say that the heart's characteristic activity is to pump blood not just because of statistical frequency – again, we can imagine states of affairs in which heart attacks were disastrously more frequent, and this would give us reason to say that hearts were malfunctioning all over the place, not that its characteristic activity had changed or that we were wrong about what

---

[3] The literature is large and growing. Influential pieces include Simmons 1979, Raz 1979a, Smith 1973, and Green 1990. The literature has been surveyed in Edmundson 1999b, 1999c, and (most extensively) in Edmundson 2004.

its characteristic activity is. We persist in the judgment that the characteristic activity is pumping blood because judgments of characteristic activity are made against a background, a privileged background of normalcy. An object's departure from its characteristic activity is to be accounted for through appeal to a change in the normal background.

To sustain the claim that law's characteristic activity is to provide dictates with which agents have decisive reason to comply, even in the face of divergences from this activity, we have to say that in such cases, the privileged background for the description of institutions such as the law does not obtain, and that departures from the activity of providing dictates with which agents have decisive reason to comply is to be explained by reference to the departure from this background. Here is the crucial move: the background from which human institutions are to be assessed, so far as possible, is one in which humans are properly functioning. But human beings are rational animals, and when properly functioning act on what the relevant reasons require. And so law would not be able to realize the end of order by giving dictates in a world in which humans are properly functioning unless those dictates are backed by adequate reasons. Thus we should say that it is law's characteristic activity to provide dictates backed by compelling reasons for action, and that law that fails to do so is defective as law.

As I said earlier, the crucial move is to hold that the privileged background of normalcy for assessing human institutions like law is, so far as possible, that in which humans are properly functioning. This conception of the normal background is, I hope, intuitively appealing, but it can also be defended in terms of the constraints under which functions are ascribed to systems and their parts. When a system has a function, and its parts also have functions, it is important to have – again, as far as possible – an account of the system's and the parts' functions according to which those functions are not at odds with one another. For to have a function is, in part, to tend toward an equilibrium state; and so for the system's and the parts' ascribed functions to be at odds with each other is to call into question either the view that the putative parts genuinely are parts of that system or the view that the functions have been correctly ascribed to the system or to the parts. For if the system's and its parts' activities are at odds with each other, then either the system or its parts will fail to tend toward its ascribed equilibrium state, and thus we should either revise our specific functional attributions to the system and its parts or reassess our understanding of one or more items as parts of that system.

The ascription of functions to systems and their parts thus proceeds in a way that generates coordination between them, and in the abstract, there is no reason to think that our judgments of the function of the system should be more or less prone to revisions than our judgments of the function of the parts of that system. But there is a class of cases in which the function of the parts does have priority over the function of the system: it is that class of cases in which the parts have a function (logically) independent of and (logically) prior to their existence as parts of that system. This is true with respect to law. In understanding the function of legal systems and of laws within those systems, there is excellent reason to treat the function of the parts as fixed, as the background by which the function of law is understood: for humans are natural objects whose basic proper functioning is prior to the various institutions in which they find or make for themselves. And so the assessment of law in functional terms rightly presupposes as its privileged background properly functioning human beings.

There may of course remain some skepticism about the notion that law is to be understood in functional terms at all, so that dictates that do not live up to those standards are defective as law. Another way to reduce this skepticism is to note that there are non-legal phenomena that also seem to call for functional analyses, the particular functional analyses of which implicate reasons for action. Consider the ("first, rough") notion of a convention as characterized by Lewis:

A regularity R in the behavior of members of a population P when they are in a recurrent situation S is a convention if and only if, in any instance of S among members of P,
1. everyone conforms to R;
2. everyone expects everyone else to conform to R;
3. everyone prefers to conform to R on condition that the others do, since S is a coordination problem and uniform conformity to R is a proper coordination equilibrium in S.

(Lewis 1969, p. 42)

This definition is a functional definition: we cannot properly understand conventions except as ways of solving problems of certain sorts. And it would not be surprising to say that some regularities of behavior are conventions, but defective: a regularity of behavior that is not universally preferred among the members of P but which can survive and be preferred by the vast majority of P, even in awareness of the existence of defectors, can be plausibly described as a convention, though in some ways a defective one. Nor would it be surprising to say that even a convention that meets Lewis's first statement of the criteria is defective: if uniform conformity to R_1 is a coordination equilibrium in S yet there is an available Pareto-superior coordination equilibrium R_2 in S, then we might think of R_1 as in one important way defective: while it does what conventions are supposed to do, it does not do it as well as R_2 would have.

Functional analysis is inescapable in dealing with convention, and there is little reason to worry about the way that functional analysis of conventions implicates practical rationality. Neither then should we balk at functional analysis of law or at the notion that the proper functional analysis of law appeals to certain sorts of reasons for compliance.

2.4 Illocutionary Acts and the Weak Natural Law Thesis

The third plausible route to the weak natural law thesis appeals to the idea that laws are or are akin to illocutionary acts. I will argue, first, that it is legitimate to understand the law as a speaker, and that a mandatory legal norm just is the law's demand to those under its jurisdiction that they carry out a certain course of action. However, it is one of the non-defectiveness conditions on demands that there be decisive reasons for the party to whom the demand is issued to comply with the demand. It thus follows that mandatory legal norms are essentially defective if they are not backed by decisive reasons for compliance: and this is equivalent to the weak natural law thesis as applied to mandatory legal norms. I will conclude the illocutionary acts argument for the weak natural law thesis by extending the argument offered for mandatory legal norms to other sorts of laws.

The Law as Speaker

It is commonplace, both in ordinary talk and in philosophical writing, to attribute to the law the performance of speech-acts of various sorts. No one is or would be puzzled by the report that United States law demands that residents pay their taxes by April 15; or by the report that United States law once declared that blacks are not and could not be citizens, but that now it does not say this; or by the report that Virginia law tells us that a valid will must, *inter alia*, be signed by two witnesses. And philosophers, though with a bit more hesitation, have been willing to treat the law and its institutions as a speaker. A central thesis of Raz's jurisprudence is that the law claims to be a practical authority.[4] While there has been a great deal of disagreement concerning the content of what Raz holds the law to claim (see, for example, Soper 2002, pp. 51–88), those responding to Raz have been mostly content to allow the legitimacy of treating the law as itself a speaker.

Now, one might complain that this way of describing the law's activities seems to presuppose a very peculiar "animism" (Moore's term: see his 1987, p. 837), or more particularly, *anthropomorphism* vis-à-vis the law by ascribing to the law claims, assertions, demands. While there have been some sketches of defenses of this way of treating the law, these sketches, while seeming to be on the right track, nevertheless require further filling out before we can be confident of the legitimacy of treating the law as a speaker. Leslie Green, for example, defends the propriety of speaking of the state's making claims to authority as follows.

Is it not a dangerous metaphor to speak of the state 'acting' and 'making claims' on us . . . ? Not all metaphors are dangerous, however, and this one has utility in avoiding

---

[4] See the discussions in Raz 1979a, pp. 29–33, 146–159, and Raz 1984a, pp. 123–131.

cumbersome circumlocutions about the activities of the officials of the state, in particular its legislative and executive officials. Of course when we say the state claims our
allegiance we are only summarizing certain politically relevant actions of officials: that
they have passed a law which purports to impose obligations on us, that the police and
courts regard these obligations as binding and will enforce them, and so on. In principle,
we could replace talk of the state as an agent with a more convoluted vocabulary of
individuals, officials, and social rules, but there would be little profit in it.

(Green 1990, p. 66)

In fairness to Green, he is clearly here only gesturing at the form such an account
would take, and such gestures are to be assessed by whether they illuminate
promising ways that a full account of the notion of the state as a speaker might
be developed; and it does seem that the appeal to the activities of officials –
real, live, paradigmatic speakers – would be a helpful way to clarify the law's
status as a speaker. But it also contains seeds of doubt. For when Green does
spell out some of what is involved in the state's making claims, he relies on the
notion that there is "a law which purports to impose obligations on us"; and
surely the notion that the law *purports* to be doing something is not a bit less
anthropomorphic on its face than the notion that the state *claims* to be doing
something.

Raz and Green are right to follow common talk in allowing the propriety of
ascribing speech-acts to the law, but it is worth examining why the ascription
of speech-acts to the law is appropriate; the propriety of such ascriptions is
central to my argument for the weak natural law thesis, and any suspicions that
this way of thinking of the law really is mere metaphor and insusceptible of
illuminating analysis will cast doubt on that argument. We can begin with the
more general question. What conditions must be satisfied for *any* entity to be a
speaker?

For an entity to be a speaker, it must be susceptible of a certain range of belief
and desire-states; it must be susceptible of a certain range of normative stand-
ings; and it must be capable of producing a certain range of events. Normal adult
human beings paradigmatically satisfy the constraints in question. They are able
to form beliefs, desires and intentions; they are able to subject themselves to
critical standards of appraisal; and they are capable of producing auditory and
visual events that express beliefs, desires, and intentions, and thereby make
themselves responsible in specific ways. For example: a paradigmatic asserter
is able to form beliefs about the propositions that he or she asserts; can express
those beliefs in virtue of his or her capacity to grasp and use certain words
and phrases; can intentionally produce the requisite words and phrases; and
can thereby make himself or herself responsible for the content and occasion
of the utterance, subject to adverse criticism for any mistaken assertion.[5] Now,

---

[5] Different views on the nature of illocutionary acts place these necessary features of speak-
erhood in different orders of explanatory importance: some views place the expression of

it is clear that the law will not be a paradigmatic speaker. *Believing that p* and *desiring that p* and *being responsible for p* are states of minded beings, and the law, unlike humans, angels, and God, does not have a mind and thus cannot possess beliefs and desires in the standard way and cannot be a responsible agent in the most straightforward sense. The question, though, is not whether the law is a paradigmatic speaker but whether it is legitimate to ascribe these features to law in any more than a metaphorical sense.

The law as believer and desirer. On the one hand, we have paradigmatic believers and desirers – that is, mature adult human beings. On the other hand, we have objects to which beliefs and desires are sometimes ascribed, but in what is a clearly metaphorical way. I sometimes say that my computer thinks that I am pushing the 'a' key when I in fact am not, or that my car wants to engage its traction control system at the slightest hint of ice on the road. But while speaking thus of my computer and my car is intelligible – everybody knows what I mean when I say these things – its intelligibility is through interpretation by metaphor. But the notion that the law believes or wants something is not metaphorical in this way. The believing and wanting of the law occupies an intermediate place between the paradigmatic believing and wanting of natural persons and the merely metaphorical believing and wanting of artifacts such as the computer and the car.

Begin with desire. What the literal desiring of the human and the metaphorical desiring of the car have in common is their teleological structure: to ascribe a desire is to hold that there is some end-state toward which the object tends, and that the object will (*ceteris paribus*) act until that end-state is realized (cf. Smith 1994, pp. 111–116). Now, in full-blooded desire, there is a typical phenomenology of desire, and the adjustment of action toward the realization of the end-state is accomplished through full-blooded belief. The car's 'desire' to activate its traction control system is not accompanied by the characteristic phenomenology of desire, nor is its realization of the goal accomplished through full-blooded belief.

Now, with respect to desiring, law occupies a place intermediate between these two extremes. Legal systems are teleological systems – all legal systems tend to order through the imposition of standards of conduct – and different sorts of legal order are distinguished by the basic ends toward which they tend and subordinate ends that they employ or refrain from employing to realize them. Thus it is at least as appropriate to say that the law wants to achieve order as it is to say that my car wants to activate its traction control system. But with the law there is a further point – that its goal-achievement is realized through the motivational systems of real, live, paradigmatic desirers. As the passage earlier

---

belief and desire as crucial, still others place the intention to bring about a certain belief or desire state in the audience as crucial, still others place the imposition of a certain normative standing as being of first importance. I have no need to enter into these disputes here.

by Green notes, the law's activities are carried out first and foremost through what Tuomela calls its "operative" members – officials – and also through those citizens who take what Hart calls the internal point of view with respect to it. The law's adjustment of its activities in order to achieve certain end-states is the result of the desires of the operative agents of the law motivated *qua* operative agents (Tuomela 1995, pp. 232–234).[6]

It is also legitimate and not merely metaphorical to ascribe to the law beliefs. Again: what is common to paradigmatic believers and to my computer is that they possess some way of representing states of affairs, which representations can be used as the basis for further representations or for the adjustment of goal-promoting activity. The common fact of representation is what makes the metaphor of belief apt in the case of the computer's representation of my having pressed the 'a' key. Now, while the law is of course not a paradigmatic believer, its having beliefs and forming judgments is not merely metaphorical, for its representations of states of affairs works through the cognitive equipment of paradigmatic believers: legal officials, whose judgments about the effectiveness of law's present activity in realizing the sought ends make possible the readjustment of the law's activities in light of those ends, as well as those persons who take the internal point of view with respect to the law.

The argument, then, is that it should be uncontroversial to ascribe to the law goals and representations, and that the particular way that these goals and representations are instantiated in law – through operative agents that are paradigmatic desirers and believers – legitimates our understanding the law's having of goals as desiring and its having of representations as believing. Now, one might ask whether it is the case, then, that it is only possible to understand the law as a speaker where the legal system has developed to the point at which there is a distinct class of operatives – legislators, judges, and so forth – through whose motivational and cognitive capacities the law functions. Without such operatives – imagine the more primitive system of norms described by Hart, which possesses primary rules of obligation but lacks rules of change, adjudication, and recognition (Hart 1994 [1961], pp. 91–92) – it would seem that there would be no basis to ascribe to the law any judgments or aims.

I do not think that this precisely follows. What follows is that ascription to the law of desires and beliefs (and the illocutionary acts ascription of which presupposes the possibility of the ascription of desires and beliefs) will be more vague and uncertain than they would be in a situation in which there is a clear set of officials responsible for the law's operations. Compare the situations in

---

[6] Suppose that I were to inform you that my car is *very* special – the way that its traction control system gets activated is that there are homunculi occupying observation posts who want the traction control to be turned on when the road is slippery and who thus activate that system when they observe that the road is slippery. I take it that this would make my claim that the car wants to activate its traction system closer to literal truth and further from mere metaphor.

primitive and developed legal systems with the cases of what Tuomela calls "joint" belief/desire and "group" belief/desire (Tuomela 1995, pp. 307–308). The conditions for group belief/desire require the presence of operative agents who can have such beliefs/desires *qua* operatives. By the presence of such agents, the conditions for ascription of a belief or desire to a group is fairly clearly defined. Joint belief/desire requires no such official capacities, but results in a less clearly defined set of conditions for joint belief or desire: if there is not unanimity among the members, it becomes unclear to what extent a joint belief or desire can be ascribed. The situation is similar in the case of the primitive and developed legal systems. In developed legal systems, a well-defined class of officials makes possible the identification of law even though there may be plenty of dissenters living under the legal system. But without a well-defined class of officials, the presence of dissenters makes it difficult to say whether there are in fact rules in place and what the goals or beliefs of the law are. (On this point, see also Gilbert 1999b, p. 144.)

The law as possessing normative standing. To speak, one must also possess the proper normative standing. To speak is to make oneself responsible in certain ways, where the sort of responsibility involved differs for different sorts of illocutionary acts. It is to render oneself subject to criticism and blame for falling short with respect to one's responsibilities.

Such responsibility is commonly ascribed to the law. The law is blamed for the content of its demands, or for what it fails to demand; it is blamed for making certain commitments, or for failing to live up to the commitments that it has made. Its general dictates and particular rulings are subject to criticism. It is not simply an unresponsive source from which dictates emerge, etched in stone and uncriticizable. Criticism can be launched and revision expected in light of the force of good arguments. Of course, it is because of the powers of the officials of a legal system, through whom the content and application of the law can be changed, that such criticism has a point. It is enough for the law to have the normative standing requisite for speaking that it can sensibly be called to account for what it says.

The law as causally efficacious. Finally, in order to speak, one must have the requisite causal powers, the power to produce the written or spoken words that are the vehicle by which the illocutionary act takes place. As the law is an institution, its capacity to intervene by producing the necessary linguistic items is through the officials occupying its institutional roles. The law has the causal power requisite for speaking because its officials have the causal power requisite for speaking.

Mandatory Legal Norms and Demands

To call the law a speaker, then, is to use the notion of 'speaker' in a way that is without a doubt extended but not simply metaphorical. It is legitimate and informative to treat the law as a speaker. As I will argue later, there are various sorts of legal propositions whose truth is interestingly connected to the performance of speech-acts by the law. But for the sake of simplicity, and for the sake of dealing first with the sort of legal rule that has historically been at the center of the dispute between natural law theorists and legal positivists, we can begin with duty-imposing laws – laws that make some conduct mandatory.

The claim that I want to make here is that duty-imposing rules essentially involve the demands of law: a duty-imposing legal rule that all members of class M ϕ is the law's demand on all members of class M that they ϕ. Here is the most straightforward argument for this view. Whenever it is by consensus true that there is a law that imposes a mandatory norm on those under it, it is also by consensus true that the law demands the conduct mandated by the norm. We acknowledge that the U.S. legal system contains a mandatory norm requiring the payment of taxes by April 15; we also acknowledge that U.S. law demands the payment of taxes by April 15. We acknowledge that the U.S. legal system contains a mandatory norm forbidding the theft of the mails; we also acknowledge that U.S. law demands that we not steal the mails. And while we acknowledge that U.S. law does not demand that we make payments toward the support of an established religion, we correspondingly acknowledge that the U.S. legal system does not contain a mandatory norm requiring the making of payments toward the support of an established religion. All of this is exceedingly obvious, and there is no need to multiply examples.

We should allow that there is a mandatory legal norm requiring ϕ-ing if and only if the law demands ϕ-ing. But the status of this biconditional is obviously not merely contingent: it is absurd to think that the demands of law and the presence of mandatory norms just happen to correspond to each other. And this connection is also clearly not a mere mutual entailment between two *independent* states of affairs: it is rather far-fetched to think that whenever there is a mandatory norm to ϕ there is also some further, distinct state of affairs, that of *the law's demanding ϕ-ing*; and whenever there is not such a mandatory norm, the law also must refrain from demanding that conduct. Given the non-contingency of the connection between the law's demands and the presence of mandatory norms, surely it is more plausible to suppose that there being a mandatory legal norm requiring ϕ-ing *just is* the law's demanding ϕ-ing.

Again: consider the sorts of analysis that have recently been offered for the existence of mandatory legal norms and compare them with those states of affairs to which I appealed in making the case for the claim that the law speaks. The law's speaking involves its having certain beliefs and desires, its making itself accountable in certain ways, and its intervening linguistically, and each of these is to be understood, at least in developed legal systems, in terms of the responses of officials acting as officials. But it seems that on any account of what the existence of a legal rule consists in, it will appeal to these very states of affairs (see, for example, Hart 1994 [1961], pp. 55–58). So a further reason to think that a mandatory legal norm requiring ϕ-ing just is the law's demanding ϕ-ing is that the very same states of affairs will appear in the analyses of both of these notions.

Again: consider the following *explanandum*. When a legal system contains a mandatory norm requiring ϕ-ing of all members of class M, we thereby know that the law *has an interest* in the ϕ-ing of the members of class M – the law *intends* for them to ϕ, *aims* at their ϕ-ing, *wants* them to ϕ. But the mere presence of a rule in a system does not give of itself any indication why we would thereby think that anyone has as an *aim* or *purpose* or *goal* that persons perform the required act. But if we think of the law's mandatory norms as being the demands of law, we would thereby render unmysterious the fact that when there is a mandatory norm requiring ϕ-ing, then we know that the law wants people to ϕ. For when one makes a demand, it is normally the case that he or she wants those to whom the demand is addressed to act on it. (It is, to use the terminology of the theory of illocutionary acts (see later in this section), a sincerity condition of one's demanding that A ϕ that one intends that A ϕ.) This gives us further reason to think that the law's mandatory norms are invariably to be identified with the demands of law.

Now, there may be some resistance to the idea that mandatory legal norms are to be understood as the law's demands. Is this not the sort of command conception of law that Hart decisively refuted in *The Concept of Law*?

It is not. It is essential to Hart's objections to the Austin-inspired command conception of law both (1) that command is taken to be the essence of law, present in every case in which there is genuine law, and (2) that the commands in question are those of a *sovereign*, some supreme, legally unlimited party to whom there is habitual obedience. And against such a view, Hart rightly notes that (1) there are types of law, most notably those that confer powers either on private individuals or on public officials, that cannot plausibly be understood in terms of the command conception, and (2) that selecting as law only those commands proceeding from such a sovereign precludes proper understanding of the way that law persists through changes in lawmaking authority (Hart 1994 [1961], pp. 26–49, 51–61). But it has been no part of the argument of this section that the mandatory legal norms, which I say are the demands of law, are the primitive normative element out of which all other legal norms are to be constructed; so Hart's criticism of the Austinian view's sole focus on command does not apply to the view that I have defended. Nor has it been any part of the argument of this section that we must identify, without reference to legal concepts, some party whose demands are the demands of law. The demands that I have identified with mandatory legal norms are not the demands of some Austinian sovereign but the demands of the law itself. So none of the criticisms that Hart levels against the way that Austinian theory appeals to the notion of sovereignty has application here.

Demands and Decisive Reasons for Action

The law's mandatory norms are its demands. The relevance of this identification is that it is through understanding these norms as demands that we can see how there are, internal to law, standards of defectiveness and non-defectiveness that make essential reference to reasons for action. For demands are one species of illocutionary act; and illocutionary acts have standards of defectiveness and non-defectiveness internal to them; and some of the standards of defectiveness and non-defectiveness for the species of illocutionary act to which demands belong make essential reference to reasons for action.

In order to make this part of the case for the weak natural law thesis, I first need to say a few things, none of them original, about illocutionary acts. Illocutionary acts are, as Searle and Vanderveken write, "minimal units of human communication" (1985, p. 1). An illocutionary act is an attempt to do something with language, an attempt to realize some state of affairs by the performance of a speech-act. Every such act can be analyzed in terms of its illocutionary force and its propositional content. Illocutionary acts may have the same propositional content yet be distinct as a result of their differing illocutionary force: commanding you to be in class on time is distinct from predicting that you will be in class on time, begging you to be in class on time, cheering your being in class on time, and so on, even though the propositional content of all of these illocutionary acts – that you be in class on time – is the same. An illocutionary force is identified and distinguished from other illocutionary forces by the conditions under which the illocutionary act partly constituted by that force is successful and non-defective: the success conditions for an illocutionary act of a certain type are those conditions that must be realized for one to perform an illocutionary act of that type at all; the non-defectiveness conditions of an illocutionary act are those conditions that are presupposed in illocutionary acts of that type and thus to whose obtaining the performer of that illocutionary act is committed by its performance.

Most fundamental to the distinguishing of illocutionary forces is the *illocutionary point*, which is the goal internal to being an illocutionary act of that type. For example, one of the fundamental illocutionary points is that of *assertion*, on which the point of presenting the proposition is to represent the world. While there are other components of illocutionary force, the illocutionary point is most basic, and defines what constitutes the success of the performance of the illocutionary act (Searle and Vanderveken 1985, pp. 51–59). No act of assertion is successful, really counts as an act of assertion at all, if it does not represent the world as being in fact a certain way.

There are, however, ways that illocutionary acts can go wrong other than through being entirely unsuccessful. One who attempts to make an assertion can fail to make any assertion through sheer linguistic incompetence, and can end up making no assertion at all. But assertions can be successful though defective: for there is a variety of ways that assertions can fall short without failing altogether to count as assertions. For aside from the illocutionary point, there are various components of an illocutionary force whose obtaining is presupposed by the speaker in the illocutionary act. Among these are the sincerity conditions – those speaker's mental states that are presupposed in an illocutionary act – and preparatory conditions – those states of the world that are presupposed in an illocutionary act. For example: in the case of assertion, it is among the sincerity conditions that the proposition asserted is believed by the speaker, and it is among the preparatory conditions that the proposition asserted has some positive epistemic status. One who asserts that p presupposes these conditions in making that assertion, and is committed to them; the clearest test of this is that it is invariably paradoxical to assert that p while denying that one believes that p, and it is inevitably paradoxical to assert that p while denying that p has any positive epistemic status for the speaker (Searle and Vanderveken 1985, pp. 17, 18–19; also Alston 1999, pp. 77–78). Nevertheless, these non-defectiveness conditions on assertion are not success conditions. To lie is to make an assertion contrary to one's mind (cf. *Summa Theologiae* IaIIae 110, 1) and to bullshit is to make an assertion without regard to that assertion's positive epistemic status (cf. Frankfurt 1988b), and lying and bullshitting *are* possible. Nevertheless, lying and bullshitting are intrinsically flawed forms of asserting, defective in their kind. To make this assessment is not to make any moral pronouncements about lying and bullshitting. It is just to say that lying and bullshitting are of the genus of asserting and are intrinsically defective instances of that genus.

There are different success and nondefectiveness conditions corresponding to speech-acts with different illocutionary forces. My aim here is to argue that it is among the nondefectiveness conditions for demands that the party demanded have decisive reasons to comply with the demand. The argument is this.[7]

1. Demanding is a species of *directive* illocutionary act: the point internal to the laying down of demands is to present an act as to-be-done.
2. When one directs another to ϕ, then one necessarily implies that the other has some reason to ϕ.
3. Though some directive acts give the addressed party the option of not acting on the directive, demanding does not give this option.
4. The features of demands noted in (2) and (3) – commitment to reasons for compliance and the non-optionality of such compliance – yield the result that when one demands that another ϕ, then one necessarily implies that the other has *decisive* reasons to ϕ.

1. Assume Searle's now-standard taxonomy of basic illocutionary points – assertive, directive, commissive, declarative, expressive. On this view, the point

---

[7] The argument that follows appears in somewhat greater detail in Murphy 2002a, pp. 24–27.

of *assertion* is to present a proposition as representing the world accurately, the point of *commission* is to present a proposition so as to commit the speaker to actualizing it, the point of *direction* is to present the proposition so as to have the addressee(s) carry out the action represented in the proposition, the point of *declaration* is to present a proposition so as to make it true by the performance of the act itself, and the point of *expression* is to present a proposition so as to express one's attitude toward the state of affairs represented by it. While, as we said, there are other components of illocutionary force – it is these other components that distinguish the various species of illocutionary acts – the illocutionary point is most basic, and defines what constitutes the success of the performance of the illocutionary act (Searle and Vanderveken 1985, pp. 51–59).

It is clear that, given this standard taxonomy of basic illocutionary forces, *demanding that p* belongs to the genus of directive illocutionary acts. But there is a problem with the way this illocutionary point has been formulated. For one can successfully make a demand even if the party demanded fails to be motivated by that demand. (We should be sure to keep clear the distinction between the success of the illocutionary act, the communication itself, and that of the perlocutionary act – what one means to accomplish by means of it.) It seems better to say that in issuing a directive, the point internal to that act is to present a proposition as to-be-done. For that is what counts as success in issuing a directive: the most basic achievement required for the issuing of a directive is that one manages to present it as to-be-done. And it is obvious that this is the illocutionary point exhibited by demands: a demand presents an action as to-be-done.

2. In performing a directive act, one invariably implies that the party addressed has a reason to perform the directed act. (Note well: to say that in performing a directive illocutionary act one implies that the directed party addressed has a reason to comply is not to say that whenever one directs another to ϕ, the other has a reason to ϕ; it is only to say that whenever one directs another to ϕ, one puts himself or herself forward as *affirming that* – at least once the directive is issued – the other has reason to ϕ.) One way to give evidence for this view is just to survey the various sorts of directive acts – pleas, demands, orders, and so on – and to note that in each case, it seems to be the case that one who performs that act puts himself or herself forward as holding that there is some reason, of some strength, to perform the directed act. But the more persuasive and more straightforward way to show that a proposition is a necessary implication of a type of speech-act is to employ the 'paradox test': to show that it is invariably paradoxical to perform that speech-act while denying that proposition. If one considers any directive act chosen at random, it is clear that it is paradoxical to perform that act while denying that the person directed has any reason to go along. Suppose that I give you the following demand to bring me a book. "There is, in fact, nothing – not even the demand that I am about to make – that gives you the slightest reason to bring me a copy of Raz's

The Authority of Law. But bring me that book!" The paradox is apparent. Even with milder directives, such as requests, it is paradoxical to deny the existence of any reason for compliance while making the request. Directives are issued by rational beings to rational beings, and thus they carry with them the implication that compliance with the directive is, in some respect, supported by reasons (Searle and Vanderveken 1985, pp. 17, 18–19; also Alston 1999, pp. 77–78).

3. In performing directive acts, and *a fortiori* in making demands, one implies that there are reasons for the addressed party to act as directed: one who directs an agent to ϕ implies that the agent has reasons to ϕ. What I want to say now is that in the particular case of demands, the reasons whose existence is implied by the directive act are decisive ones. To show this we need to note a component of commanding acts that does not hold of all directive acts. Some directive acts allow the addressee the option of non-compliance; others do not allow such an option (Searle and Vanderveken 1985, pp. 198–199). A request, for example, allows the one to whom the request is addressed to opt out, while an order, by contrast, does not. In this broad division of directives, demands clearly fall on the side of the non-optional. One can, after all, non-paradoxically say "I request that you do this, though you may refrain if you choose"; one cannot non-paradoxically say "I demand that you do this, though you may refrain if you choose."

4. Together, the fact that (a) demands display a non-optionality feature, and (b) all directive acts, including those of making demands, imply the existence of reasons for action on the part of those addressed gives us grounds to believe that the reasons for action implied by demands are of a specific sort – that is, decisive ones. In making a demand, one implies that there is no option other than compliance. But how can rational beings be left with no option other than compliance unless the reasons that favor compliance are decisive ones? To confirm this result, we can again appeal directly to the paradox test: one can non-paradoxically say "I hereby request that you ϕ, while recognizing that you can reasonably, all things considered, refrain from ϕ-ing"; one cannot non-paradoxically say "I hereby demand that you ϕ, while recognizing that you can reasonably, all things considered, refrain from ϕ-ing." The reasons for action implied in all directive acts and the strength of the directive force partially constitutive of demands together entail that in demanding one implies the existence of decisive reasons for compliance.[8]

---

[8] One might wonder whether this puts the point too strongly. Think of the variety of unreasonable demands made by small children on parents, for example – are we to suppose that these demands carry the implication that the parents have decisive reason to comply? Well, yes, we are. Whether an illocutionary act has certain implications is not a feature of the performance of an act of that type on any given occasion, so it is not as if the fact that the child knows not of decisive reasons is any strike against the claim that demands imply decisive reasons for compliance. An important feature of illocutionary act-types, and of terms in a language, is that one can have greater-or-lesser mastery over them, and this

The Argument for the Weak Natural Law Thesis as Applied to Mandatory Legal Norms

Here, then, is the argument for the weak natural law thesis as applied to duty-imposing laws. Assume that there is a duty-imposing law that all those in class M ϕ. There being such a law just is the law's demand that all those in class M ϕ. But the law's demand that all those in class M ϕ is defective unless there is decisive reason for those belonging to class M to ϕ. But that is all that is required for the weak natural law thesis: for according to that thesis, the law is backed by decisive reasons inasmuch as any dictate that is not backed by decisive reasons either is not law or is defective precisely as law.

The Argument for the Weak Natural Law Thesis Extended

The argument for the weak natural law thesis is most straightforward in the case of mandatory legal norms. But not all legal norms are of this sort: some confer rights, others powers. One might simply restrict the natural law view so that it applies only to mandatory norms: on this restricted view, all that the natural law theorist is interested in claiming is that duty-imposing laws are backed by decisive reasons for action. It is these norms that have been of most interest to those defending the natural law thesis, after all. And one might wonder in what sense norms that confer rights or powers can be 'backed by decisive reasons,' so that these norms are defective if they fail to be so backed. Even if the natural law thesis as applied to mandatory norms is highly contentious, its sense is clear enough: for a mandatory norm to be backed by decisive reasons is for there to be decisive reason for compliance with that norm. But it is not nearly so clear at first glance what sense the natural law thesis would carry in the case of these other legal norms.

One way that the natural law thesis might be extended to other sorts of norms is by holding that rights-conferring and power-conferring norms are simply very complex mandatory norms. This is a view criticized thoroughly by Hart, and I shall not revive it here.

The approach that I will take is based on the idea that once we take seriously the notion that the law is a speaker, there is no reason to suppose that the only sort of illocutionary act that the law performs is that of demanding. Demanding is an act with a directive illocutionary point. But it might well be that the law not only issues directives: it might also make assertions, commitments, and declarations. There is little reason to require or even expect a one-to-one correspondence between fundamental sorts of illocutionary acts and fundamental

---

greater-or-lesser mastery is fixed in part by the extent to which one grasps the implications of performing those illocutionary acts or using those terms. It is, in fact, part of what makes some children's demands so amusing that they imply the presence of reasons for compliance that are so obviously not present at all.

sorts of legal norms, but if we are looking for an account of the key differences between duty-imposing and other sorts of legal norms, along with an account of the different ways in which reasons for action might be involved in these norms, we can begin by looking at illocutionary acts other than those of the directive sort.

Let us begin with right-conferring norms. The hypothesis that I have suggested might be brought to bear on such norms in the following way. When there is a right-conferring legal norm – at least where the right is not merely the shadow cast by a mandatory legal norm – the law has *made a commitment*, in the specifically illocutionary sense of 'making a commitment.' There being a legal norm conferring a right on those in class M to ϕ is just the law's performing a commissive act, an act of committing itself to act in a certain way with respect to the ϕ-ing of those in class M. (At least this will be true for a certain class of ϕ-ing's – those that protect the interests of those in class M, or protect a choice of those in class M, or whatever. The view that I am suggesting can be adopted by those who accept Choice (for example, Hart 1955, pp. 175–191) or Interest (for example, Raz 1986, pp. 165–192) theories of rights.

Suppose, for example, that we hold that there is a legal right to free speech. On this view, for there to be a right to free speech is just for the law to commit itself to treating citizens in a certain way with respect to their speaking – to refrain from hindering them in certain ways, to prevent other citizens from hindering them in certain ways, and so forth. (The precise content of the commitment will of course depend both on the sort of Hohfeldian right at stake and on what we take the content of 'free speech' to be.) Or suppose that there is a right not to be deprived of one's property without due process of law. I say that for there to be a legal right not to be deprived of one's property without due process of law is just for the law to commit itself to treating citizens in a certain way with respect to their holding of property – not to take their property from them without due process of law. There being a right-conferring legal norm is the law's committing itself to act in a certain way.

The arguments for understanding right-conferring norms along these lines are, *mutatis mutandis*, the same as those for understanding mandatory norms as the law's demands. First, we do recognize that there is a legal right if and only if the law makes such a commitment; and as it is ridiculous to think of these states of affairs as only contingently co-realized or as mutually entailed but distinct, we should think of them as one and the same. Second, if we were to elaborate upon what states of affairs would have to be realized for it to be true that there is a legal right, the list that we would come up with would be the same as the list we would come up with were we to elaborate upon what states of affairs would have to obtain for it to be true that the law commits itself to do something. And, third, when we know that there is a legal right, we know that the law has some sort of aim, the aim to promote the conditions for citizens' action or to protect the conditions for that action or at least not to hinder that action, and our knowing this is very well-explained by the fact that it is a sincerity condition on speech-acts of commitment that one intend to perform the actions to which one has committed oneself.

Now, if the presence of a right-conferring norm is just the law's commitment, then we can provide both an account of what it would mean to extend the weak natural law thesis to right-conferring norms and an argument for its truth in the case of right-conferring norms. For, like demanding acts, commissive acts have non-defectiveness conditions that involve reasons for action. But while the reasons for action whose existence is a preparatory condition for demands are reasons for the party addressed to act, the reasons for action whose existence is a preparatory condition for commitments are reasons for action for that very speaker. One who commits himself or herself to ϕ in circumstances C presupposes that upon making that commitment he or she will have decisive reasons to ϕ in circumstances C. (The proof of this claim of presupposition is just the paradox test: it is paradoxical to commit oneself to ϕ in circumstances C while allowing that, even upon performance of that illocutionary act, one could perfectly reasonably refrain from ϕ-ing in circumstances C.) But if that is the case, then to the extent that the course of action to which one is committing himself or herself is an act that he or she will not have decisive reason to perform, even upon making the commitment, that illocutionary act will be defective.

A legal norm conferring upon those in class M a right to ϕ is defective, then, if the law does not have decisive reason to protect (etc.) the ϕ-ing of those in class M. Note well: to say that such a norm is defective if there is not decisive reason to protect (etc.) the ϕ-ing of those in class M is not to say that there might not be, prior to the establishing of the norm, no such decisive reasons. The claim is that the norm is defective if there is not, even including the reasons brought about through the generation of the norm, decisive reason to protect (etc.) citizens' ϕ-ing.

Here is an example. Suppose that it is true that one can never have decisive reason to protect another's performance of a morally vicious act. (That is, one can never have decisive reason to act under the description 'protecting A's performance of ϕ-ing,' where ϕ-ing is a morally vicious action.) And suppose that it is true that doing violence to one's spouse in order to bring one's spouse's will into line with one's own is a morally vicious act. And suppose further that there is some jurisdiction in which the law has explicitly granted a right for husbands to treat their wives in this way. On the weak natural law thesis as applied to right-conferring laws, this right-conferring legal norm would be essentially defective as law. For the law has in this case committed itself to protecting the choice to abuse one's wife, and this commitment presupposes that it will thereupon have decisive reason to protect the choice to abuse one's wife. But given the supposition that this practice is morally vicious, then the law cannot have decisive reason to protect this action. And so any legal norm granting a right to it would be defective precisely as law.

Next, powers. In order to explain how the natural law thesis can be brought to bear on powers, it is necessary to bring to light the way that the illocutionary act of *declaration* is ubiquitous in law. Declaration is a speech-act in which a state of affairs is brought about through the very performance of the speech-act: declaring p makes it the case that p. Law makes use of declaration in making it clear what legal meaning a term bears: the law declares that murder is intentional malicious homicide, and that burglary is breaking and entering with the aim of committing a crime, and so forth. Now, legal declarations are of themselves not of much interest. What makes legal declarations of interest is their practical effect: if the law declares that if something is an x, then it is (counts as) a y, this is of interest insofar as the law either demands that those in class M act some way with respect to y's or makes a commitment to act some way with respect to y's. The legal declaration that breaking and entering for the purpose of committing a crime is (counts as) burglary would be idle if it were not conjoined with the law's demand that we not perform acts of burglary.

I suggest that legal powers ought to be understood as a conjunction of a certain sort of legal declaration with a legal commitment or demand that bears on the object of that declaration. When there is a legal power, the legal declaration involves an action that is up to an agent, and the agent can choose to perform that action in order to trigger the corresponding legal commitment or demand. So a legal power is a legal declaration that under conditions C an x is (counts as) a y, where C is some action up to an agent, along with a legal commitment (the law will ϕ with respect to y) or a legal demand (those in class M will ϕ with respect to y).

This is very abstract. Here is an example: consider the legal power to make wills. According to the account that I have offered, this legal power consists in a legal declaration and a legal commitment. The legal declaration is that an expression of one's intentions as to the disposal of one's property after one's death, written down in a certain form and signed by the testator in the presence of two witnesses (etc.) counts as a *will*. The legal commitment is to enforce the provisions of wills. By carrying out the action described in the declaration of what a will is, agents can trigger the law's commitment to carry out certain of their wishes.

For legal powers to be backed by decisive reasons is to be understood in terms of the part of the legal power that is constituted by a legal commitment or demand. For 'being backed by decisive reasons' is a wholly practical notion, and a legal declaration is not susceptible of practical criticism insofar as it is taken up in a legal demand or a legal commitment. There is no basis to criticize a declaration of what counts as a will except insofar as the law is committed to carrying out the intentions expressed in wills. And one could on this basis hold that a certain legal rule pertaining to wills is defective precisely as law: for if the law were to commit itself to executing wills the provisions of which one could not commit oneself to enforcing, the law would exhibit an intrinsic defect.[9]

The Raz Thesis Rejected

One might claim that the argument for the weak natural law thesis through appeal to the character of legal norms as illocutionary acts is unnecessarily circuitous: by appeal to the basic thesis of Raz's jurisprudence, I could have made a much quicker argument to the same conclusion. Raz holds that the law necessarily claims to be authoritative. He does not hold that the law necessarily *is* authoritative – in fact, he denies it, holding that modern legal systems lack the authority to which they essentially aspire (Raz 1979a, 1984b). If true, the view that the law necessarily claims authority could serve as a premise in a straightforward argument for the weak natural law thesis. For if we agree with Raz that law necessarily claims authority for its dictates, then it follows that law sets for itself a certain normative standard, and if it fails to measure up to that standard, then it is defective, and defective precisely as law. This is why some positivists think that the Razian claim that the law claims for itself authority is a Trojan horse, not to be admitted into the positivist stronghold, lest it be exploited for natural law purposes (cf. Kramer 1999, and Goldsworthy 1990).

While one might construct an argument for the weak natural law thesis by relying on the Raz thesis as a premise, I have declined to do so. The Raz thesis is that law essentially claims to be authoritative; the corresponding thesis upon which I rely in the argument for the weak natural law view is that the law is committed to there being decisive reasons to comply with its dictates. There are two clear differences between Raz's view and my own.

The first is that the Raz thesis is a thesis about a proposition that the law necessarily *asserts* – namely, that it has authority. The premise upon which I rely is a thesis about a proposition that the law necessarily *is committed to* when it makes demands, regardless of whether it ever bothers to make that commitment explicit. When Raz's thesis is taken strictly, it is very implausible, and the evidence that he offers for it is not nearly sufficient to justify it. Raz

---

[9] How are sanctions to be offered an illocutionary act analysis? On a simple view, a rule stipulating a sanction could be a legal commitment: for there to be a rule stipulating sanction S for offense O is for the law to have committed itself to inflicting S on those who have performed offense O. It is clear from the preceding arguments how a rule stipulating a sanction could be defective as law: if there could not be adequate reason, even upon the making of a commitment, for the law to inflict such a sanction on an agent who commits that offense, then the rule is defective as law. (If, for example, torture is a sanction that there could not be adequate reason to inflict on an offender, then any legal rule that stipulated torture as the official response to some offense would be defective as law.) There are some complications, though: as I argue later (6.1), punishment is constituted also by authoritative dictates, and no proper analysis of rules stipulating sanctions would be complete without taking this into account.

appeals to the way that judges and other officials formulate the demands of law: they treat its demands as *duties* or *obligations*, they describe themselves as *authorities*, they designate as *offenders* and thus *guilty* those who fail to comply. But it seems quite clear that there could be a legal system in which officials do not designate themselves as authorities, do not describe the requirements imposed as duties or obligations, and do not describe lawbreakers as offenders and thus guilty. I am not imagining here what Kramer has in mind – that is, a regime of stark imperatives backed only by force (Kramer 1999, pp. 83–89). Rather, I have in mind a much more benign situation in which the law is in fact authoritative, everyone believes it to be such, and no one bothers to make it explicit. In such a regime it would be false to say that the law claims to be authoritative. It claims nothing of the sort; it has not stated its opinion on the matter. (See also Himma 2001, Dworkin 2002, pp. 1661–1667, and Soper 2002, pp. 79–87.) That is why I refrain from framing the premise upon which I rely in the argument for the natural law thesis in terms of what the law asserts, framing it instead in terms of what the law is committed to: not every proposition to whose truth one is committed by performing an illocutionary act is a proposition that one has asserted by performing that act.

Now, one might say that if this is the difference between the thesis that I defend and Raz's own thesis, then the difference is slim indeed. For surely Raz would be happy enough with the acknowledgment that necessarily the law is committed to the view that it is authoritative. But there is a further difference. Raz holds that the proposition that the law asserts is that it is *authoritative*; I hold that the proposition to which the law is committed is that it is *backed by decisive reasons for action*. These are importantly different notions: the law's being authoritative entails its being backed by decisive reasons for action, but its being backed by decisive reasons does not entail its being authoritative. For the law to be authoritative, two things must be the case: there must be decisive reasons to adhere to the law (Raz takes it that these must be protected reasons– that is, both first-order reasons to adhere to the law's demands and second-order reasons not to act on reasons against adhering to the law's demands), and these decisive reasons must include the fact that the law requires that conduct (cf. Murphy 2002a, p. 15, and Murphy forthcoming). But it seems to me that we lack an adequate basis to take Raz's step past the claim that the law is committed to its being backed by decisive reasons for compliance to the claim that these reasons for compliance include the law's demands themselves.

I say this for two reasons. The first is just that once we allow that mandatory legal norms are just the demands of law, there is no basis to suppose that every legal system must hold that each such demand bear authority.[10] All that is

---

[10] Compare Hart 1983b, p. 10: "It seems to me unrealistic to suppose that judges in making statements of legal obligation *must* always either believe or pretend to believe in the false theory that there is always a moral obligation to obey the law. It seems to me that such

implied in the giving of a demand, I have argued, is that there is some set of reasons that militates decisively in favor of compliance. One who makes a demand is not committed to those reasons being of any particular sort. They might include the demander's say-so, but they might not: they might include sanctions, either specified or unspecified; they might include independent moral reasons; they might include independent prudential reasons. We know from the fact that a demand was issued that the demand is defective unless there are decisive reasons to comply with it; we do not know that it is defective simply because the demander lacks authority.

The second reason for refraining from affirming the view that the law is committed to its being authoritative requires us to return to the example of the legal system that issues a number of duty-imposing rules but never makes any explicit claims about its authority. The question is: what are we entitled to say about that system's commitment or non-commitment to its status as authoritative simply from the fact that it issues such rules? Surely the answer is that it depends: it depends on what the legal system lays down as rules. Suppose that every duty-imposing norm that the legal system in question includes requires an action that is independently required by practical rationality. All of the legal system's rules simply reproduce the contours of natural practical reasonableness, in its more uncontroversial regions: the law forbids intentional killing of the innocent, torture, rape, and so forth. We would have no basis for holding that the law is committed to its being authoritative. It could be that the reasons for action that back the law's demands are not those of the law's say-so but of morality itself. Raz is right that every legal duty is purported to have some reason-giving source, but this does not commit the law to the claim that there is a single reason-giving source – its own say-so – for all of its rules.

Now, one might object that even if I have offered reasons to doubt Raz's thesis, doing so harms my own natural law position. For I have held that there is no privileged class of reasons that the law is committed to holding out as providing a decisive basis for compliance; the reasons might be authority reasons, or independent moral or prudential reasons, or reasons resulting from the threat of sanctions. But it would be, one might say, certainly a non-standard natural law view that holds that the decisive reasons that allegedly back compliance with the law may not at all be reasons of the law's authority but instead reasons from the independent rational force of moral norms or reasons from the brute force of legal sanctions.

It does not strike me as much of a route for criticism of my argument as a means to defend natural law jurisprudence that the reasons for action allegedly supporting compliance with legal norms might derive from independent moral

statements may be better construed as stating what may be properly *demanded* of their subjects by way of action according to the law which the judges accept as setting the correct standard of legal adjudication and law enforcement" (emphases in original).

concerns (such as is at least plausible in the case of norms forbidding rape, murder, or torture) rather than from the law's authority (such as is at least plausible in the case of norms concerning tax payments and traffic rules). Perhaps a more promising line for the critic is the possibility that these reasons derive from sanctions. But it seems wrong to think that the silence of the law on the source of the reasons by which its norms are backed provides help for the critic of natural law theory. For, first, the source of the reasons for action by which the law claims to be backed is really not the central source of dispute between natural law theorists and their critics. The positivist's separation thesis has never been formulated merely as the claim that it is among the truth conditions for any proposition of law that the law actually be authoritative; rather, that thesis is always formulated in terms of entailment by or conformity with or consistency with moral or practical principles generally (see 1.2). And even if the premises employed in my argument allow that the reasons to adhere to legal rules are provided by sanctions, that thesis still remains capable of underwriting the weak natural law claim that there are some actions that could not be required by a non-defective legal norm. For it would remain possible that there are some rules such that *no* sanction would be sufficient to make adherence to them practically reasonable. For example: Aquinas, who thought that the killing of the innocent is always and everywhere wrong (*Summa Theologiae* IIaIIae 64, 6), would say that a law that required such killing is gravely defective as law, because there could never be adequate reason, under any conditions, to kill the innocent. Thus, even if the law's commitment to the claim that it is backed by reasons for compliance were silent on the issue of the source of the reasons – even if the reasons for obedience to law were *stipulated* to derive from sanctions – the internal connection between law and reasons for compliance would still support natural law jurisprudence. For if there are some acts that, *no matter the sanction*, one could never have decisive reason to perform, then any law that dictated their performance would be defective.

Second: even if the theory of illocutionary acts has no implications on the source of the reasons for compliance in the case of demands, there may be a basis in something like considerations of charity for holding that the law *characteristically* does not base its claim to be backed by reasons on sanctions. Here the anthropomorphic language of the laws making claims and being committed to certain propositions gets stretched a bit, and it is easier to proceed by analogy. Suppose there to be a person (Jane, for example) who imposes a large number of rules on a large class of people. Jane has some coercive power: if she chooses, she can inflict suffering on certain people. She also has some information-gathering capacities: to some degree she can find out who is adhering to the rules and who is not. Now suppose that Jane's rule-imposing acts are sincere: she in fact believes that the presuppositions of her acts of rule-imposition are true, and so she believes that in each case, those on whom she imposes rules have decisive reasons to act on those rules in each instance that those rules apply.

Yet, her capacity to inflict sanctions for disobedience is severaly limited. She can catch only a limited number of those that commit infractions, and no one can tell in advance whom she will catch and whom she will not. Given the sincerity of her rule-imposing acts and her knowledge of the limitedness of her capacity to give reasons for action through sanctions, it seems charitable to hold that her belief in reasons for compliance springs not from her coercive power but elsewhere – either from the content of what she lays down, or from her authority. The upshot, of course, is that if we remain willing to use the language of law-imposing rules, making claims, being committed to propositions, and so on, then considerations of charity may well lead us, in the vast run of cases, to take the law's claim to be backed by reasons to extend to the further claim that the reasons involved are not, or are not simply, those provided by sanctions.

2.5 The Relation between the Function and Illocutionary Acts Arguments

I have defended two routes to the weak natural law thesis: the function of law argument (2.3) and the illocutionary acts argument (2.4). The former asserts that a function of law is to provide dictates backed by decisive reasons for action; the latter asserts that laws are to be identified with illocutionary acts a non-defectiveness condition of which is that they be backed by decisive reasons for action. These arguments seem to be of very different kinds, and it might seem a coincidence, and indeed a suspicious one, that I deem both of them successful.

But it is no mere coincidence. We can give a plausible account of why it is the case that if the function of law argument is successful, then the illocutionary acts argument must be successful as well. For if the function of law argument is correct, then a function of law is to provide dictates that are backed by decisive reasons for action. We might think of these dictates simply as rules. But legal systems are instantiated by the thought, judgment, action, and speech of real live human beings. It is central to the existence of a legal system that its dictates be expressed as the demands of actual persons, whether that of the ordinary folk who use the dictates to guide their conduct and to criticize others' (and their own) actions or that of the legal officials whose specific role it is to apply those dictates to ordinary citizens. It is thus inevitable that a system whose function is to issue dictates backed by decisive reasons for compliance and whose function is executed by the speech-acts of rational beings like us should produce illocutionary acts the non-defectiveness conditions of which include that they be backed by decisive reasons for compliance.

Again, recall the reason-backed rule machine (2.3). Suppose that the design of this machine were instantiated not by silicon chips but by homunculi. If these homunculi sought out the relevant information, formed judgments about what the handle-pullers have decisive reasons to do, and then expressed that judgment – either through a straightforward statement of the form 'you have decisive reasons to ϕ', or through an ought-statement ('you ought to ϕ'), or through a demand ('ϕ!') – then it would obviously be the case that we would have reason to say both that the machine performed an illocutionary act, and that this illocutionary act either presupposed or asserted the existence of decisive reasons for the handle-puller to comply with the dictate. But these points hold with respect to law as well: given the particular roles that human beings play in carrying out the functions of legal systems, we have a basis for saying that the law performs illocutionary acts, and we have reason to think that these acts, if non-defective, are backed by decisive reasons for compliance (2.4). It is thus unsurprising and non-suspicious that both the function of law and the illocutionary acts arguments are successful routes to the weak natural law thesis.

2.6 The Weak Natural Law Thesis, the Strong Natural Law Thesis, and Legal Positivism

Law that is not backed by decisive reasons for compliance is defective as law. The weak natural law thesis is true. Should the natural law jurist go on to defend the stronger thesis – that a law unbacked by decisive reasons for action is no law at all? No: the arguments that I have offered for the weak natural law thesis gives us reason to doubt the strong natural law thesis.

The function of law argument (2.3) does not give anyone reason to accept the strong reading, and indeed it gives us reason to doubt it. Moore sets up the functional kind argument as an argument for the strong natural law thesis (though he does not consider the weak natural law thesis as an alternative). But it seems false to suppose that, whether on Moore's functional kind argument or on the emendation I suggested, the strong natural law thesis would be the result. The law cannot carry out its function if it is not backed by decisive reasons for compliance, on this view, but why would we think that there is no law unbacked by decisive reasons for compliance rather than merely that all such law is defective? There is, after all, nothing more ordinary than things that have the function of ϕ-ing but which at the moment are not ϕ-ing and, in their present condition, cannot ϕ: witness broken alarm clocks, broken arms, and so on. A broken alarm clock is an alarm clock; it is just a defective alarm clock. To have one's arm broken in a skiing accident is not to lose an arm in a skiing accident. The functional kind argument should aspire to no more than the weak natural law thesis.

The same holds true with respect to the illocutionary acts argument. Consider again the claims that lies and unjustified assertions are essentially defective. It would obviously be too strong to say that lies are no assertions at all, or that unjustified assertions are no assertions at all. In order to recognize them as lies, and as unjustified assertions, one needs to be able to recognize them as assertions, as representations of the world as it is. And it would obviously be wrong to say that one could not use lies and unjustified assertions effectively for his or her particular purposes. One can lie and bullshit successfully. But it is for all that *not* too strong to say that such assertions are all defective in their very nature. To engage in assertion is to engage willy-nilly in an activity with its own internal teleology, and to assert insincerely or without justification or falsely is to fail to live up to the standards for flawless assertion. That is why 'lying assertions are no assertions at all,' while not literally true, is recognizably an exaggeration of something literally true; 'rude assertions are no assertions at all' is neither literally true nor a recognizable exaggeration of something literally true.

One interesting feature of this case is that, generally, our criteria that one is making an assertion are matters of natural and social fact: Are his or her lips moving? Are the sounds that are coming out recognizable as words? Do the words form a grammatical declarative sentence? Is the context of utterance such that folks in such contexts that utter such sentences characteristically mean to be making assertions? And so forth. The criteria that we use for determining whether an assertion has been made are characteristically non-evaluative. And this is no accident: the goods of being able to form beliefs on the basis of others' testimony could not be realized if we had to engage in normative epistemology in order to find out whether someone's utterance counted as an assertion. But while the criteria employed for registering the making of an assertion are largely factual, the criteria for determining whether an assertion is free of defect require an appeal to epistemic and semantic values: Is the appeal to justification implicit in making an assertion made good? Is the appeal to truth implicit in an assertion made good? Is the appeal to sincerity implicit in making an assertion made good?

Now, I want to say that this sort of pattern reappears when we consider illocutionary acts other than assertions. It is important that our criteria for determining whether a directive has been issued be largely factual: for part of the point of directives is to change people's views of what is to be done, either by changing the balance of reasons, or by presenting those reasons, or by making those reasons more vivid, more motivationally effective.[11] It is important that our criteria for determining whether a commissive has been performed be largely factual: for part of the point of one's performing a commissive is to alter what one is to do, how it is reasonable for one to act. So once we allow that duty-imposing and right-conferring laws are to be understood in terms of demands and commitments, we should further allow that whether there are such laws in place is something that is determined largely by natural and social facts. For, like

---

[11] Note the variety of ways that demands can guide action other than by adding reasons for action: they can influence both one's cognitive and one's volitional response to reasons for action that already exist. This is the basis on which I would criticize Shapiro's argument for hard positivism (1998).

assertions, demands and commitments are illocutionary acts, and our criteria for the presence of an illocutionary act are largely straightforwardly a matter of natural and social fact. It is important that our criteria for the existence of laws be largely a matter of natural and social fact: if we had to do moral philosophy in order to know whether there is a law, a great deal of the law's capacity to solve practical disagreement by the laying down of standards of conduct would be undermined (cf. Raz 1985), and much of our capacity to arrange our affairs by relying upon the law's commitments would be undermined as well. Thus the natural law theorist should concede to the positivist the separation thesis (1.2) and reject the stronger of the two jurisprudential natural law theses.

2.7 The Agenda for Natural Law Political Philosophy

The agenda for natural law political philosophy, as I mentioned in 1.1, is set by natural law jurisprudence. Natural law jurisprudence focuses on the conditions of non-defective law, and specifies those conditions as including that those under the law have decisive reason to comply with it. Natural law political philosophy asks: under what conditions do citizens have decisive reason to comply with the law? How is it possible for law – something made by folks of not-that-much-greater-than-average intelligence and certainly not-that-much-greater-than-average moral virtue – to be binding, to be the sort of norm that is backed by decisive reasons for compliance?

One answer, as we hinted in 2.4, is for the law simply to reproduce the contours of natural practical reasonableness, so that what is required by nature is recapitulated in the law. But, as we also hinted at the end of that section, this state of affairs is far from characteristic. Most of what we encounter in developed legal systems seems to be a contingent setting of norms rather than a reproduction of what is fixed by nature prior to the operating of social institutions. The norms of reason display *normative openness*: quite a lot of how we ought rationally to act is underdetermined by natural practical rationality. But while this normative openness can be a source of great human good – it is what makes possible human creativity in structuring one's own life and setting one's own priorities – it is also a source of tremendous difficulty in the structuring of a common life, in which agents are attempting to coordinate their actions with one another. Even if agents share a common end and wish to act in concert to realize it, there may be disagreement between them about what plan of action to follow; and the normative openness of practical reason may ensure that neither of the disagreeing agents is in error. Even if agents share, at some abstract level of description, a common end, and wish to act in concert to realize it, there may be disagreement between them about how that abstractly cast common end is to be specified as a concrete objective; and the normative openness of practical reason may ensure that neither of the disagreeing agents is in error (cf. Murphy 2001a, pp. 252–254). Law is one way to structure such agents' common life: law aims to set a decisive standard for common action and thus rules out (reasonable) practical conflict in certain classes of cases. Law aims to close off some of the normative openness that generates practical conflict among even reasonable agents.

To put the problem bluntly, though: how is non-defective law possible? How can law be a standard for conduct with which there are decisive reasons for compliance when law goes beyond what natural practical rationality alone can prescribe? How can a common standard of conduct provided by the law, a standard that is not uniquely endorsed by natural practical rationality, come to determine decisively what one ought to do? The natural law view holds that it is through the law's standing in a privileged place with respect to the *common good* of the political community that it comes to have this unique status. In the next chapter, we look for an account of the common good that enjoys the elevated normative status necessary to fulfill this role.

3

The Common Good

3.1 The Common Good in Natural Law Political Philosophy

As we saw in 2.4, the status of law as a giver of demands proves not that the law is committed to the view that it is authoritative but only to the view that its dictates are backed by decisive reasons for action. But, as we saw in 2.7, given the normative openness of practical reason and the rational desirability of a basis for common action among agents, the characteristic case of non-defective law will be that in which law is established as authoritative. We thus turn to the second key natural law thesis (0.1): that the law's reason-giving power flows from the common good of the political community. When law is authoritative, the natural law theorist wants to say, it has that status because of the way that the law is situated with respect to the *common good* of the political community. The common good is, according to this view, some state of affairs (perhaps a very complex one!) that is *good*, something that there is reason to promote, honor, respect, and so on, and is *common*, having this value for all members of the political community.

It is worth pausing for a moment to note that the commonness criterion implies that Hobbesian conceptions of the common good are, at most, deviant natural law conceptions of the common good. Recall the situation that Hobbes describes as the "natural condition of mankind." In the natural condition of mankind, human agents are predominantly self-interested, roughly equal in mental and physical capacities, in a condition of moderate scarcity, and lacking any coercive political authorities. This condition, says Hobbes, is guaranteed to be a state of war, and the lives of the denizens of the state of nature terrible and short. Hobbes holds, though, that even given the radically disparate aims of those in the state of nature, they must come to realize that peace is good, and will recognize that the only way to achieve peace is to contract together to institute a nearly absolute political authority – the sovereign – that has the right and power to apprehend and punish all those who engage in behavior that threatens the peace. Now, do we not have adequate grounds to hold that in

Hobbes's natural law view, there is a common good – peace – that serves as the central premise for subsequent reasoning about the source, nature, and form of political authority?

There is surely some sense in which peace is a common good for Hobbesian agents, but it is a very weak sense. The reason is that, appearances aside, there is not a single state of affairs that the parties in the state of nature take as an object of common, reasonable pursuit. What each party in the state of nature wants, given Hobbes's description of those agents, is not *peace as such*, or *peace for all of us in the state of nature*, but rather *peace for him or her*. The state of affairs aimed at by each party, that is, has an essential self-reference; it is a wholly agent-relative end. At no point does the Hobbesian agent have a reason to promote the condition in which all agents are in a state of peace; he or she has a reason only to promote the condition in which he or she is in a state of peace.[1] If all agents act in this way, Hobbes thinks, general peace will prevail. But there is no robust sense in which the general peace is a common good for Hobbesian agents.[2] I will, then, treat it as a point in favor of the natural law credentials of a conception of the common good that it fulfill the 'commonness' desideratum more fully than a Hobbesian conception does.

So the natural law view holds that the law's authority is to be explained in terms of a good that is genuinely common to the members of a political community. There are, then, two tasks to be accomplished if one aims to provide an account of the authority of law within the constraints set by the natural law conception. First, one needs to show that the common good is up to the challenge – that there is a conception of the common good of the political community that can carry the normative burden that the natural law view assigns to it. Second, one needs to show how the law is, or can be, related to the common good thus conceived so that the law will bear authority. The second task will be the focus of our attention in the two chapters that follow. In this chapter, we will look into the question of how we ought to understand the common good, given the role that it must fulfill of providing the normative force for the law's authority.

The three main candidate conceptions of the common good that I will consider are the *instrumentalist*, the *distinctive good*, and the *aggregative*. On the instrumentalist view, the common good consists in the presence of those conditions that are necessary or helpful means for members of that community to realize their own worthwhile ends. On the distinctive good view, the common

---

[1] Some writers think that Hobbesian agents, either in accepting the laws of nature or in entering the covenant to obey the sovereign, are transformed such that they do share ends in this way. This is at least a plausible reading of Hobbes, though it raises different argumentative difficulties for him. At any rate, 'Hobbesian' is meant here to indicate a type of view of the common good, of which Hobbes's actual view may or may not be an example.

[2] I discuss this Hobbesian case with respect to the basic good of community in Murphy 2001a, pp. 126–127.

good consists in the obtaining of some intrinsically good state of affairs that is literally the good of the community as a whole (as opposed to simply the goods of the members of that community). On the aggregative view, the common good consists in the realization of some set of individual intrinsic goods, characteristically the goods of all (and only) those persons that are members of the political community in question. My aim for the bulk of the remainder of this chapter (3.2–3.5) will be to exhibit the strength of the credentials of the aggregative conception for filling the role assigned to the common good by the natural law account, and to argue that the instrumentalist and distinctive good conceptions gain their plausibility only by way of the aggregative conception. The chapter will conclude (3.6) with the generic natural law account of the way that the law's authority flows from the common good, an account whose appropriate specification we will consider in Chapters 4 and 5.

3.2 The Argument for the Aggregative Conception of the Common Good

The case for the aggregative conception of the common good is a simple and straightforward one. Consider any individual A within a political community, and consider the state of affairs in which A is flourishing – that is, is enjoying the goods that genuinely make human life go well (0.2). That state of affairs is a reason for action that members of the political community should acknowledge: in the crafting of law or policy, the effect that the proposed law or policy would have on A's flourishing is relevant with respect to that law or policy. That a law or policy would promote an A's good is a reason to adopt it; that a law or policy would thwart A's good is reason to reject it.[3] There may be other considerations, of course, that outweigh, or in some way exclude, the reason to adopt or reject the law or policy that is based on its effect on A's good. But that does not call into question the fundamental relevance of A's good in political matters.

So the state of affairs in which A is flourishing is a fundamental reason for political action within A's political community. Now consider the state of affairs in which A, and one other individual B, are flourishing. The state of affairs in which A and B are both flourishing is an even stronger reason for political action, and in the most straightforward way: the state of affairs *A and B are flourishing* includes all that is of importance in the state of affairs *A is flourishing*, and more as well. To construct the normative ideal of the aggregative common good, one merely carries out this process of inclusion to its limit, including all of the goods of the members of a political community in the common good of that political

---

[3] This is of course fully compatible with the point that a great deal of one's flourishing cannot be directly brought about through law or policy.

community. The common good aggregatively conceived is that state of affairs in which all of the members of a political community are fully flourishing.

There is nothing epistemologically suspect about the aggregative common good. Given the general human capacity to grasp the fundamental elements of well-being (0.2), there can be little objection on such grounds: for, on the aggregative view, the idea of the common good is built upon the idea of well-being, upon the theory of prudential value. And since, as far as I can tell, every normative political theory develops, or at least assumes, a conception of individual well-being, a conception of the common good construed aggregatively does not on any view add an epistemological burden to political thought that was not already present.

One might claim that the problem with the aggregative common good is not that we cannot understand it, but that we can understand its demands rather too well, and we can see that what it lays before us is an unrealizable ideal. There are stronger and weaker versions of this objection. On the stronger version, the aggregative common good is an incoherent ideal, because there are some goods essential to human flourishing whose realization involves others' failing to flourish. (Consider, for example, the (false) view that among the essential human goods is that of dominating other members of one's social group; on such a view, the vision of a community in which all of the members of that community are fully flourishing would be an incoherent one.) On the weaker version, the aggregative common good is coherent but practically out-of-reach: the wide variety of aspects of the good, the finiteness of resources, and the limits of human will and ability to pursue the good ensure that the aggregative common good is not a feasible ideal.

I do not accept the view that the human good is such that one human's flourishing essentially involves others' failure to flourish. But even if I were to grant this possibility, it seems to me that the response to both the stronger and the weaker versions of the objection should be the same. I concede that either the nature of the human good or the nature of the human good in conjunction with the circumstances of action within a political community entails that the aggregative common good is unrealizable. But this does not preclude the aggregative common good from serving as both the starting point for correct political deliberation and the basis of whatever normative force is possessed by the law or policy of a given political community. The aggregative common good can serve as a *regulative ideal*, perhaps unrealizable in practice, but the basis on which realizable objectives and binding common norms can be justified.

Consider as an analogy the notion of one's own individual good as that condition in which one is fully flourishing. If this notion were objected to with the proposition that, given the multiplicity of human goods, the tensions that can exist among them, and the limits of human time and energy in pursuing one's own good, it is impossible for one to realize one's own good thus conceived, that would not be much of an objection. For two responses are readily available.

First, insofar as I settle on a further practically realizable, feasible conception of my own overall good, it is as a limitation or truncation of my overall good in this more robust sense. Second, insofar as I am bound to promote some goal or adhere to some norm in light of my own good, it is ultimately in virtue of the normative ideal of one's overall good that I am so bound. If the unrealizability of one's fully flourishing is no objection to identifying one's overall good with that condition in which one is fully flourishing, then the unrealizability of every community member's fully flourishing is no objection to identifying the common good with that condition in which every community member is fully flourishing.

Nor is there a basis for objection on the grounds that the aggregative common good is insufficiently *common*. While the common good is built up out of individuals' goods, the common good thus conceived is the same for all citizens: while the common good is constituted by individual goods, all reasonable agents should recognize it as an end worth seeking, and under the same description. It is not a Hobbesian common good (3.1), which is simply the result of various agents' realizing the necessary conditions for promoting their own ends. When asked why a Hobbesian common good is worth pursuing, reasonable agents will answer differently: A will answer that it serves *A's good*, B that it serves *B's good*, and so forth. When asked why the aggregative common good is worth pursuing, reasonable agents will give the same answer: A will answer that it serves *A's good and B's good and C's good (etc.)*, B that it serves *A's good and B's good and C's good (etc.)*, and so forth. That the 'material' of the common good is individual goods does not make the aggregative common good less than common. (Or so I say: but see 3.4 for a response that a defender of the distinctive good conception might offer.)

Further, this conception of the common good seems a promising candidate to serve the role assigned by the natural law account to conceptions of the common good – that is, to provide a normatively weighty basis from which we can account for the law's authority. It seems clear that if one accepts the point that an individual's good provides all members of the political community with a reason for action, the aggregative common good, which includes the goods of *all* members of the political community, will be a very strong reason for action indeed. (Whether the reasons for action it provides are sufficiently weighty to provide *decisive* reasons for compliance with the law – which is necessary for law to be non-defective (2.7) – is the subject of Chapter 7.)

3.3 Against the Instrumentalist Conception of the Common Good

The aggregative conception of the common good that I defend has two main rivals: the instrumentalist account and the distinctive good account. Let us begin with the instrumentalist view. John Finnis's account of the common good identifies it with a broad obtaining of states of affairs that are instrumentally valuable for the flourishing of the citizens of the political community. Finnis holds that the common good is constituted by "the whole ensemble of material and other conditions, including forms of collaboration, that tend to favour, facilitate, and foster the realization of each individual [in that community] of his or her personal development" (Finnis 1996, p. 5; also Finnis 1980, p. 147).[4] While on Finnis's view, the common good is good only instrumentally – that is, as a means to the promotion of the genuine goods in which citizens can participate – we should not (as the definition makes clear) confine the common good's character only to material means: the common good also includes the preservation of certain institutions (for example, marriage) as well as a moral environment that is conducive to citizens' flourishing (see also George 1993).

Surely the instrumentalist picture is epistemically not much more suspicious than the aggregative view: if we can, as the aggregative conception assumes, say something informative about the content of the human good, we should be able to say something informative about certain sorts of conditions in which citizens are better equipped to pursue their good. But it seems to me that its response to the questions of allegiance and commonness shows that the instrumentalist account is parasitic upon the aggregative conception.

Why should we be interested in promoting the common good instrumentally conceived? There are two answers suggested in Finnis's work. The first is implausible and *ad hoc*. The second indicates that the normative force of the common good instrumentally conceived flows from the normative force of the common good aggregatively conceived.

In order to understand one of the answers that Finnis might offer for the reason to promote the common good, we need to say a few words about what he understands the structure of correct practical thinking to be. On his natural law view, as on the natural law view briefly considered in the Introduction (0.2), the first principles of practical reasoning are a number of *basic goods*, things that are worth pursuing for their own sakes.[5] These basic goods are aspects of agents' well-being, ways that agents are made better-off. What governs our choices and commitments with respect to plans of action to respond to these goods are *principles of practical reasonableness*, which rule out certain possible plans of action or ways of forming plans of action on the basis that acting or choosing in these ways is incompatible with full practical reasonableness.[6] Now, Finnis

---

[4] In providing such an account, he takes himself to be following John XXIII, *Mater et Magistra*, §65, in which the common good is said to be "the sum total of those conditions of social living whereby men are enabled more fully and readily to achieve their perfection."

[5] Finnis's list in his 1980 includes life, knowledge, aesthetic experience, play, practical reasonableness, friendship and community, and religion (pp. 86–90). In later writings, he has altered his account in a couple of important ways: (1) he has widened play to include the skillful performances involved in work; and (2) he has included as a distinct form of good the special form of interpersonal communion he calls 'the marital good.'

[6] Finnis's list in his 1980 includes requirements to form a coherent life plan, to exhibit appropriate commitment to and detachment from that plan, to exhibit no arbitrary preferences

holds that one of these principles of practical reasonableness is that agents are bound to favor and foster the common goods of their communities (Finnis 1980, p. 125). If, then, the common good of the political community is this complex instrumental good, then we might answer the allegiance question by appealing to the principle of practical reasonableness that agents are bound in reason to foster the common good of their communities, including their political communities.

The immediate question to be asked is, of course: what is the warrant for the principle of practical reasonableness that the good of one's communities is to be fostered? His official view is that the principles of practical reasonableness are self-evident and underivable. I take him to be claiming something like the following: one who understands the nature of the basic goods can immediately recognize that these principles specify (and thereby rule out) inappropriate responses to these goods. Thus, not every minimally rational agent will affirm these principles: those agents that have a false view of the features of the basic goods will tend to affirm claims that are in tension with the correct principles of practical reasonableness. Thus, in defending these principles, Finnis's main task is to lay bare the features of the basic goods to which these principles specify appropriate responses, and to criticize rival conceptions of the basic goods.[7] But we get nothing like this sort of defense of the principle requiring the fostering of the common good of one's communities; in fact, we get no defense of it at all. It is simply laid down as a principle of practical reasonableness. Perhaps this manner of proceeding would not be objectionable if the defense of it were obvious or the principle itself so evident that it needed no amplification. But neither of these is the case.

First, the characteristic defense of principles of practical reasonableness involves an appeal to the features of basic goods: after all, these are the first principles of practical reasoning, from which all practical warrant flows. But if Finnis means to use this principle to underwrite a rational requirement to promote the common good of the political community, then another line of defense will have to be found, for the common good of the political community is by Finnis's lights an instrumental good, not a basic good. This is highly problematic, since no practical thought is reasonably governed by reference

---

among the basic goods, to exhibit no arbitrary preferences among persons that can participate in these goods, to act efficiently within the constraints set by the other principles, to
respect every basic good in every act, to foster the common good of one's communities,
and to follow one's conscience (pp. 103–126).

[7] To take just a couple of examples: in arguing for a principle of impartiality among those
that can enjoy the basic goods, Finnis emphasizes the agent-neutral character of the basic
goods; and in arguing for the claim that it is always wrong to intend to destroy an instance of
a basic good for the sake of a distinct instance of a basic good, he argues that the rejection of
the view is predicated on the commensurability of these instances of basic good, but that in
fact distinct instances of basic good are incommensurable. See Finnis 1980, pp. 106–109,
118–125.

to instrumental goods alone; it is reasonably governed only by the intrinsic goods, specified or unspecified, to which the instrumental goods can serve as instruments.

Second, the principle is far from evident. As a requirement of practical reasonableness, not just a principle stating what is a basic good, it is supposed to say more than that being in community with others is a good thing. That being in community with others is a good thing is indeed affirmed by Finnis when he holds that friendship and community are basic goods (Finnis 1980, p. 88). But that there is some reason to enter into and promote friendship and community is a much weaker claim than the claim that we are morally bound to foster the common good of our political community. We should want to hear more about how and why this principle controls our practical reasoning.

The placement of the principle concerning the fostering of the common good of one's communities strikes me as mysterious within the wider context of Finnis's views on the theory of practical reasonableness, and thus I think that an appeal to this principle is not a helpful way to explain the allegiance that reasonable citizens will have to the common good instrumentally conceived. There is, however, a far more straightforward way to explain the allegiance owed to the common good instrumentally conceived. The extent to which we should be interested in any instrumental good is the extent to which we are interested in the intrinsic good or goods to which it is an instrument. It seems, then, that if we are to understand the allegiance owed to the common good instrumentally conceived, we will have to appeal to the good to which the common good instrumentally conceived is instrumental. Given Finnis's description of the common good as the conditions that the individuals of that community can draw upon in order to flourish, it appears that it is the overall flourishing of citizens in community that provides the normative force of the common good instrumentally conceived. But if that is what provides it, then I do not see the advantage in offering an instrumentalist conception of the common good, for the aggregative conception in the background is doing all of the normative work.

A similar point can be made with respect to the commonness desideratum. Whether or not the common good instrumentally conceived is genuinely common or common only in (for example) a Hobbesian way is going to depend on the end to which that good is instrumental. If the reason that I should be interested in the common good instrumentally conceived is that its realization enables me to promote my own good, and the reason that you should be interested in the common good instrumentally conceived is that its realization enables you to promote your own good, then in promoting the common good thus conceived we do not aim at a common end: what each of us is really aiming at is just that aspect of the common good that is good for each of us individually. Only by seeing the common good instrumentally conceived as for the sake of something like the common good conceived aggregatively can its commonness be validated. But, again, if we can confidently say that the instrumentalist account fulfills the commonness desideratum only by connecting that account to the aggregative conception, there seems to be strong reason to affirm an aggregative conception rather than an instrumentalist conception of the common good.

My main line of argument for the superiority of the aggregative conception to the instrumentalist conception of the common good is, then, that the instrumentalist view is parasitic on the aggregative conception. Now, I am not sure that a defender of the instrumentalist view need deny this. What the defender of such a view would have to go on to say is that there are distinct reasons to keep with the instrumentalist conception. The defender of the instrumentalist conception can admit, that is, that with respect to the issues of normative force and commonness, the instrumentalist view leans on the aggregative view, while holding that there are other grounds to identify the common good of the political community in the instrumentalist way.

Let's return to Finnis. In *Natural Law and Natural Rights*, he vacillates between an aggregative conception and an instrumentalist conception of the common good of the political community, while in later work he explicitly adopts the instrumentalist conception. As far as I can tell, he offers two reasons for adopting the instrumentalist view: first, that the common good aggregatively conceived is not a realizable end; and second, that the common good instrumentally conceived is able to provide an account of limited government. But it seems to me that neither of these arguments provides grounds to move from the aggregative to the instrumentalist view.

Here is the realizability argument.

If the object, point, or common good of the political community were indeed a self-sufficient life, and if self-sufficiency (*autarcheia*) were indeed what Aristotle defines it to be – a life lacking in nothing, of complete fulfillment – then we would have to say that the political community has a point it cannot hope to achieve, a common good utterly beyond its reach. (Finnis 1996, p. 7)

The argument is, as it stands, unsatisfactory. The first thing to be said in response is that the conception of the common good that Finnis offers – that whole set of material conditions, and so on – is utterly beyond the reach of the political community as well. We might think about it this way. What would it be for the common good in the instrumental sense to be wholly realized? Something like the following: that for every reasonable aim a citizen might have, the only thing that would prevent the citizen from achieving that end would be that citizen's lack of a will to achieve it. This is far beyond the reach of any political community. Now, the response might be: surely it cannot be achieved, but it can be achieved to a greater extent than the aggregative common good can be achieved. I am not sure that this is true – I am not sure that the comparison involved makes much sense – but even if it were, it would not seem to me to be that great an objection. As I argued in (3.2), the notion of the common good, like the notion of an individual's good, serves as an *ideal* – perhaps not something realizable in practice, but nevertheless the starting point for deliberation.[8]

The other main argument that Finnis puts forward in favor of the instrumentalist conception is that this conception seems better suited to providing a principled rationale for limited government. Finnis seems to understand by 'limited government' a government whose actions are constrained not only by the basic principles of natural practical reasonableness, which principles apply to all agents, but also by principles of *antipaternalism* and *subsidiarity*. There are a variety of understandings of antipaternalism, some of which Finnis would reject. At the very least, though, antipaternalism is the principle that political authority is not to be exercised solely in order to prevent a competent agent from acting unreasonably. Subsidiarity, the other constraint on government Finnis wishes to defend, is the principle of Catholic social thought that political authority is not to take over the provision of goods that lower-level associations are able to provide for themselves.[9] But if one were to affirm the aggregative conception of the common good, it might be thought that one would find oneself committed to the advocating of (for example) criminalization of self-regarding immoral behavior simply as such – not because of further undesirable social effects, including the deterioration of a moral environment in which vice is discouraged, but simply because acting in a practically unreasonable way is bad for the agent that acts in that way, and thus damaging to the aggregative common good. Further, the aggregative conception seems to leave inadequate room for subsidiarity, according to which the proper role of government is that of "assisting individuals and groups to co-ordinate their activities for the objectives and commitments they have chosen, and to do so in ways consistent with the other aspects of the common good of the political community" (Finnis 1996, p. 6). The instrumentalist view is better suited to a conception of government in which government cannot be simply paternalistic and cannot, even in principle, take over the tasks of lower-level associations. For if the aim of political authority is to promote the common good, and the common good is in principle restricted to instrumental goods, political authority cannot reach beyond the provision of instrumental goods in a way that would justify paternalism or take away the proper tasks of individuals or groups.

All of this strikes me as the wrong way around. The attractiveness of the antipaternalist and subsidiarity principles should be, on a natural law account, explicable in terms of the good; we should not have to pare down the theory of the good in order to generate an argument for antipaternalism and subsidiarity. A theory of the common good should not have to be rigged in order to generate these two results; even if in developing a theory of the common good the

---

[8] This view of the common good as ideal is also articulated in Cochran 1978, p. 236, where Cochran ascribes this conception of the common good to Yves Simon.

[9] For its classic formulation, see Pope Pius XI's *Quadragesimo Anno* (1931), §79.

direction of our inquiry is shaped by antipaternalist and prosubsidiarity intuitions, our finished account should provide some explanation from the nature of the good to the antipaternalist and prosubsidiarity principles. Indeed, it seems clear that whether or not one should accept antipaternalist and prosubsidiarity principles as part of the central story of political authority's proper functioning will depend on one's theory of intrinsic goods, those goods that constitute the aggregative common good.

Here is an example that might help to make this clear. Suppose that one is firmly committed to a Benthamite understanding of the good – that all goods are, at root, individual, and reducible to pleasure absent pain. The only things worth pursuing on this view are pleasures, and the only things worth avoiding are pains. Now it seems to me that a Benthamite account of the political order would have very little use for the antipaternalism and prosubsidiarity principles. If the only things of value are pleasures and pains, what does it matter whether they are provided through paternalistic measures by the state? If the only things of value are pleasures and pains, what does it matter whether they are provided by political institutions, or by families, or by trade unions, or by individuals? What difference could it possibly make? A Benthamite could support antipaternalism or subsidiarity as an empirical generalization about the best means to generate pleasures and avoid pains. But for the Benthamite to have an *in principle* preference for lower-level associations' producing pleasures and avoiding pains for themselves would be bizarre. And if a Benthamite declared that the common good of the political community should not be understood in terms of pleasure and pain but in terms of the conditions by which individuals can realize pleasures for themselves and avoid pains for themselves, we would have very little idea what the Benthamite was up to. The conception of intrinsic good that the Benthamite is working with would make any principled appeal to antipaternalism and subsidiarity unintelligible.

What makes the imagined Benthamite's appeal to antipaternalism and subsidiarity unintelligible is Bentham's theory of intrinsic goods. Similarly, we might say, what would make the antipaternalism and prosubsidiarity principles intelligible is a different theory of intrinsic goods. Natural law accounts of the human good, of which Finnis's is a premier example, tend to be sufficiently rich that – unlike on Bentham's view – many of the goods that are affirmed include agent's deliberations, judgments, choices, and actions (see, for example, Finnis 1980, pp. 59–99, and Murphy 2001a, pp. 100–135). One could offer some support for the antipaternalism and prosubsidiarity principles by appeal to one or another of these basic goods. One could offer at least a weak antipaternalist rationale on the basis of there being a *prima facie* reason against any legal restriction on conduct: that there is a good involved in deliberating one's way to a practical conclusion, and the existence of a legal rule cuts off or at the very least restricts the relevant range of deliberation. (A good – though by no means the only – reason for not having legal rules against all lying is that it is a good thing to reach and act on the deliberative conclusion that one is not to lie without having any legal apparatus determining one's practical thinking in this matter.) One could offer at least a weak prosubsidiarity rationale on the basis of there being a *prima facie* reason against stripping from individuals the responsibility to carry out tasks that they can fulfill on their own: that there are goods involved in deliberation and judgment, in intelligent, challenging work, and so forth (0.2). (See, for an argument along these lines, Wolfe 1995.)

Now, a defender of the instrumentalist view might say that this is something like what he or she had in mind all along – that while the common good aggregatively conceived provides for the normative force and the commonness of the common good, sound practical thinking governed by the features of the aggregative common good indicates that the common good instrumentally conceived is the uniquely appropriate *proximate* ideal for political deliberation and action. Once we see clearly the nature of the aggregative common good, we will see that promoting and honoring it requires that we restrict ourselves to the instrumental common good as the object of political deliberation and action. If this turns out to be so, then the defender of the aggregative view would have no objection. But it seems to me that we have grounds to doubt that things will turn out so neatly. Surely there will be occasions when the difficult questions of the following sort arise, not just as matters of idle speculation but as serious practical issues. One might ask: "Even if deliberative freedom is important, aren't some self-regarding actions so evil or debasing that they are the appropriate object of state action, even apart from their effects on specific other-regarding obligations or on the moral environment more generally?" Or: "Even if there are goods realized through letting functions be carried out at lower levels, are there not other goods – perhaps goods of community – that are instantiated or at least fostered by placing citizens 'in the same boat,' as it were?" These are questions that cannot be answered at the level of the instrumental common good; we would have to move back to the level of the aggregative common good, the good of persons in community, to have a hope of answering them reasonably and assessing their relevance for particular political decisions. No matter how much we can rely on the instrumental conception of the common good in ordinary political thinking, the aggregative conception will retain at least its background influence and almost certainly will on some occasions have to be relied upon more directly in dealing with difficult questions about the appropriate scope and exercise of political authority.

3.4 Against the Distinctive Good Conception of the Common Good

The instrumental conception of the common good yields to the aggregative conception. But there is within the natural law tradition of theorizing about politics a rival understanding of the common good that, like the aggregative conception, understands the common good in terms of intrinsic rather than instrumental goodness. What distinguishes this rival conception – what I call a 'distinctive good' view – is that it holds that the common good is not composed out of the various goods of the members of that community. Rather, the good is the good of the community *as a whole*, what perfects the political community as such.

I think that Aquinas offers this sort of picture of the common good, though I admit that his remarks on the nature of the common good of the political community are not completely unambiguous. As I understand him, for Aquinas the common good consists of "justice and peace"(*Summa Theologiae* IaIIae 96, 3), where justice and peace are conditions of the community entire. Justice consists in that state of the community by which a proper relation between persons, a certain kind of equality, is preserved (IIaIIae 57, 1). Peace consists both in the absence of discord among citizens and the presence of a proper ordering among them (IIaIIae 29, 1). A political community's being in good condition as a whole consists in its being just and well-ordered. (For further discussion, see Murphy 1997a and Finnis 1998b.)

Now, the common good thus conceived does seem to be sufficiently accessible to be an object of political deliberation. Aquinas does think that we can have access to truths of natural justice, and that we can concern ourselves with the most appropriate way to determine the particulars of these principles of justice for the concrete circumstances of common life in which we find ourselves (*Summa Theologiae* IIaIIae 57, 1–2). And these goods might be taken to be common in a strong sense: as perfecting the whole community, they belong to no one in particular, but to the community itself. I want to argue, though, that the distinctive good conception runs into difficulty with respect to the normative role criterion: it is unclear why we should treat the distinctive good of the political community as an object of rational allegiance. In order to see how it runs into difficulty on this score, though, we need to get clearer on the different ways that one might understand the distinctive good view.

For clarity on the differing understandings that one might offer of the distinctive good view, let us consider briefly an objection that might be leveled against aggregative conceptions of the common good. There is a straightforward sense in which the aggregative view is individualistic: for, on that view, the common good is made up of the goods of individuals.[10] But such conceptions are deeply flawed, one might argue, because they fail to recognize the importance of *irreducibly social* goods, goods that involve not one agent but two, or many (for

---

[10] It should go without saying that the individualism of the aggregative conception is not egoism. One often finds, though, in accounts of distinctive good conceptions of the common good arguments that seem to be of the form: if one rejects the distinctive good conception of the common good, one must be going in for a conception of the common good as mere means to one's own private good; but this latter conception of the common good is an absurd, vicious, etc. form of egoism; therefore, etc. But there is nothing remotely egoistic about the aggregative conception of the common good.

thoughts along these lines, see Taylor 1997b). The aggregative conception, by not including these irreducibly social goods in the common good of the political community, is both at odds with the natural law tradition and implausible in itself. The distinctive good conception, by contrast, affirms the possibility of irreducibly social goods; indeed, its key thesis is just that the common good is one of these irreducibly social goods.

It seems to me important, though, to recognize that there is more than one way that a good can be said to be social, and to be clear on the way that the distinctive good view is supposed to be superior to the aggregative conception, we need to make explicit at least two of these senses. Consider a statement of the form 'x is good for y,' where x ranges over states of affairs and y ranges over 'parties', where a party is a person, a group of persons, or an institution whose offices are occupied by persons. Now, suppose that one were to claim that x is an irreducibly social good. There are at least two ways that this claim could be understood. First, it could mean that the state of affairs x is irreducibly social. For x to be irreducibly social is, roughly, for x to involve more than one person (that is the 'social' part), and for x not to be divisible into two or more states of affairs that do not include all of the persons involved in x (that is the 'irreducible' part). Second, it could mean that party y is irreducibly social. Again, for y to be irreducibly social is, roughly, for y to involve more than one person and for y not to be divisible into two or more parties that do not include more than one person. To claim that x is an irreducibly social good is therefore an ambiguous claim: it can mean either that the good itself is social (this is the first sense) or that the being that is made better-off by x's obtaining is a social unity (this is the second sense).

Given these clarifications, it cannot be a point against the aggregative conception of the common good that that conception rejects the existence of goods that are social in the first sense while the distinctive good conception affirms the existence of goods that are social in the first sense. Most natural law theorists hold that (for example) friendship, community, and religion are basic goods (0.2), but these goods are irreducibly social in the first sense of that notion: the goods of friendship, community, and religion cannot be broken down into states of affairs that are asocial.[11] The aggregative view, then, could include within its conception of the common good goods that are irreducibly social in the first sense, insofar as these irreducibly social goods are aspects of the fulfillment of individual persons.

Indeed, it seems to me that a number of defenders of the distinctive good view affirm the thesis that while the common good perfects the community as such, the practical force of the common good arises from its role in perfecting

[11] There would be trouble for the natural law theorist that denied the existence of goods irreducibly social in this sense, though, but defenders of such a position are few and far between.

individual members of the community. As I mentioned, on Aquinas's view the common good consists of justice and peace, which perfects the community as a whole. But if I understand his view of the relationship between an individual and the common good of that individual's political community correctly, the individual's good includes not just his or her private good but the broader goods of family and political community, and Aquinas understands the allegiance claimed by the common good in terms of its place in one's own overall good (for relevant texts see *Summa Theologiae* IaIIae 19, 10; IIaIIae 26, 3; IIaIIae 26, 4 ad 3; IIaIIae 31, 3 ad 2; IIaIIae 47, 10; I argue (briefly) in Murphy 1995, pp. 863–865, that this is Aquinas's view). And recent advocates of distinctive good views like Aquinas's have often asserted that the common good is common through its perfecting the community as a whole yet perfects each individual member of that community. Louis Dupré endorses the "classical definition" of the common good as "a good proper to, and attainable only by, the community, yet individually shared by its members" (1993, p. 687). When Ralph McInerny emphasizes the "shareability" of the common good, he is drawing our attention to the fact that the realization of the common good is something that perfects each member of that community (1988b, p. 90).

Now, if the defenders of the distinctive good view want to say nothing more than that the common good is irreducibly social but is worthy of pursuit as a constituent of the good of individual members of that community, then it seems to me that the defender of the aggregative view can affirm this claim as well. One might think, on the basis of the agreement between the aggregative and the distinctive good view on this point, that we have reached an argumentative impasse between these two views. But that does not seem to me to be correct. First: if we affirm that the obtaining of the common good is a constituent of the good of each and every member of the political community, we still have to provide an account of what the defender of the distinctive good view wants to say about the source of allegiance to the common good. Does the defender of the distinctive good view want to say that for each member of the political community it is the contribution to his or her own good that makes pursuit of the common good worth carrying out? Or does the defender of this view want to say that for each member of the political community it is the contribution not only to his or her own good but also to the good of the other members of the political community that makes the common good something to be promoted by him or her? If the former option is chosen, then it looks as though the distinctive good theorist's account of the common good has become, strangely enough, Hobbesian. It may be a logical truth that the common good is shared by members of the political community; it would be, on this view, a logical impossibility for me to gain the benefits of the common good's being instantiated without others' gaining them as well. But the end of my actions would be just the promotion of a just, peaceful order for myself; it is at my perfection alone that my actions are aimed. We have thus lost an important element of the commonness of the common good, that it should be shared as an end by reasonable agents within the political community.

Suppose, on the other hand, that the defender of this version of the distinctive good view allowed that it is not only insofar as the common good perfects oneself, but also insofar as it perfects the fellow members of one's political community, that this good is a reasonable object of pursuit. On this reading of the distinctive good view, what would separate the defender of the distinctive good view from the defender of the aggregative view would be only the scope of their accounts of the content of the common good: the defender of the distinctive good view would hold that only justice and peace – conceived as perfecting each member of the political community – should be included within the common good, while the defender of the aggregative view would hold that not only justice and peace, but also the non-social (and even social but non-political) goods of each and every member of the political community should be included within the common good as well. Given that the difference between these views is only one of scope, there seems to be a powerful argument for preferring the aggregative view to this version of the distinctive good view: since other goods besides the distinctive common good of justice and peace are reasons for action, grounds for the community to make one decision rather than another, then the common good aggregatively conceived provides all of the reasons for allegiance than this distinctive good view provides, and more as well. It has a greater claim to guide action than this version of the distinctive good view can offer, and thus it would be an unmotivated watering down of the common good aggregatively conceived to affirm this understanding of the distinctive good position.

When the source of the allegiance to the common good as distinctive good is held to be its status as a constituent of individual members' goods, the distinctive good conception of the common good places itself into a sort of direct competition with the aggregative conception that the distinctive good view cannot win. It would avoid this sort of direct competition by affirming that it is the common good's status as an irreducibly social good of the second type that provides, on its own, the source of members' reasonable allegiance to the common good. On this latter reading, the idea is not that the community's being just and peaceful is a part of each and every member's good and therefore part of the common good; rather, the idea is that justice and peace is good for *the community as a whole*: it perfects *a body of persons organized politically*. It is therefore – and without necessary recourse to additional premises – an end that members of the political community have reason to pursue and promote. There is thus a sharp contrast between this view and the aggregative view: the aggregative view understands the common good wholly in terms of what fulfills individual persons, while this version of the distinctive good view understands the common good wholly in terms of what fulfills the political community as a social unit.

It might at this point be suggested, in an attempt at reconciliation, that the common good consists *both* in the goods of individual persons *and* in social goods in this latter sense. If it were agreed that it makes sense to speak of such distinctive goods, and that these distinctive goods are as such fundamentally relevant to reasonable action, then one could run an arbitrariness argument against an aggregative view that affirms goods that fulfill persons but not goods that fulfill irreducible social units: it would be arbitrary to allow the former but not the latter into one's conception of the common good, if both are fundamentally relevant to deliberation. But it seems to me that we should reject the fundamental relevance to deliberation of this kind of irreducibly social good. On the welfarist view of practical rationality that I have defended elsewhere (Murphy 2001a, pp. 139–156), all fundamental reasons for action must be framed in terms of individuals' well-being, and so to refer to what makes an irreducibly social unit better-off is to place oneself at odds with this natural law view's welfarism. But to rule out this kind of distinctive good view by an appeal to welfarism is to ignore the possibility that this natural law view's welfarism might be meaningfully and importantly challenged by appeal to this second kind of distinctive social goods. We need, then, to provide some account amenable to a welfarist view by which we can explain the appeal that the distinctive good view has had for many natural law theorists.

My ground for saying that we should reject the fundamental relevance to deliberation of irreducibly social goods in this sense is *not* that it is not meaningful to ascribe irreducibly social goodness to certain states of affairs. One can speak of a team's good condition, or a university's, or a chess club's, and one can talk about what is good for a team or university or club in ways that can be understood only by appeal to this irreducibly social goodness. Moreover, such statements can be true: it is true that a university's having intelligent faculty, motivated students, well-designed facilities, and wealthy and nostalgic alumni is good for that institution. So claims about certain states being good for some social units – such as the claim that justice and peace is good for the political community as a whole – can be intelligible and correct. But this concession to the distinctive good view does not yet offer any grounds for the defender of that view to argue against the aggregative conception. For claims about what is good for some entity do not always have fundamental practical or moral importance, do not always of themselves furnish reasons to choose or act one way rather than another. To take a clear example: whether a vacuum cleaner is in good or bad condition is of no fundamental practical importance – it can only be made practically relevant by appeal to other reasons for action, reasons that are themselves fundamental or appropriately connected to reasons that are fundamental. I want to make the same claim with respect to the distinctive good view: that while it can be meaningful and correct to hold that certain states of affairs are good for the political community as a whole, our reasons to promote these states of affairs are explicable wholly by way of those goods included within the aggregative conception of the common good. Any allegiance that the distinctive good version seems to claim derives from what is involved in reasonably promoting, honoring, and respecting the aggregative common good.

Let us take as a test case Aquinas's conception of the common good as the distinctive good of justice and peace. Start with justice, and with a basic distinction between two ways that justice can function in deliberation. Justice can function as a *constraint*: one's deliberation will be guided such that one does not act unjustly. Justice can function as a *goal*: one's deliberation will be guided such that one's actions promote the obtaining of justice. Now, whatever the differences may be between the aggregative and distinctive good conceptions, that justice should serve as a constraint on political deliberation is not, or need not, be at issue between them. The defender of the aggregative conception can, that is, affirm that political deliberation must adhere to the constraints of justice in reaching deliberative conclusions. The difference between the distinctive good and the aggregative conceptions concerns the way that justice should function as a goal in political deliberation. For there to be an important difference between these views, the value of justice as a goal cannot be reducible to the overall good of citizens in community.

Here is what I have in mind. Suppose that one affirms the following: that it is a human good for one to respond properly to others' good. This is part of the good of practical reasonableness, or excellence in agency (0.2). Part of what would make me well off is to act in a reasonable way with respect to others. Now, imagine a political community in which I, and everyone else in it, act in a reasonable way with respect to others' good. We are, roughly speaking, honoring everyone's rights, what is due to each of us with respect to our goods.[12] Clearly, this state of affairs is worth pursuing. But given the claim that to respond reasonably to others' good is an aspect of one's well-being, it seems that (1) the importance of this state of affairs can be understood in the terms provided by the defender of the aggregative conception, (2) the aggregative conception is superior in that it includes other relevant goods as well, and (3) the common good of the community as a whole adds little or – I would say – nothing to the point of pursuing justice within a community.

1. The capacity of the aggregative conception to provide an account of the point of the pursuit of justice as an end is straightforward, given the claim that practical reasonableness is a basic good. If it is a basic good, then the state in which an agent acts reasonably with respect to others is an instance of a basic good, something that makes that agent well-off. But if it is something that makes the agent well-off, it is part of the agent's individual good, and thus part

---

[12] I don't assume here that what counts as responding reasonably to others' goods can be determined 'atomistically – that is, in isolation from the way that others act. What I am suggesting here is that we can see a *value* in such reasonable response apart from merely as an aspect of a good of the community as a whole.

of the common good of that community aggregatively conceived. To the extent that justice can be broken down into proper responses by one agent to another, its value can be captured by the aggregative conception of the common good.

2. To the extent that the value of justice can be captured by the aggregative conception of the common good, the aggregative conception is superior to a view that focuses on justice alone. For there are other aspects of well-being besides reasonable response to others' good: it is arbitrary to focus on just relations to the exclusion of other goods. And, besides, since justice involves responding properly to others' good, it would be very peculiar to deny the importance of others' good in an account of the common good that makes justice central.

3. The extent to which the value of justice can be captured by the aggregative conception is great. When we consider the choiceworthiness of justice as a goal, we should probably consider the extent to which its choiceworthiness is bound up with making individuals well-off – both intrinsically, to the extent that responding reasonably is a basic good, and instrumentally, to the extent that agents are often made worse off by injustice. Now ask: what is added to the choiceworthiness of justice by noting that "and what's more, it perfects the community as a whole"? It seems to me that very little normative pull indeed is exerted by this addendum.

We may be briefer with respect to the distinctive good of peace. Its instrumental value in promoting agents' well-being has always been clear. Further, we might add that there is a genuine intrinsic good in not being in discord with one's fellows: this is the negative aspect of the good of friendship. The argument follows the same course as the argument against the importance of the distinctive good of justice: that the good of peace can be accounted for in terms offered by the aggregative conception of the common good; that the aggregative conception is less arbitrary by allowing all other aspects of well-being into the picture; and that once the choiceworthiness of peace provided by individuals' good is bracketed, there seems to be little or nothing left for the distinctive good of peace to account for.

The distinctive good view rightly says that we sometimes speak of there being a good that is of the community as a whole. There are many other things besides political communities of which we may speak of their distinctive good: football teams, universities, families, trade unions, and so forth. But while nothing in my treatment of the particular features of Aquinas's representative distinctive good account commits me to anything more than that the distinctive good account of the common good that he offers takes its reason-giving force from the aggregative view, I am willing to generalize the point not only to other distinctive good theories of the common good but to distinctive good theories of all of these associations and institutions. To whatever extent the distinctive good of a football team, university, and so on is worth promoting, respecting, honoring, the reasons to act in these ways derive not from the distinctive good of that association but from the good of the persons whose lives that association affects.

Inasmuch as a distinctive good view distances itself from the good of persons, its normative hold on us is loosened. It is a virtue of the aggregative conception that it retains its normative hold through being entirely person-regarding.

A final point. I have challenged the distinctive good view practically, holding that it does not seem that the distinctive goods of the political community as such provide us with reasons for action and that to the extent that they appear to provide such reasons it is only because of the way that these distinctive goods enter into the individual well-being of its members. There is, however, a very direct way to challenge the distinctive good view – metaphysically. Consider, for the sake of comparison, one of Parfit's lines of criticism of the self-interest theory of rationality: that personal identity is not some further fact, holding in an all-or-nothing fashion; rather, there are simply more-or-less strong psychological and physical connections between earlier and later person-stages (Parfit 1984, pp. 307–347). Parfit wields this thesis about the nature of personal identity against the self-interest view: the self-interest view presupposes that the relationship between my present and later selves is one of strict numerical identity, and inasmuch as it is not strict identity, but rather a matter of more-or-less psychological continuity, the self-interest theory's absolute insistence on a pattern of concern in which I care as much about my later self as I do about my present self and in which I give entire priority to my later self over any other party is irrational.

One could use this sort of metaphysical line of attack against the distinctive good view in a much more direct challenge. There is a difference, one might say, between what exists strictly speaking and what exists only loosely speaking, and human persons fall on the former side of this divide while communities and associations fall on the latter. Since only what exists can have a good, individual human persons can, strictly speaking, have goods; communities and associations can have goods in only a loose sense. And since it also seems to me that what is of fundamental practical importance must be referred to what is good really, and not just to what is good in a manner of speaking, a distinctive good conception of the common good just could not have the normative force that an aggregative conception has.

3.5 Utilitarianism and the Aggregative Conception of the Common Good

My argument in favor of the aggregative conception of the common good is that we have strong reasons for allegiance to the common good thus conceived, and that the other conceptions of the common good claim our allegiance only through the normative force of the common good aggregatively conceived. Before we turn from the problem of characterizing the common good to a statement of the principle invoking the common good on which the natural law account of the law's authority will be based (3.6), I want to consider a difficulty that those hostile to the aggregative conception might press against it: it concerns the issue of whether the aggregative conception, just because it is aggregative, is therefore open to the most serious criticisms to which the utilitarian view is open. The aggregative conception of the common good, like the utilitarian notion of the overall good, is welfarist. The argument for the choiceworthiness of the common good aggregatively conceived in political matters mirrors the utilitarian argument for the choiceworthiness of the overall good in all practical matters: it is a characteristic form of utilitarian argument to proceed aggregatively, noting that if one takes an individual's good (characteristically one's own!) to be a reason for action, then non-arbitrariness commits one to accept others' goods as reasons for action, and thus the aggregate of all persons' goods as the ultimate object of practical concern (cf. Sidgwick's *Methods of Ethics*, pp. 379–382; and also the terse argument in Mills's *Utilitarianism*, p. 34).

Regardless of the merits of the aggregative conception, then, it might be thought to be a serious concern for that conception that the correspondence between it and the utilitarian view of morality entails that the discontents of utilitarianism are bound to become the discontents of the aggregative view of the common good. The central problem here is *subordination* – that, as the utilitarian view implies, objectionably, the individual's good must be subordinated in an inappropriate way to the overall good, the aggregative conception too must imply that the citizen's good must be subordinated in the same way to the good of the political community. Rawls puts the point this way in his discussion of utilitarianism as a principle governing the distribution of goods by the basic structure of society. On the utilitarian view, "society is rightly ordered, and therefore just, when its major institutions are arranged so as to achieve the greatest net balance of satisfaction summed over all the individuals belonging to it" (Rawls 1971, p. 22). But, as he notes:

> The striking feature of the utilitarian view of justice is that it does not matter, except indirectly, how this sum of satisfactions is distributed among individuals. . . . The correct distribution . . . is that which yields the maximal fulfillment. . . . Thus there is no reason in principle why the greater gains of some should not compensate for the lesser losses of others; or more importantly, why the violation of the liberty of a few might not be made right by the greater good shared by many. It simply happens that under most conditions, at least in a reasonably advanced stage of civilization, the greatest sum of advantages is not attained in this way. No doubt the strictness of the common sense precepts of justice has a certain usefulness in limiting men's propensities to injustice and socially injurious actions, but the utilitarian believes that to affirm this strictness as a first principle of morals is a mistake. (Rawls 1971, p. 26)

On Rawls's view, the central mistake of utilitarianism is its failure to "take seriously the distinction between persons" by holding that a sacrifice of one person's good can be simply compensated by a greater good realized in another.

Given the similarity between the utilitarian picture of the overall good and the aggregative conception of the common good, the aggregative conception must be prone to this weakness as well.

If we do grant that these implications are obnoxious – and I do grant that – then a defense of this objection to the aggregative view will have to fulfill two tasks. It will first have to show that the aggregative conception of the common good does not immediately commit the defender of that view to endorsing the utilitarian mode of deliberating about how to advance the common good. Second, it will have to show that there is an alternative, more reasonable mode of deliberating about how to advance the common good that is not subject to the criticisms to which utilitarianism is susceptible.

We find in utilitarianism the following sensible line of thought. The highest end in ('ideal') moral deliberation is, on the utilitarian view, overall well-being. But we cannot realize everyone's well-being to the logical limit. Choices have to be made about whose good to promote and in what ways. Since everyone's well-being counts, everyone is to 'count for one, and only for one.' The only relevant differences are the amounts of well-being that we can realize in the various options before us. If these are the only relevant differences, then the most obvious strategy is that of maximization: if the only thing that ultimately matters is agents' well-being, then what could be as reasonable as a strategy of maximization, of promoting as much well-being as one can? Certainly, in some cases, this may involve sacrificing some agents' good for the good of others – either letting their good languish, or even in destroying it, for the sake of the greater good. But their being sacrificed is, after all, a result of the tough choices that agents have to make rather than their good being discounted in any way in deliberation.

To fulfill the first task – to show that the defender of the aggregative conception of the common good need not be subject to the criticisms leveled against utilitarianism's willingness to subordinate agents' good in objectionable ways – all that needs to be done is to show that affirming the overall good as the proper end to promote does not commit one to a maximizing theory of practical reasonableness in deliberation. And this seems clear enough: for the defender of a maximizing strategy of deliberation must appeal to at least three other theses to justify the move from the overall good as a starting point in deliberation to the conclusion that maximization is *a*, let alone *the only*, reasonable strategy to determine how to go about responding to that good (cf. Murphy 2001a, pp. 142–156).

First: the defense of the maximizing conception of reasonableness presupposes that what is right, or reasonable, is entirely a function of the nature of the good – that is, that the only guidelines to deliberation are those that can be gathered from the intrinsic features of the goods that one has reason to promote. But this can be sensibly denied: one might claim, instead, that there are side-constraints on reasonable action that do not derive simply from the character of the good (see, for example, Dworkin 1977b, pp. 90–94). These side-constraints may very well limit the areas in which maximization is a reasonable deliberative strategy.

Second: the defense of the maximizing conception presupposes that what is right, or reasonable, is always best understood in terms of promotion of the good. But this can be sensibly denied: one might claim, instead, that there are modes of reasonable response to goods other than that of promotion. What I have in mind here is primarily expressive action, that of honoring, respecting, or otherwise expressing one's relationship to them.

Third: the defense of the maximizing conception presupposes that what is right, or reasonable, can be determined by a weighing or summing of goods that are instantiated in different agents' lives; it presupposes, to the extent that it aims to govern deliberation, commensurability. But this can be sensibly denied: one might claim, instead, that the goods of different lives are incommensurable, and as such cannot be placed on a common scale to be weighed off against each other.

The point, then, is that there are a number of claims that one has to affirm in addition to the claim that the common good of the political community is the aggregate of individual members' goods in order to arrive at the admittedly objectionable maximizing view of practical reasonableness. One has to affirm the priority of the good to the right; one has to affirm promotionism – that is, the view that the only reasonable response to goods is that of promotion; and one has to affirm the commensurability of different agents' goods. The rejection of any of these blocks the easy route to a maximizing view of practical reasonableness.

The natural law view that I affirm would not reject the first of these three claims – it shares with utilitarianism the view that the good is prior to the right, or the reasonable – but it would reject the second and the third (0.2). The second of these is the hardest to elaborate; theories of practical reasonableness along promotionist lines are well-developed, while the theory of reasonable expressive action is still quite underdeveloped (but see Anderson 1993). (I will have more to say about expressive action in Chapter 6, in the discussion of rationales for legal punishment (6.6).) On the third point: one of the key features of the natural law view discussed in the opening chapter (0.2) is the emphasis on the incommensurability of distinct persons' goods. It is this incommensurability that, on the view I hold, rules out the intentional destruction of some agent's good in order to promote some other agent's good (cf. Finnis 1980, pp. 120–121, and Murphy 2001a, pp. 204–207); and so it is clear that at least some forms of subordination – those that involve intentional, instrumental destruction of some agents' goods for the sake of others' – can be ruled out consistently with the adoption of an aggregative conception of the common good.

Even with this restriction in place, though, we are still left with deep questions about how we are to deliberate about how to advance the common good. We seem to be left with nothing more than that the good of each member of the community is worth realizing, yet with respect to their value each is unique, non-fungible, irreplaceable. How could we possibly deliberate in a reasonable, non-arbitrary way about how to promote the common good when (1) all individuals' goods are included in that good, (2) not everyone's good can be fully realized, yet (3) none of their goods can be sensibly weighed against the others?

One important source of political judgment can be found by noting that even through maximization is ruled out, the requirement of impartiality remains in force. All of these goods have a place in the common good; none can be dismissed. What we need is something to make the requirements of impartiality more vivid, a way to try to ensure that decisions about how to advance the common good are made in a way that is impartial among the various goods that make up the common good. Here is an example. The defender of the aggregative conception of the common good looking for such a procedure might turn to a suitably modified Rawlsian account, in which the requirements of impartiality in promoting the common good can be modeled by way of an agreement of parties, each of which represents an agent's good.[13] Surely the details of the agreement situation will differ: the natural law theorist would surely allow that distributions might be affected by the intrinsic unreasonableness of some agents' ends, as agents in such an original position would be aware that there is such a thing as worthwhile and worthless plans of life, and that there are other principles of practical reasonableness that constrain their agreement. But the agreement situation is a helpful model, since we know that rational agents can come to agreements that are non-arbitrary in content even when they do not place their ends on a common scale to be weighed off against each other (cf. Gauthier 1986).

Of course, there is no reason to think that how the aggregative common good should be determined for the sake of common action must be entirely decided by the demands of practical reasonableness. As an analogy: think of one's own ideal individual good, the condition in which one is enjoying to the logical limit all of the aspects of well-being that make one's life go well. Surely this is an ideal unrealizable in practice, an ideal that will have to be pruned and molded if one is to pursue in a fruitful way a realistically attainable vision of a good life. But even if deliberation will take one some way in deciding how to reshape this ideal for the sake of action, there is no reason to think that deliberation will take one all the way: at some point, choices undetermined by reasons have to be made.

---

[13] Rawls suggests that the original position is appropriate because of persons' equality, but this strikes me as misleading, or at least not dispositive. If they are equal, why shouldn't we treat citizens' systems of ends as equally valuable, and then proceed to trade them off against each other? The separateness-of-persons point does not seem to help here. After all, each of the one-dollar bills in my wallet is separate from each of the others, but fungible with each of the others; there is nothing unreasonable about trading them off, of 'sacrificing' one in order to gain three, and so forth.

And so it may well be – indeed, it seems obvious that it must be – that how the unrealistically ideal aggregative common good will yield a realistic, proximate object of common political pursuit will be a matter for free political choice. But even here it is not as if it will be a matter of indifference which political structures are in place that will determine what counts as the public's choice on matters related to the common good. It may be, for example, one of the demands of impartiality that all citizens have an equal share with respect to the making of discretionary choices about the determination of the common good (cf. Christiano 1996, pp. 59–93, and Richardson 2002, p. 243). And so some of the rational constraints with respect to the determination of the common good may concern not how agents are to reason with respect to the question of how to determine it for the sake of common action but what procedures should be in place for deciding such questions once the resources for rational deliberation run out.

The discontents of utilitarianism, then, are not the discontents of an aggregative conception of the common good. We can affirm the aggregative conception of the common good while rejecting a maximizing conception of practical reasonableness; and this combination of views need not lead to mere arbitrariness in deciding how to act in response to the common good.[14]

3.6 The Common Good Principle

I have argued that the conception of the common good that best captures the normative appeal of the common good and its commonness as an end among reasonable members of the political community is an aggregative conception. Now, it is by appeal to the idea that citizens are bound to promote the common good of their political communities that standard natural law theories have made their case for political authority – that is, for a requirement of reason to adhere to the law of one's political community. Thus, by the articulation of the normative appeal of a certain conception of the common good, we lend some plausibility to the principle that each member of the political community is required in reason to promote the common good.

---

[14] Surely, one might say, commensurability has to enter the picture somewhere: at some point, the political process is going to yield the decision that a resource should be allotted to A rather than to B, and that is to say that the contribution to A's good offered by the resource is more important than the contribution to B's good offered by the resource. Perhaps so, but the standards of commensuration here are posterior to the decision procedure: the only basis for saying that the contribution is better in one case than another is that the decision procedure yields that result. This sort of commensurability is completely unlike utilitarian commensuration, which holds that we can, *prior to the adoption of such a scale,* compare the value of agents' goods. (See Finnis 1980, p. 115.) After all, since the principle of utility makes reference to a comparison of goods, the comparison must be logically prior to the principle. But in the alternative procedure I am suggesting, there is no such logical priority.

The argument for the aggregative conception of the common good drew on the reason-giving force of the common good thus conceived, and so if that argument was a good one, there is little reason to be suspicious of the notion that the common good of one's political community is something that one has strong reason to pursue and promote. The difficulties that arise concern the way the common good as an end on the one hand measures up against more particular ends to which one might be devoted, and on the other hand measures up against more cosmopolitan aims. I will discuss these questions at some length in Chapter 7, but for the moment I want to bracket questions of these distinct and conflicting ends to which an agent might have allegiance, noting only that the defense of a common good principle thus formulated is key to the natural law view's dealing with the *particularity* requirement on theories of political obligation (cf. Simmons 1979, pp. 30–35; Green 1990, pp. 227–228). An account of political authority must, that is, explain the presence of a *special tie* to one's own laws, not just to those of any political community, or any minimally just political community. The reason that one is bound to adhere to these laws, and not those in some other political community, is that one is bound to act for the common good of one's own political community in a way that one is not bound to act for the common good of other political communities, and so just as one has a special responsibility to *this* community's common good, one has a special responsibility to adhere to *this* community's set of laws. We cannot, consistent with the main thrust of the natural law account, forgo a principle of acting for the common good with an agent-relative cast (*one is bound to act for the common good of one's political community*) in favor of a similar principle with a more agent-neutral cast (for example, *one is bound to act for the common good of political communities in general*), for that would be to leave the natural law view without a way to satisfy the particularity desideratum.

Each person in a political community is bound to act for the common good of that community. Since it is possible that sound practical thinking may recognize limits on how far the agent must extend himself or herself in seeking the common good, we may say, without begging any questions, that this principle can also be stated in the following way: *each person is bound to do his or her share for the common good*. I will call this practical principle, upon which the natural law account of the law's authority is based, the *common good principle*. What, then, does the natural law view take to be the relationship between a citizen's being bound by the common good principle and that citizen's being bound to adhere to the (non-defective) law of his or her political community? The idea is this: that adherence to the law is a constituent of doing one's share for the common good, such that (1) in adhering to the demands of the law, one is to some extent fulfilling the practical requirement to do one's share for the common good, and (2) if one does not adhere to the demands of the law, one is *ipso facto* failing to act properly with respect to doing one's share for the common good. The natural law political theorist is not claiming that every reason to act for the common good is exhausted by the content of the civil law, or even that what is a matter of minimal reasonableness with respect to acting for the common good is exhausted by the law. The claim is that at least part of what is a matter of minimal reasonableness with respect to acting for the common good is that one adhere to the dictates of the civil law. One likely is under requirements with respect to the common good that go beyond the demands of the law, but one will invariably go afoul of the common good principle if one fails to obey the law.[15]

Now, one might think that such an account of the law's authority is bound to be a non-starter, due to the tight structural similarities between this sort of account of the law's authority and utilitarian 'public interest' accounts that have been roundly criticized. Suppose that one were to affirm a crude act-utilitarian account of political authority by asserting that each act should promote the public happiness and that obedience to law is required because it is necessary to promoting the public happiness. Now, some have responded to such accounts by noting that there are clear cases in which obedience to law does not promote the public interest, and so the act-utilitarian account fails because it establishes an obligation to obey the law only when such obedience is optimific (see Smith 1973, pp. 964–965, and Simmons 1979, pp. 47–49). This criticism is, I think, wrongheaded, because there is no reason to suppose that an account of political obligation cannot be limited in some way – that citizens are bound to obey all laws that are not unjust, for example. (I discuss this point further in Murphy 1997b, p. 134, and Murphy 1999, p. 78.) The more important point, which the defectively formulated criticism suggests but does not make explicit, is that in the act-utilitarian account no normative weight is carried by the existence of the law. The act-utilitarian view has this problematic feature because in attempting to account for the obligation to obey the law (1) it appeals to an end, the public interest, that can be characterized independently of anyone's decisions, and which is such that various states of affairs can be ranked with respect to the extent that they realize this end, and (2) what it is to do one's share in promoting this end is similarly independently characterizable, as simply whatever one can do to realize a state of affairs that best approximates the public interest. Thus what the law says (or assumes) about the content of the common good, and what one should do to help realize it, is normatively impotent.

But whatever the vices of a natural law account that appeals to the common good aggregatively conceived, they do not include the law's normative impotence, for such a view would reject the propositions (1) and (2), with the result that the law can make a genuine difference normatively speaking. Against (1): on the aggregative view, the common good is an ideal, one that is impossible

---

[15] The law may fail to require something that duty requires toward the promotion of the common good for good reasons: it might be burdensome or unjust to enforce, for example. See *Summa Theologiae* IaIIae 96, 2.

to realize in practice (3.2); the proximate object of political action – the common good that can be reasonably hoped for – will be what we will call a *determination* of the common good ideally conceived. As I will use the expression, a 'determination' of some objective O is some objective O* that stands to O either as a realizable approximation to an unrealizable ideal or as a more precise specification of a vague objective. (So, lowering the crime rate may be a determination of eradicating crime (making an ideal objective realizable), and lowering the crime rate by 20 percent may be a determination of lowering the crime rate (making a vague objective more precise).) In both cases, an objective the adequate realization of which is indeterminate becomes more determinate through truncation or 'precisification.' Not only *objectives* can be the objects of determinations; *principles* as well can be. An overly demanding principle might be determined in order to provide a realistic basis for choices, and an overly vague principle might be determined in order to provide a clearer guide to action.[16]

The status of the common good as such an unrealizable ideal means that in politics, the best that we can do is to settle upon some determination of the common good for the sake of common action. But candidate determinations of the common good cannot be readily ranked, though, as approximations to the common good ideally conceived, and thus must be fixed upon partly by practical norms other than those of sheer maximization (for example, impartiality norms, norms of coherence, and so on; see 3.5) and partly by acts of free but reasonable discretion.

Against (2): what counts as doing one's share in acting for the common good, even assuming a particular determination of the common good aggregatively conceived, is itself something that requires determination; what justice requires one to do in acting for the proximate common good may be specified in a number of incompatible ways, each with its own distinctive merits (so that the determination decision is not arbitrary, or at least not arbitrary through indifference), yet such that the distinctive merits of each do not entail a uniquely correct solution. There is an openness in the common good principle, then, that makes room for the law to carry some weight in how one is to act in doing his or her share in acting for the common good, and that is why the law in the natural law account need not suffer from the normative impotence from which the law suffers in the act-utilitarian account. (For a discussion of normative openness in natural law views, see Murphy 2001a, pp. 252–254.)

The natural law account of authority of law holds, then, that the law live up to its pretensions to authority by providing a partial determination of what one is to do in fulfilling the common good principle. The idea of political authority

---

[16] The notion of determination appears in *Summa Theologiae* IaIIae 95, 2. I am also indebted to my colleague Henry Richardson's discussion of specification (and various relationships between principles that are akin to it): see his 1990 and 2000.

as determining the common good principle is extremely important. There is a tension in the theory of political authority between two poles. On the one hand, political authority must display a certain content-independence (cf. Green 1990, pp. 36–59), so that within a certain range of otherwise eligible proposals for action, the law's picking out a certain one determines that the selected proposal is the one to act on. The most natural way to explain content-independence is to provide an account on which the mere fact that an act is prescribed by law invariably adds normative weight to the performance of that act. On the other hand, if we explain content-independence in this way, we leave ourselves open to an argument that Raz levels against the very idea of political obligation. Raz claims that if there were an obligation to obey the law, then it would follow that the duty not to murder is stricter and weightier if the law proscribes it than if it does not. But since the duty not to murder is not made stricter and weightier by the existence of law, there is no such obligation (see Raz 1984b, p. 142). One might quibble with Raz over whether this implication is counterintuitive, but I agree with Raz on that point; what I deny is that the content-independence of political obligation entails that normative weight is added with every law. The point of the law's authority, on this view, is to fix some of the content of the common good principle, to settle, in part, how agents are to act on the common good principle. If, then, there are some acts the performance of which or the refraining from which are simply *entailed* by the common good principle, then no extra normative weight need be added to their performance or non-performance by the existence of a law prescribing or proscribing them: they are part of any minimally acceptable determination of the common good principle. If, as I think, acts of murder, rape, torture, assault, and fraud are all, in themselves, failures to do one's share in acting for the common good, there is no need for law to determine the common good principle to include refraining from these acts. The law does not set aside these acts as not to be done; that is done already by the common good principle on its own.[17] So Raz's objection fails against such understandings of the obligation to obey the law. But content-independence – at least, any version of content-independence worth wanting – is preserved: within the range of reasonable potential determinations of the common good and citizens' shares in acting for the common good, it is the law that settles, at least in part, which determination will count as doing one's share to act for the common good.

But while this emphasis on the role of the law in partially determining the requirement to do one's share to act for the common good makes clear both how

---

[17] So Aquinas, in distinguishing civil laws that are derived from the natural law simply by way of logical deduction from the natural law and the given features of the situation (derivation by *deduction*) and those that are derived from it by a free decision (derivation by *determination*), says that the former have their force from the natural law but the latter from the civil law alone (*Summa Theologiae* IaIIae 95, 2).

the natural law view differs from utilitarian 'public interest' accounts and how certain worries about the content-independence of the requirement to obey the law can be handled, it also brings into relief the central problem that confronts natural law accounts of political authority. The practical requirement to adhere to the demands of the law is supposed to be based somehow in the practical requirement to do one's share in acting for the common good. But both *the common good* and *one's share in promoting it* are in need of determination. That leaves unanswered a crucial question, though: why does the law have the *privileged* place in rendering determinations of the common good and of the citizen's share in acting for it? Think of it this way: imagine a citizen confronted by a law. The citizen asks, conscientiously, why he or she is bound to adhere to this law. The answer comes back: because you are bound to do your share in acting for the common good, and the law tells you what must be done in order for you to do your share. The citizen grants the principle invoked and asks for a demonstration from the principle to the conclusion that this law must be followed. But in place of a demonstration, he or she receives an explanation that includes both deductions and descriptions of acts of free, discretionary choice with respect to the content of the proximate common good and justice in acting for the proximate common good. "But wait," the citizen says. "That isn't a demonstration. What needs to be explained is why I must act on the particular determinations of the common good, and of justice in promoting it, rendered by the civil law. Even if I were to grant for the moment that I will have to act on *some* determination of the common good and of my just share in acting for it, I haven't yet been given an account of why I am failing to live up to the principle of acting for the common good if I act on my own determinations, or on my friends', or on anyone's besides the law's."

This is, I believe, the central problematic of the natural law account of political authority. What is at issue is, first, how *any* particular (non-entailed) determination of a general normative principle can become authoritative for an agent, so that the agent is failing with respect to that general normative principle if he or she fails to act on that determination, and second, why it is the *law's* determinations of the general principle to do one's share in acting for the common good that are authoritative for the agent. Some natural law theorists want to say that the authority of the law's determinations can be accounted for simply by the fact that the law possesses a certain *salience* with respect to the coordination problem that citizens face in trying to act for the common good through unified action. I will examine such an account in the next chapter (4.6).

4

The Natural Law Rejection
of Consent Theory

4.1 Consent and Natural Law Theories, Classical and Contemporary

There is a popular but false story concerning the connection between the rise of consent theories of political authority and the fall of natural law theories of political authority. The story is, to put it crudely, that the rise of consent theory in the modern period coincided with, and came as a result of, the fall of the natural law theory that dominated during the medieval period. Neat though it is, the story errs doubly, for it supposes both that consent did not play a key role in natural law theories of political authority offered in the medieval period (a supposition falsified by close inspection of the view of Aquinas, the paradigmatic natural law theorist; see Murphy 1997a) and that natural law theory did not play a key role in the consent theories of political authority offered in the modern period (a supposition falsified by close inspection of the views of Hobbes and Locke, perhaps paradigmatic consent theorists; for Hobbes as a natural law theorist, see, for example, Murphy 1995, and for Locke, see, for example, Tuckness 1999).

It is bad history to set up natural law and consent theories of political authority as unqualifiedly antagonistic to each other. But it is not an unfair description of the accounts of political authority offered by contemporary natural law theorists to say that these accounts were developed in self-conscious opposition to voluntaristic accounts of political obligation, and that their formulations rule out as normatively unnecessary a citizen's consent to adhere to the dictates of the civil law. If we are blinded by the bad history, we might think it altogether natural or obvious that a contemporary natural law view would eschew any basic appeal to consent. But the fact that a number of predecessor natural law theories saw no inconsistency in grounding their accounts of political authority both in the natural law and in consent should give us pause, and provides us with some motivation to inquire further into whether the rejection of consent within a natural law account of political authority is the most plausible line for the natural law theorist to take.

It is no exaggeration that the fundamental criticisms of the consent theory of political authority acknowledged by contemporary natural law theorists derive entirely from Hume, however much they have been elaborated and sharpened by recent writing on the subject. In "Of the Original Contract," Hume makes several distinct points against consent theory: first, that consent theory is *ab initio* an unpromising account of political authority, at odds with both *de facto* authorities' and citizens' views of their relationship; second, that the conditions necessary for the application of the moral principle upon which the consent theory relies are not realized in actual political communities; and third, that the consent theory is at any rate a dispensable account of our political bonds, which can be explained without any mention of consent. Our political obligations are better understood by reference to the public good rather than by reference to the binding power of consent, and it is a good thing, too, as the consent view fails to deliver the account of political authority that it promises.

The negative part of Hume's critique has been nearly universally embraced by contemporary writers on political authority. They have been concerned to show both that consent theory is in principle an implausible way of accounting for the law's authority and that even if its in principle plausibility were allowed, the prevailing conditions in actual political communities fail to trigger the application of the consent principle. On the other hand, the positive part of Hume's argument – in which he tries to show that the appeal to consent is unnecessary, given the requirements of the public good itself – has been less universally embraced. For most recent work on political authority has been unrelentingly negative: the critique of consent theories has been but one facet of a sustained attack on a variety of accounts of political authority (cf. Smith 1973, Simmons 1979, Raz 1979a, Green 1990). But those who have been interested in systematically defending a natural law position on ethics and politics have not been a part of this trend, holding instead that the broadly Humean picture is correct, that the need for law in promoting the public good is sufficient to account for law's authority.

What I will argue in this chapter is the following. Given the conception of consent theory with which Hume and contemporary writers on political authority are working (4.2), their criticisms of consent theory (4.3–4.4) are damning, and writers in the natural law tradition are right to accept this critique as conclusive. (Indeed, there is even reason – as I argue briefly in 4.5 – to think that the basic natural law political thesis is simply *incompatible* with the consent approach.) But the 'salient coordinator' account of political authority (4.6) that natural law theorists have taken from Hume and modified for their own purposes fails (4.7), and its failure suggests that the natural law account of political authority needs help of the sort that consent theory promised to give. The moral that I draw from this chapter is that if there is to be an account of political authority answering to the fundamental natural law thesis that the authority of law derives from the common good, then it will be an account that employs consent-type elements – though, given the decisive criticisms of standard consent views, these elements will have to be interpreted or arranged in something other than the standard way. The formulation of this alternative consent theory is the task of Chapter 5.

4.2 The Argument from Consent

The consent theory of political authority is to be distinguished from hypothetical contract views, views on which political authority is justified through its being the object of an agreement that would be made by individuals in some idealized choice situation. As Green rightly notes, such views do not genuinely share the voluntarism of consent theory (Green 1990, p. 161–162), according to which it is one's *actual* consent that makes it the case that one is tied by bonds of political obligation.

While the argumentative motivations for affirming a consent theory of political authority are various, we can get at the common line of thought behind consent views by thinking of the consent account in two stages: first, as a model of how political authority might be realized in some community; and second, as an argument that this model applies broadly in actual political communities.

The argument that consent (or promise, or agreement – I shall not distinguish between such views; though see Raz 1981) is a possible basis for political authority is the following. While there is widespread variation among moral philosophers on the catalog of correct moral principles and on the extent to which these principles are binding, there is wide agreement that, at the very least, one can become bound to perform some action by one's own promise to carry out that action. Again, there are various explanations to be offered for why this is so, and no one view is dominant (see, for example, Anscombe 1969; Rawls 1971, pp. 344–348; MacCormick 1972; Raz 1972; Scanlon 1998). But on each of these views, the relevant points are that the sort of consent that these authors have in mind involves the performance of a speech-act under certain specific conditions, and that those who perform that speech-act are obligated to perform the promised act. Consider, for example, the account of promising offered by Rawls. On Rawls's view, we must distinguish between two kinds of rules: "rules of promising" and "the principle of fidelity" (Rawls 1971, p. 346). A rule of promising is a social rule, a "constitutive convention" that can be applied to determine whether or not a promise has been made. The "basic rule" of promising is that "if one says the words 'I promise to do X' in the appropriate circumstances, one is to do X, unless certain excusing conditions obtain" (Rawls 1971, pp. 344–345). Uttering those words constitutes a promise under the conditions that

one must be fully conscious, in a rational frame of mind, and know the meaning of operative words, their use in making promises, and so on. Furthermore, these words must be spoken freely or voluntarily, when one is not subject to threats or coercion, and in situations where one has a fair bargaining position, so to speak. A person is not required to perform if the operative words are uttered while he is asleep, or suffering delusions, or if he was forced to promise, or if pertinent information was deceitfully withheld from him.   (Rawls 1971, p. 345)

Rawls emphasizes that these rules of promising are not moral principles, though: they are "on a par with legal rules and statutes, and rules of games" (Rawls 1971, p. 345). In order for one to reach the conclusion that one has at least a *prima facie* moral reason to act in accordance with what one promises, there must be invoked a principle of fidelity, some moral principle that enables one to deduce from the fact that one has performed a speech-act that falls under certain rules of a practice the moral conclusion that one ought to perform the actions that those rules require.

Now, not everyone holds to such a two-level view. Scanlon, for example, does not think of the rules of promising as a practice being taken up in toto and made binding by some principle of fidelity: he understands the requirement to keep promises as simply an application of a rule against manipulation, where the practice of promising typically figures centrally in the manipulator's plan of action (Scanlon 1998, pp. 296–309). But nevertheless the consent theory of political authority works similarly on both accounts. On both accounts, what matters is that one can become bound to perform some action by the performance of a speech-act of a certain sort under certain specific conditions. If one promises to ϕ, then under the proper conditions – conditions that have to do both with the agent making the promise and the character of the act that one is promising to perform – one is obligated to ϕ.

The great utility of promising is the wide range of actions to which one can commit oneself by promising. Particularly important for the consent account is that one can commit oneself to actions whose description is *open* – that is, the nature of the promised performance is not entirely set at the time of the promise, but remains to be filled in at some time between the time of the promise and the time of the performance. I might sell you a dog under the constraint that you promise to give me my pick of the litter, should the dog ever give birth. What you are required to do to keep your promise remains to be seen: it may involve nothing at all (if the dog never has puppies), or it may involve my receiving a puppy in the next year, or in the next three years. What is more, what you must do to satisfy your promise depends on my later say-so: given a first litter of puppies, I might choose one, or another, of the puppies, and you would be required to yield to me whichever one I chose. So some promises are open, in that what constitutes the promised action is to be determined later; and of these open promises, some party can determine by his or her choice as to what constitutes the promised action.

It seems to most plain that we can undertake obligations by promising, and that these obligations can be open in the way described. On this basis, the defenders of the argument from consent hold that it is possible for political authority to be established by means of a universal, open-ended promise by members of a political community to adhere to the dictates laid down by some person, persons, institution, or set of rules. So long as the parties make their promise in conditions apt for binding – they are not under duress, they have an adequate understanding of the facts of their situation, they are aware of the normative consequences of their actions, they are adequately mature and capable of making life decisions for themselves – political authority can be realized through consent.

On what basis, though, can we say not only that this is a *possible* way for political authority to be realized but is *actual* as well? The consent theorist can appeal in a limited way to the situations of those who have expressly consented to be ruled by the prevailing political institutions: certain naturalized citizens, certain political officeholders, certain members of the military. But the main effort to show that consent theory is generally applicable is by appeal to *tacit* consent. Tacit consent is not to be confused with hypothetical consent. Hypothetical consent is no consent at all: to consent hypothetically is merely to have the dispositional property *being such that if one were placed in preferred situation S, then one would consent.* Tacit consent, by contrast, is *actual* consent, expressed in a non-standard, not overtly expressive way. Our paradigm cases of consent occur in contexts in which it is perfectly clear that the primary purpose of the action is communicative. Tacit consent occurs other than in these paradigm contexts. It occurs either when one refrains from engaging in a communication of the standard sort or when one performs an act that is not a paradigmatically communicative act. So one might claim that in a context in which there is a common understanding that citizens are bound to adhere to the dictates laid down by the existing government, a refusal to dissent explicitly from their common understanding counts as expressing one's willingness to become bound by such obligations. Or one might claim that there are various acts – voting, seeking and receiving government benefits, paying taxes, even simply remaining in residence – that may not appear to be paradigmatically communicative acts on their face, but that do turn out to meet the conditions by which speech-acts generate promissory obligations and that by and large the citizenry has engaged in.

4.3 Against Consent Theories: Implausible *Ab Initio*

The most widely acknowledged criticisms of consent theories of political authority appeal to the absence of the acts of consent that would trigger the relevant moral principles. But there are concerns about consent theories that can be articulated even prior to an examination of the conditions in actual political communities, concerns about whether it seems at all likely that any such account can succeed. One might wonder why it is worth examining such criticisms: for, after all, surely we would do better simply to go straight to the question of whether the conditions in actual political communities justify the view that citizens generally have consented to be ruled, rather than to bother asking in advance whether the examination of such a question is likely to yield a positive result. But there is nevertheless good reason to devote some attention to whether the consent theory is an initially plausible view. For it may turn out that the question of whether acts of consent are sufficiently general in present political communities does not admit of a clear answer, and it may turn out that how we ought to interpret this result depends on how we ought to construe the burden of proof in the case of consent theory. And, further, even if it turns out that there is good reason to reject the view that citizens generally consent to be ruled, the independently established dubious character of the consent view provides a basis to accept this conclusion at face value, as a conclusion that is not at odds with common sense.

Begin with Hume's initial observations on consent theorists:

> Would these reasoners look abroad into the world, they would meet with nothing that in the least corresponds to their ideas, or can warrant so refined and philosophical a system. On the contrary, we find everywhere princes who claim their subjects as their property, and assert the independent right of sovereignty from conquest or succession. We find also everywhere subjects who acknowledge this right in their prince, and suppose themselves born under obligations of obedience to a certain sovereign, as much as under the ties of reverence and duty to certain parents. . . . It is strange that an act of the mind, which every individual is supposed to have formed, and after he came to the use of reason too, otherwise it could have no authority – that this act, I say, should be so much unknown to all of them that over the face of the whole earth there scarcely remain any traces or memory of it.   ("Original Contract," p. 359)

Hume puts forward two related difficulties for consent theory in this passage, neither of which requires us to examine the conditions of political communities to see whether citizens generally perform speech-acts of the sort that generate promissory obligations. The first is what I will call the *self-image* objection. Hume expresses it in terms of the relation between princes and subjects, but the criticism can be expressed independently of a particular form of governance. The idea is that consent theory is at odds with the self-image both of the rulers and of the ruled. The self-image of rulers is not that of those whose authority depends on the consent of those whom they purport to rule. Rather, rulers suppose that all those that are under their jurisdiction – where jurisdiction is, at least nowadays, defined territorially – come under their rightful governance. The law does not condition its demands on whether there has been consent to its rule, even where its range of operation is extensive. The self-image of the ruled is not that of those whose obedience is owed as a matter of consent: most of the ruled have not considered whether the authority of law might be based on their consent, thinking it instead as simply a brute matter of birth or one's present residence. So the consent view fits poorly with the self-image of both the governors and the governed: neither seems to think and act as if the law's authority results from and depends on the consent of the ruled.

The second objection we may call the *knowledge* objection. This objection can be, and is used by Hume as, support for the self-image objection. But it is a strong criticism in its own right. On the consent view, one comes under the authority of law through one's own promise. But promises, especially those of moment and performed during one's adulthood, are things of the sort that one tends to remember. Surely consent to be governed by law is both momentous (given the range of authority typically claimed by law) and performed during one's adulthood (given the conditions that must be realized for consent to be morally binding). The only other promise that most adults make during their lifetimes that would be similar in scope and importance to the promise that the consent theorist suggests that we have made is the marriage vow. Marriage vows are, however, characteristically (!) remembered by married people. However tense the actual moment of the vow might have been, people who are married know that they made their marriage vows: they can remember making them. But most people do not remember making a promise to adhere to the law's demands, and so it seems extremely unlikely that they have made such a promise.

If the self-image and knowledge criticisms are sound, then it is clear that there is an initial burden of proof against the consent theory of political authority. Any doubts about the success of an argument that people have generally consented to place themselves under the authority of law are not to be resolved in favor of the view that consent has in fact occurred. And if, upon examination of the conditions in present political communities, there are strong reasons to think that there is not widespread consent, we should not have our confidence in this conclusion shaken on account of its being contrary to ordinary views on the matter.

4.4 Against Consent Theories: The Paucity of Consent

The success of consent theory as a general account of political authority depends on very widespread consent to be ruled. But very few of us – perhaps only naturalized citizens and those who have taken oaths upon entering some sort of public office – have ever expressly consented. As Smith points out, this is just a "brute fact" (Smith 1973, p. 960; see also Simmons 1979, p. 79, and Raz 1979a, p. 239). Hence, the doctrine of *tacit* consent, whereby one expresses his or her consent to obey the law by some means other than the usual written or spoken words. In *Leviathan*, Hobbes claims that such significant acts include that of voluntarily entering "into that Congregation of them that were assembled" to discuss the covenant (*Leviathan*, ch. 18, p. 90) as well as that of living openly under a government's protection (*Leviathan*, Review and Conclusion, p. 391); Locke and Rousseau also fix on residence as the significant act (*Second Treatise*, §119; *Social Contract*, IV, 2). Others have appealed to voting (Plamenatz 1968, pp. 168–171) and to making use of publicly funded and publicly produced facilities.

Simmons's treatment of tacit consent is rightly widely cited for its careful demolition of tacit consent theories, though there are points at which his criticisms are formulated so as to make them more restricted than they were intended to be. On Simmons's understanding of tacit consent theories, consent is tacit when it is exercised by refraining from doing something – paradigmatically, by refraining from expressing dissent: "Consent is called tacit when it is expressed by remaining silent and inactive" (Simmons 1979, p. 80). The conditions that Simmons proposes must be satisfied in order for tacit consent to be binding[1] presuppose this understanding of tacit consent. But if theories of tacit consent built on the absence of dissent were his only target, he would have left untouched theories of tacit consent on which the act of consent is indeed an intervention of some sort – voting, or accepting public benefits – rather than the refusal to intervene. And it would seem strange to restrict the notion of 'tacit consent' to failures to dissent: for the plain sense of 'tacit' is just that of being expressed without language rather than being constituted by a refraining from making some linguistic expression. If there is such a thing that is tacit consent, it is consent realized in an act that is not primarily linguistic; it need not be consent realized in a refusal to perform a primarily linguistic act.

Why should we reject the notion that residence, or voting, or use of the roads, or any such act as these constitutes tacit consent? We should reject this notion because generally residence, voting, and so on do not share the features of the performance of the speech-act 'I promise to ϕ' that figure in our view that the performance of the speech-act 'I promise to ϕ' can bind one to compliance. The first is that uttering 'I promise to ϕ' and refraining from uttering 'I promise to ϕ' are both, of themselves, low-cost options. It is very *easy* both to make and to refrain from making a promise. I am not talking about the costs of satisfying the obligations resulting from promises, or about the losses that one might sustain by refusing to make a promise on some occasion. I am talking only about the boring part, the mouthing of the words themselves. The second is that, through being acquired by uttering 'I promise that . . .' and thereupon predicating a future action of oneself, promissory obligations allow one to bind oneself extremely explicitly. No doubt future turns of events can arise that one did not foresee, and that can make the fulfillment of one's promises more onerous than one imagined it would be. But if the matter is sufficiently

---

[1] Simmons holds that for tacit consent to be significant and binding, (1) the individual must be aware that forbearing from a certain action is an expression of consent; (2) there must be a definite period of reasonable duration for the individual to perform that action, and thus to express dissent; (3) the point at which dissent is no longer accepted must be made clear; (4) the action by which dissent is expressed must be reasonably easily performed; and (5) the consequences of the dissent cannot be extremely detrimental to the potential consenter (Simmons 1979, pp. 80–81).

important, one can be precise enough with the content of one's promise that for the vast run of plausible scenarios, one can tell what constraints one is under as a result of the making of the promise. The third is that the practice of undertaking promissory obligations through the uttering of the characteristic 'I promise' phrasing is widely understood and accepted: it is clear to almost everyone the central ways of promise-making and, in broad outline at least, the obligations that attend on it.

If any of these features were absent, the attendance of obligations upon the performance of the acts characteristic of promising would be seriously in doubt. With respect to the first feature: if, for example, a large portion of the population were such that their horrifying pain could be quelled only by going through the standard behavioral motions of promise-making, it would be very hard to believe that they would generally bind themselves to performance by making those utterances. It is crucial to the binding character of promising that promising behavior itself be a matter of near-indifference, mattering only for the normative effects that one means to produce by engaging in it. With respect to the second: it would be very hard to believe that one could bind oneself by promises if it were not at all clear what one was binding oneself to. This general point seems to be behind certain knowledge and maturity conditions on binding promises, and seems to be what motivates certain concerns about our ability to bind ourselves to extremely long-term commitments. With respect to the third: promises are public matters; they require uptake; there must be a mutual understanding of the practice, of the fact that by using these words one means to place oneself under an obligation, for one to make oneself bound by means of it.

These three features of the speech-acts characteristic of promising are essential to the binding character that promises have. If any set of actions were to lack these features, then we would have strong reason to doubt that the performance of that set of actions could bind one in the way that the making of a promise binds one. The difficulty with the tacit consent theories of political authority on offer is that the acts that they put forward as expressions of consent lack these features, and so it is extremely implausible to think that they could constitute valid consent. For, first, the acts that are on offer are not those of relative indifference. Residence is the most obvious case of this. Whether one remains in residence in a particularly political community is not a matter of relative indifference. Thus, if residence were understood as consent, then there would be a heavy cost in not consenting. Thus Hume:

Can we seriously say, that a poor peasant or artisan has a free choice to leave his country, when he knows no foreign language or manners, and lives from day to day, by the small wages which he acquires? We may as well assert, that a man, by remaining in a vessel, freely consents to the dominion of the master; though he was carried on board while asleep, and must leap into the ocean, and perish, the moment he leaves her. ("Original Contract," p. 263)

Simmons notes further that even if the poor and oppressed were granted material aid in leaving their country, many goods are "non-transportable": home, family, and friends are for many the most important things, even if they can only be enjoyed under a state of tyranny (Simmons 1979, pp. 99–100). The same would be true of the acceptance of various benefits: it would be most inconvenient not to use public roads, or not to avail oneself of public utilities, or not to make use of the services of the police or fire departments. Even voting, for the negligible effect it has on the outcome of most elections, is obviously not an indifferent matter to the voter, regardless of whether one understands the value of voting in terms of asserting one's equal control over political outcomes or simply in terms of promoting good consequences (see, for example, Christiano 1996, pp. 88–89; and Parfit 1984, pp. 73–75).[2]

Second, it is not at all clear what one would be consenting to by remaining in residence, or by accepting public benefits, or by voting. The rule for determining the action to which one is binding oneself by saying 'I promise to ϕ' is a simple one: it is (minor complications aside) ϕ-ing. But there is no such rule for determining what action one would be agreeing to perform by remaining in residence, or by voting, or by accepting public benefits. As the rationale for holding people bound by their own consent is that they can see what they are binding themselves to and can avoid being bound if they choose, that there is no clear answer what people would be binding themselves to if we understand residence (etc.) as an act of consent gives us reason to doubt that it is such an act.

Third, it seems clear that none of these acts is conventionally understood as an attempt to place oneself under an obligation of obedience (cf. Smith 1973, pp. 960–961). Residence has no such conventional meaning. Voting might seem more plausible, but even there it seems that voting, while a conventional sign of approval and perhaps acceptance, is far more limited in scope: it signifies at best willingness to accept this particular proposal, at middle a preference for this proposal to the others on offer, and at worst nothing at all (in the case of merely strategic voting).

It is hard to see that there could be a practice of imposing obligations on oneself that took these acts to be expressions of consent, and it is hard to see why one would think that there is any reason to suppose them now to be such expressions. Simmons offers one explanation. In diagnosing why philosophers

---

[2] It is sometimes said that tacit consent views run afoul of the duress condition. This is not so. The duress condition can kick in only if one makes a demand that another consent or else face certain consequences (cf. Raz 1981, p. 126). But this need not be the case. The unpleasantness of not consenting need not be something that is used to get consent. That is why the unpleasantness of not consenting (having to leave, not getting to vote, not getting to use public benefits) bears on the act-indifference issue, not on the duress issue.

have fallen into error concerning the extent to which persons in political communities consent to obey their political authorities, he writes:

> It is easy to be misled . . . by what I will call the "attitudinal" sense of "consent"; "consent" in this sense is merely having an attitude of approval or dedication. . . . But this sense of "consent" is quite irrelevant to our present discussion, where we are concerned exclusively with "consent" in an "occurrence" sense, i.e. with consent as an act which may generate obligations. An attitude of approval or dedication is completely irrelevant to the rights and obligations of the citizen who has it. When a man consents, he has consented and may be bound accordingly, regardless of how he feels about what he has consented to. (Simmons 1979, p. 93)

Green similarly notes the ambiguity, and emphasizes that in considering the merits of a consent theory of political authority, we need to keep focused on the sense of consent that is "performative and active" (Green 1990, p. 160). 'Consent' is no doubt often used loosely to mean any sort of acceptance of or approval of or acquiescence with some rule-making person or institution. But the widespread presence of consent in this sense – used loosely enough, 'consent' might be a necessary condition for any society that we take to have a legal system at all – is not what the consent theorist needs: the consent theorist needs the presence of consent in the specific speech-act, obligation-generating sense. And it seems clear that in *that* sense, consent is a relatively rare phenomenon.

4.5 Against Consent Theories: Incompatible with the Natural Law View

According to the criticisms that we examined in the previous two sections, the appeal to consent is *prima facie* a singularly unpromising view of our political bonds, and turns out in fact to have come to very little by way of explaining political authority. It is, at any rate, far from clear that any defender of a natural law view could adopt any version of the consent theory described in 4.2.

Here is what I mean. Recall that the generic understanding of the natural law account of the authority of law (3.6) holds that when the law is authoritative, one who fails to adhere to the law's dictates will be failing to do his or her share with respect to the common good of the political community. It is hard to see how one could hold this view while also holding that the authority of law results from the performance of a speech-act of consenting to be ruled. For when one is obligated to ϕ by way of a promise, the reason that one has for ϕ-ing is just the promissory obligation: the fact that one promised to ϕ plus the moral requirement that binds one to keep one's promises is a complete reason to ϕ. So if one is bound to adhere to the law's dictates by way of a promise, then the reason that one has for adhering to the law's dictates is just the fact that one promised to do so plus the moral requirement that binds one to keep one's promises. It does not look like the authority of law is at all being accounted for here by the requirement to do one's share with respect to the common good of the political community.

Another way to put the point is this. Suppose that with respect to doing one's share for the common good, there are at least two courses of action, A_1 and A_2, that are eligible determinations of 'doing one's share for the common good.' One makes a promise to adhere to the demands of the law, and the law demands that one carry out A_1. But one instead carries out A_2. There is no doubt that one acted wrongly: one violated a promissory obligation. But it is not at all clear why we should describe this situation as a case in which one failed to do one's share for the common good. If accused of not doing his or her share for the common good by carrying out A_2 rather than A_1, one could reply: "I don't know what you mean. The requirement to do one's share for the common good does not militate in favor of A_1 over A_2. The promise that I made militates in favor of A_1 over A_2, but that does not automatically imply that if I fail to follow A_1, then I am falling short with respect to the common good."

Here is an analogy. Suppose that I have an imperfect duty to help those in need. Bob and Larry are both in need, but I lack the means to help both. You are fond of Bob, and extract from me a promise to devote the means at my disposal to helping Bob. For some reason, though, I help Larry. It would be obviously false to say that I have gone wrong with respect to my duty to help those in need by breaking this promise. It would be obviously false even if my promise had not been to you, but to Bob. It may be cruel of me to promise to help Bob and then to fail to help him, but my breaking this promise does not show that my performance of this imperfect duty has somehow gone awry.

This line of argument suggests that there is no way to reconcile the natural law view that the law's authority comes from the common good with the claim that the law's authority comes from consent. Consent in this sense is itself the operative reason for action; the normative force of the common good cannot 'flow through' the consent to confer authority on the law.

4.6 Against Consent Theories: Unnecessary (the Salient Coordinator Account)

Hume's case against the consent theory of political authority does not rest merely on the negative claims that consent theory is *a priori* unpromising and *a posteriori* indefensible. He argues further that it is a useless view, for the requirements of allegiance to the dictates of public authority stands on the same ground as that on which the principle of consent itself stands, that is, public benefit.

[Some] moral duties are such as are not supported by any original instinct of nature, but are performed entirely from a sense of obligation, when we consider the necessities of human society and the impossibility of supporting it if these duties were neglected. It is thus *justice*, or a regard to the property of others, *fidelity*, or the observance of promises, become obligatory and acquire an authority over mankind....

The case is precisely the same with the political or civil duty of *allegiance* as with the natural duties of justice and fidelity.... A small degree of experience and observation suffices to teach us that society cannot possibly be maintained without the authority of magistrates, and that this authority must soon fall into contempt where exact obedience is not paid to it. The observation of these general and obvious interests is the source of all allegiance and of that moral obligation which we attribute to it.

What necessity, therefore, is there to found the duty of allegiance, or obedience to magistrates, on that of fidelity, or a regard to promises, and to suppose that it is the consent of each individual which subjects him to government, when it appears that both allegiance and fidelity stand precisely on the same foundation and are both submitted to by mankind on account of the apparent interests and necessities of human society? ("Original Contract," p. 367)

There are two separable claims here. The first claim is that the allegiance that we owe to *de facto* political authorities is due to the requirements of the achievement of the public good: experience has taught us that the public good cannot be achieved without general adherence to the dictates of such authorities, and general adherence to the dictates of such authorities cannot persist unless there is "exact obedience" to them.[3] The second claim is that the ground for adherence to one's promises, express or tacit, is the same as the ground for adherence to the dictates of the public authority: the promotion of the public good. So the consent theory of political authority is doubly redundant. For the requirement to adhere to the dictates of political authority is adequately explained by the necessities of the public good, and so there is no need of consent; and what is more, the ultimate basis for adhering to one's promises is the same as the ultimate basis for adhering to the dictates of political authority, so the appeal to consent could be no more explanatorily interesting than the direct appeal to the public good.

Now, the second of these strategies is ill-founded. For, even if we were to grant Hume that the requirement to adhere to one's promises is grounded in the promotion of the general good – which is itself dubious – the fact that one must appeal to the general good to explain why promises should be kept would not be sufficient to show that a general promise to adhere to the dictates of political authority is not needed to adequately account for those dictates' binding force. This is obvious. The fact of the general promise to obey could be what makes it the case that the public good can be promoted only by obedience. (Compare this with *any* promise: surely Hume would not say that, on the assumption that the requirement to keep promises is ultimately grounded in the public good, his

---

[3] It is hard to believe that Hume really thought this.

promise to pay the butcher for his meat is otiose in the explanation as to why he owes the butcher money.)

But the failure of the second of Hume's two redundancy arguments does not even suggest the failure of the first. Though Hume's remarks here are not as clear and well-worked-out as we might like, what is not made explicit in "Of the Original Contract" had already been made explicit in the *Treatise of Human Nature*. The most obvious reason to have government is the Hobbesian reason – that a strong authority is needed to impose sanctions on those unreasonable persons who act viciously with respect to their fellow citizens. But Hume emphasizes that government is needed not just for the use of force to hinder injustice, but also to make possible a coordination of action that tends to the general good: "government extends further its beneficial influence; and, not contented to protect men in those conventions they make for their mutual interest, it often obliges them to seek their own advantage, by a concurrence in some common end or purpose" (*Treatise*, III, 7). This is a role that government would have even if a citizenry were generally practically reasonable: for their being practically reasonable would not be enough on its own to make "a thousand persons" agree on a set of schemes for the promotion of the common good. Thus government has a coordinating role, making possible agreement on action for mutual advantage.

This Humean appeal to the coordinating possibilities of government action has been taken up by contemporary natural law theorists with such firmness that it is now the standard natural law position. The central idea in these writings is that (1) even in a political community composed entirely of practically reasonable agents there is a need for an authority to coordinate action for the common good, and (2) the law is the salient candidate to fill the role of authority coordinating action for the common good. Given these premises, the defender of this view holds that in any political community in which there is a legal system that issues directives toward the achievement of the common good, those under this legal system are bound to adhere to its directives.

The coordinating role of government has the central place in Yves Simon's natural law theory of authority. Simon frames his account of political authority around the issue of whether political authority finds its justification only as a result of human defectiveness – in particular, practical unreasonableness (Simon 1962, p. 22).[4] Simon's rationale for holding that political authority is not justified merely by its role in dealing with unreasonableness is that, even for citizens who reasonably aim at the common good of their community, there

---

[4] This is also a central issue in Aquinas: it appears when Aquinas asks whether political authority would have existed had humans remained in a state of innocence. Aquinas's answer – an answer that undoubtedly influenced Simon's view – was that it would: political authority would not be needed to punish wrongdoers but it would nevertheless be needed to direct subjects to the common good (*Summa Theologiae* Ia 96, 3).

is a "plurality of genuine means" to achieve it (Simon 1962, p. 47). But one or another of these different means must be settled upon in order for collective action to be most effective in its pursuit of the common good: and as a *de facto* political authority can in fact serve this coordinating function, those reasonable citizens who seek the common good have reason to adhere to its decisions about how the common good will be pursued.

The most well-elaborated version of this argument has been offered by Finnis. Basic to his view, as to Hume's and Simon's, is that the existence of a genuine political authority – some person, group of persons, set of rules, and so on whose dictates are capable of coordinating action for the common good by making prescriptions that make a normative difference – is some-thing that is needed within a political community. The basis for this is just that the common good is variegated, and different reasonable citizens may settle on different determinations of the common good and of each citizen's proper role in promoting that good (Finnis 1980, pp. 231–232). Citizens may, with equal reasonableness, appeal to the common good and justice in promoting it as the source of their determinations; but since these determinations are, though constrained by practical reasonableness, also the product of free, discretionary choice, different citizens' determinations will be incompatible with each other, and cannot serve as bases for common action. Practically reasonable agents will see, then, that it would be a good thing if they were to have reasons for adhering to some common standard for conduct, if there were a standard that were authoritative for their action to promote the common good. For, after all, given any realistically attainable determination of the common good that might be put forward as a proximate aim of common action, that determination can be better promoted by practically reasonable citizens in a community where practical authority exists than where it does not.

As Finnis understands it, the existence of a common good to be pursued and the availability of a number of ways of reasonably promoting it in common gives rise to a coordination problem, which is in some ways analogous to coordination problems as defined technically within game theory. In game theory, coordina-tion problems are "situations of interdependent decision by two or more agents in which coincidence of interest predominates and in which there are two or more coordination equilibria," where a coordination equilibrium is a situation in which the combination of the players' actions is such that no one would be better off if any single player, either oneself or another, acted differently (Lewis 1969, pp. 24, 14). The classic example is, unsurprisingly, Hume's: two people want to get from one side of a river to the other by rowing; they can get across only if both row in tandem; there are a number of different rowing 'patterns' that they can establish. The main point is that they just need to settle on one: it does not particularly matter which. Crucial, then, is the identification of one of the available solutions as *salient*, either by making an agreement or by noting features of a solution that exist prior to agreement. If a solution is salient, then a player can expect that others will act on it, and thus, by the definition of a coordination problem, no player will have reason to depart from that standard. To reconsider Hume's case: an agreement between the two rowers can easily make a certain pattern of rowing salient. But a pattern might be salient even in the absence of an agreement. If the two rowers cannot communicate with each other, but can see (and can know that the other sees) a large metronome, mounted to the rowboat and ticking away, there is an obvious pattern of rowing to which to conform.

Now, in attempting to make a similar argument for the law's status as salient coordinator, defenders of the natural law account are not suggesting that everyone's *actual* purposes are such that adherence to law is a coordination equilibrium. This would be clearly false, given the existence of persons who are uninterested in the realization of the common good. The appropriate restriction to place is to concern ourselves entirely with those *practically reasonable* persons that are intent on acting on the common good principle: these persons share an end – the realization of the common good. Given that they share an end, and that the law offers a salient point of coordinated action, can we not say that those acting on the common good principle are bound in reason to adhere to the law?

Even with this constraint placed on the ends of the citizens involved, the fact that the common good admits of multiple reasonable determinations, each better than another eligible determination in some respects but worse than it in some other relevant respects, undercuts the possibility that the law's mere salience can underwrite an account of the obligation to obey it. For given such a good as the aim of political action, it seems hardly likely that an eligible determination of that good will be such that, even if everyone else acts for its sake, there would not be some other eligible conception of the good that would be more closely approximated by an agent's departing from the common standard. To make this more concrete, imagine again the practically reasonable citizen confronted by a law, asking for the argument from the principle that the common good be promoted to the conclusion that this law is to be obeyed. Perhaps the law in this citizen's political community dictates that each citizen pay 10 percent of his or her income in taxes, and of the collected income tax, one-third will be spent on defense, one-third on welfare, and one-third on promotion of the arts. Suppose that everyone else in that political community is willing to go along with the tax scheme, and that the distribution of the tax monies is guaranteed to follow the proposed pattern. Our practically reasonable citizen, though, would prefer a different determination of the common good, one that emphasized welfare over defense and the arts, and thus thinks that the common good would be better achieved if he or she withheld his or her tax and spent it directly on contributions to homeless shelters, soup kitchens, and the like. Why, this citizen might ask, should the existence of the law's rival determination of the common good be dispositive of what he or she must do in order to act on the principle of doing one's share to promote the common good? It seems clear that there is, in this best-case compliance scenario, rational motivation for unilateral departure from the common standard, even for a fully practically reasonable citizen concerned for the common good. This sort of salient coordinator view lacks an account of the authority of the law's determination of the common good, given the presence of rival eligible determinations that can make unilateral defection reasonable.

As far as I can see, Simon's work on political authority offers no answer to this question. Finnis, however, recognizes it, and insists, contrary to the views of those that suppose that coordination arguments go a long way toward accounting for any authority that the law possesses, that the fact that the common good might be reasonably specified in various ways undermines most coordination arguments. Yet nevertheless he labels his own natural law view a coordination account. His view is distinguished from the type of coordination argument that he criticizes by the type of salience that the law is held to possess. In the coordination problems of game theory, the salience of the standard consists merely in its being unique in some way, and indeed the solution "does not have to be uniquely good; indeed, it could be uniquely bad" (Lewis 1969, p. 35). The law, by contrast, has its salience not simply in virtue of its standing out, its 'catching the eye,' so to speak, but in virtue of its superior capacity to carry out in a reasonable way the determinations that must be made. Here is the key passage from Finnis:

The law presents itself as a seamless web. Its subjects are not permitted to pick and choose among the law's prescriptions and stipulations. It links together, in a privileged way, all the persons, and all the transactions, bearing on [one's] present and immediate future situation. It also links all the people and transactions which have borne on [one's] well-being or interests in the past. And finally, it links too all the people and transactions that may bear on [one's] future interests and well-being as [one] moves into other occupations, into retirement, old-age, illness, and death.   (Finnis 1984, p. 120)

Raz is unable to see Finnis's discussion here of the seamlessness of the law as anything other than question-begging: "For [Finnis], if this is how the law presents itself, then this is how we ought to take it. To be sure, if we have an obligation to obey the law, then the conclusion does indeed follow. But one cannot presuppose that we have such an obligation in order to provide the reason . . . for claiming that we have an obligation to obey. This would be a vicious circle indeed" (Raz 1984b, p. 150). This, I think, misses the thrust of Finnis's argument. What Finnis is arguing for is the law's normative salience with respect to filling the need for an authoritative standard in pursuing the common good. Its salience consists in its capacity, as a result of its considerable scope, to deal with the problems of justice that invariably attend the pursuit of an end as massive as the common good. We are all, so the natural law view holds, bound to pursue and promote the common good, to do our share in helping to realize it (3.6).

In acting to promote it, we will need some common determination of it. But in fixing on a common determination of the common good in a reasonable way, we will have to keep in mind that the benefits and burdens constituted by or attendant upon the realization of the common good will have to be justly distributed. This too is a problem for determination: we will need to render determinations of distributive principles in order to settle on a determination of the common good. Now, we will also have to decide what each person's just share in promoting the common good is. But surely if we are to reach in a reasonable way determinations about what each person's share is, this will have to be related both to the benefits that one will receive in the realization of the common good as well as the burdens that will be laid on one's fellow participants in the action toward the common good. And once again, this will require determination. We need to keep in mind, further, that how a person is benefited and burdened at a particular time is not dispositive of the justice or injustice of the scheme; we will have to look at how these burdens and benefits are distributed over an entire life, so that no one is required to shoulder excessive burdens at a particular stage of life, and so that over the course of one's whole life the benefits and burdens are equitable. And, finally, we need to realize that the law promises a particularly salient way of solving the coordination problem inasmuch as we may be concerned not only that the standard for common action be eligible with respect to its intrinsic features, but also with respect to the way that it was put into place. A scheme of cooperation that is in itself just can be rejected on the grounds that (1) even though eligible, it is not the one that one would have preferred, and (2) the way that it was put into place was itself unfair or discriminatory. But a well-functioning legal system, non-discriminatory and working in accordance with the rule of law, removes any reasonable ground for complaint on that score.

It is not, then, that the law presents itself as a seamless web, and therefore that's how we should take it: the idea is that it is the very comprehensiveness of the law's scope and the method by which law is put into place that makes it peculiarly appropriate to determining the requirement to do one's share in promoting the common good. The law regulates the whole life of the community, and this makes the law normatively salient to fill the role of authoritative specifier of the principle to do one's share in promoting the common good. There may be, no doubt, other candidates: systems of customary rules, perhaps. In simpler societies, a system of customary rules may be able to perform this function quite well. But in a society of any complexity, the need to make adjustments in how the common good is specified and promoted picks out the law, with its "prospect of combining speed and clarity in generating practical solutions to constantly emerging and changing coordination problems, and in suggesting devices by which such solutions can be generated" (Finnis 1984, p. 136), as peculiarly appropriate to serve as the practical authority by which the common good is pursued.

I will treat Finnis's view as the most plausible version of the salient coordinator account for our purposes. On this view, authority is needed for the promotion of the common good, or else practically reasonable agents will be at loggerheads with one another, rendering incompatible determinations of the common good. The law is particularly well-suited to serve as a practical authority with respect to the common good, due to its capacity to render determinations over the broad range of human life necessary for reasonable determination of the principle to do one's share to promote the common good. Since there is a need for authority in promoting the common good, and a system of law is the normatively salient institution for guiding the promotion of that good, where there in fact exists a legal system that is willing and able to promote the common good by rendering at least minimally reasonable determinations of the principle to promote the common good, one is bound to adhere to those of its determinations that are at least minimally reasonable for acting on that principle. There is no need for any appeal to the consent of the ruled, for the normative salience of the law is, without any appeal to consent, sufficient to establish its authority.

4.7 The Refutation of the Salient Coordinator Account

There is much in Finnis's view that any natural law account of political authority should accept. The natural law theorist should agree on the need for authority in coordinating practically reasonable agents in acting for the common good. Since each agent has a duty to do his or her share for the common good, each agent should do his or her share in putting into place such an authority. Further, the natural law theorist should agree with Finnis about the normative salience of the law as candidate to fill this role as practical authority. While there are genuinely difficult issues concerning the existence of worthwhile ends that compete with the common good for the attention of fully reasonable agents, I will continue (see 3.6) to bracket these concerns for the time being. (We will return to them in Chapter 7.) As I see it, the key question for the defender of the salient coordinator account is whether the acknowledgment of the need for a genuinely authoritative institution to guide action to the common good, and a strong argument that the law is uniquely suited to serve this function, is sufficient to show that where the law exists, citizens are under a practical requirement to adhere to it.

I say that it does not. For an institution to be authoritative is for its dictates to at least partially constitute decisive reasons for action in a certain domain (Murphy 2002a, p. 15, and Murphy forthcoming). The salient coordinator account is supposed to show that with respect to the promotion of the common good, the law's dictate that agents ϕ constitutes a reason for them to ϕ. It would be a good thing for a political community to have a practical authority to guide action toward the common good, for otherwise members of that community will (reasonably) act on their conflicting determinations of the common good and justice in promoting it. The presence of such an authority would give members of that community reasons to act on a common determination, and not to act on their own determinations, or what they would render as their own determinations. And the law is the best thing that can be made to be practically authoritative. *But the fact that authority is needed, and that law is the best candidate to serve this role, does not actually make the law authoritative.* It does not show that citizens are acting wrongly by failing to act in accordance with the law's dictates. At most, it shows that if citizens fail to do their part to make the institution authoritative – perhaps by consenting to it, or something of that sort – then they are acting unreasonably. This is a very important conclusion, but it is *not* the conclusion that there is an obligation to obey the law. There still exists a gap that is not crossed: that it would be a good thing for the law to be authoritative does not mean that the law is in fact authoritative.[5]

The slide from the need for authority to its presence appears even more clearly in Finnis's sympathetic (to a point) reconstruction of Aquinas's account of authority within the family, and so it would helpfully illustrate the point that I am making to consider it here. He writes:

Aquinas ascribes a limited governing responsibility and authority to the husband. Every complex co-ordination requires unanimity or, in default of unanimity, authority. In dealings with children, domestic servants, and persons outside the family, a rule requiring agreement between the spouses for every binding decision would sometimes result in paralysis and default to a very bad outcome. The responsibility of making decisions in default of agreement between the partners, where the partnership's common good is seriously in issue and dissolution of the partnership is not a reasonable option, may be assigned by prior agreement – a possibility that Aquinas neglects to consider – but failing that must in the last analysis rest with someone identifiable independently of agreement.   (Finnis 1998a, p. 172)

Finnis goes on to consider, and criticize, Aquinas's reasons for identifying the husband as the authority in such cases. But we may raise the same criticism of the argument for authority in the family as for authority within the political community: from the fact that it would be a good thing for authority to exist to solve a coordination problem, and even assuming that a clear best candidate for this role exists, it does not follow that that clearly best party is an authority.

---

[5] I thus reach the same conclusion about Finnis's version of the natural law account of political obligation that I reached concerning Jeremy Waldron's natural duty of justice account (Waldron 1993). Waldron argues that we are all bound to promote justice, and justice cannot be secured unless institutions function to ensure that the principles of justice are satisfied. Since those institutions will not function well unless those to whom those institutions apply accept the supervision of those institutions, those to whom such institutions apply are bound to comply with them. In response (Murphy 1994) I argued, a bit too tentatively, that it is unclear whether Waldron's premises imply that justice demands that we adhere to the law, or that justice demands that we make the law authoritative over us. I now think that it shows *at most* the latter, just as Finnis's view shows at most that the common good demands that we make the law authoritative over us.

It follows, at most, that steps ought to be taken to make that clearly best party the authority that will settle those coordination problems when they arise. Does that mean, as Finnis's argument on Aquinas's behalf suggests, that without an authority in place, the result of disagreement must be "paralysis," sometimes "defaulting to a very bad outcome"? Yes, perhaps: the bad consequences of the absence of authority do not simply bring authority into existence, though the threat of such consequences makes the need to bring authority into existence more pressing.[6]

Now, one might respond: given what has been granted so far – that practically reasonable citizens will do their share in bringing authoritative institutions into existence to guide action toward the common good – it can be pointed out that it follows that in any community populated by practically reasonable citizens, the law will be authoritative: for it follows that such citizens will do their parts to put into place such an authority, and will thereupon be obligated to adhere to its determinations. But that can be conceded without lessening the force of the objection to Finnis's view. The fact that a community of practically reasonable citizens will be under a requirement of obedience to law does not show that the requirement of obedience to law is independent of consent, or some other voluntary obligation-generating act: rather, it might show that practical reasonableness requires one to submit to a political authority by performing some relevant obligation-generating act, and since practical reasonableness requires this, it follows that a community of practically reasonable citizens in sufficiently apt political conditions will have performed just such acts. The 'law as (normatively) salient coordinator' view does not close the gap, does not show that the mere presence of law is enough to render the law's determinations of the principle to promote the common good authoritative in the absence of something like consent.

Natural law political philosophy cannot explain how fully fledged law – law backed by decisive reasons for action – is possible simply by appeal to the way that the law is necessary to coordinate action for the common good. If the natural law thesis is that the law's authority is to be explained by way of the requirements of the common good, coordination is not going to be enough for the story. It may seem that we have already ruled out the possibility that consent theory can provide any help (4.3–4.5). But this is wrong. The problem with consent theory is not with its main idea – that consent is normatively effective in realizing political authority, both in principle and in fact – but with the particular understanding of consent theory assumed both by the critics and defenders of the consent view. I present an alternative consent account in the next chapter.

---

[6] Compare: in the absence of an adequate number of life rafts, shipwrecks often default to a very bad outcome. But that does not bring an adequate number of life rafts into existence; they must be brought into existence in light of the possibility of shipwrecks.

5

A Consent Theory of the
Authority of Law

5.1 A Non-Standard Consent Account

The salient coordinator account of the authority of law, upon which natural law theorists have of late relied, fails to explain why citizens ought to adhere to the law's dictates rather than to defect unilaterally when so doing would better approximate the determination of the common good that they prefer (4.6). While Finnis's robust coordination account, on which the law is a normatively salient coordinator, explains why we ought to make it the case that the law's determinations of the common good principle are authoritative, that account cannot show that the law is in fact authoritative (4.7).

The aim of this chapter is to explain how citizens' consent can make the law authoritative over them, in a way that is nevertheless consistent with the central thesis of natural law political philosophy – that the law's authority derives from the common good of the political community. The possibility of such an account might be challenged at the outset. Simmons claims, as we saw in 4.4, that the only sense of 'consent' in which consent generates requirements of compliance is consent in the *occurrence* sense – that is, consent that is constituted by the performance of a speech-act. All other senses of consent are *attitudinal*, in which consent consists merely in an attitude of approval toward the law or toward the *de facto* authorities, and such consent generates no requirements of compliance. The difficulty, then, is to articulate a third sort of consent, one that does not consist in the performance of any speech-act but that is capable of producing practical requirements that would make the law authoritative. The form of consent to which I will appeal is consent in the *acceptance* sense, a practical stance in which one adopts open-ended determinations of practical requirements, determinations to be filled in by the decisions or dictates of other parties, as those upon which one will act in order to satisfy those requirements. Such consent is, I will argue (5.4), like consent in the occurrence sense in that it is capable of binding one to action; such consent does not, however, require the performance of some speech-act in order to be binding. So there is at least some opening for this consent account to succeed further than the standard consent account does.

Here is the basic argument from consent in the acceptance sense. That citizens are bound to adhere to the demands of law arises from the common good principle (3.6), the requirement to do one's share with respect to the common good of the political community, The common good principle admits of a variety of determinations, ways that one can make that principle more concrete for the sake of action, and there are very good reasons for adopting some particular determination of that principle, a determination that is potentially shared by others in the political community as well. When one reasonably adopts a determination of a practical principle, then one ought to adhere to that determination. And so one who reasonably adopts a reasonable determination of the common good principle is bound to adhere to that determination. But in a decent political community, at least one reasonable determination of the common good principle includes acting in those ways that the law in that community prescribes. So one whose determination of the common good principle includes 'doing what the law prescribes' is bound to act in accordance with its prescriptions. To the extent that there exists this general acceptance of the law as determiner of the common good principle, citizens are bound to adhere to the law.

This is both a natural law account and a consent account. It is a natural law account because the practical principle that citizens flout by failing to obey the law is the common good principle. So the account satisfies the natural law thesis that the authority of law derives from the common good of the political community. It is a consent account because it is due only to the consent of the citizenry – their acceptance of the law as determiner of the common good principle – that the law's determination of the common good principle becomes *privileged, the* way to carry out the demands of the common good principle.

As is obvious, there are a number of claims that need to be defended in order for this consent account to be a plausible one. It has to be shown that it is plausible to think of the common good principle as the practical principle in terms of which the law is authoritative (5.2). It has to be shown how determinations of a general principle can become *the* way for one to act on that general principle (5.3). It has to be shown that it is possible to adopt open-ended determinations, determinations whose content is to be filled in by others' dictates, and that it can be reasonable to do so; and it has to be shown in particular that it is reasonable to adopt an open-ended determination of the common good principle that includes doing what the law tells one to do (5.4). And, it has to be shown to what extent this non-standard consent account can succeed in establishing the authority of law (5.5–5.7).

5.2 Law and the Common Good Principle

The common good principle is a singularly promising practical principle from which to begin an account of the law's authority. For law is comprehensive, regulating all matters of practical import within a political community, yet law apportions the responsibilities for realizing its comprehensive goals, giving specific directives to easily identifiable classes of people. It aims to realize a wide-ranging state of affairs, but it does so by placing people under specific requirements.

The common good principle is like this. It is comprehensive, for it is concerned with acting for the common good: and the common good, as I argued earlier, should be understood as that comprehensive state of affairs in which every person's good is fully realized (3.2). But it does not merely affirm the importance of this good: it tells each person to do his or her share with respect to it (3.6). So there is an isomorphism between law and the common good principle that makes the common good principle a singularly promising principle from which to begin an account of the law's authority.

There are two relevant differences between the law and the common good principle. The law need be no more than a *partial* set of directives: it does not purport to exhaust the requirements that a citizen is under with respect to the common good. The law is a fairly *precise* set of directives: while law may well make use of notions that are open textured ('vehicle') or that require employment of evaluative concepts ('reasonable'), the requirements that it imposes on citizens are more easily understood and thus more capable of guiding conduct than the common good principle alone.

As we have seen (3.6), it is the second of these features that sets the crucial question of the natural law account of political authority. That the law aims to provide no more than a partial determination of the common good principle raises no serious questions: it indicates only that civic virtue requires more than the law requires. The hard question is why citizens are ever bound by the determination of the common good principle offered by the law.

5.3 How Can Determinations Bind?

How can law, as a determination of the common good principle, be binding, so that one fails to act properly with respect to the common good principle if he or she fails to act in accordance with the law? A prior question is: how can *any* determination of *any* practical principle become authoritative for an agent, so that he or she fails to act properly with respect to that principle if he or she does not follow that determination?

Any attempt to show that one could ever be violating a practical principle P simply by failing to act on one's own (non-entailed) determination of P seems bound to founder against the argument considered in 4.5. To recall that argument: let A and B be minimally acceptable, incompatible determinations of P, and let ϕ-ing be the act dictated in A, and ψ-ing the act dictated in B. Suppose that one renders A as the determination of P, yet ψ-s instead of ϕ-ing. How could the agent have violated P by ψ-ing, since ψ-ing is the act dictated by B, which is *ex hypothesi* a minimally acceptable determination of P?

One might offer a solution along the following lines. One could firmly resolve to act on A as a determination of P, and since one ought to keep one's firm resolutions, one would be acting wrongly with respect to the fulfillment of P by acting in accordance with B rather than A. But this is equivocating: even if we grant that one would be acting improperly somehow in acting on B, that does not mean that one is violating P; rather, one is acting improperly simply because one is violating the requirement to keep one's firm resolutions, the content of one of which refers to the fulfilling of P, and *not* because one is violating P itself. And so it may seem that any attempt to make a determination of P an *authoritative* determination of P will do so not by making it the case that one will violate P by acting on any other determination than that one but rather by making it the case that one will violate some other practical requirement by acting on a different determination of P.

So long as we proceed on the assumption that the only way to violate a practical principle P is to act in a way that is incompatible with the *content* of P, the conclusion is inescapable that no one of a range of minimally acceptable determinations of P can ever become privileged with respect to the fulfillment of P. But there may be other ways to violate a practical principle besides that of acting in a way incompatible with its content. What I have in mind is that one might act in a way vis-à-vis P that is incompatible with its status as a practical principle, as something that is to guide conduct. While this papers over a dispute, especially relevant with respect to some consequentialist positions, on how practical principles should figure in the deliberation of a reasonable agent, I want to say that a reasonable response to certain practical principles requires not just that one's conduct be consistent with the principle but that one act on the principle, so that one is flouting it by failing to have one's course of deliberation properly shaped by it. It seems to me that it is this sort of flouting of a practical principle that takes place by failing to act in accordance with one's determination of that practical principle.

In order to see how one flouts the practical principle with respect to which one has formed a determination by failing to act on one's determination of it, we should step back to see why one forms determinations in the first place. Consider the following scenario. (I discuss a very similar case in Murphy 2002a, pp. 161–162.) Suppose that you have agreed to carry out the terms of a very wealthy, very eccentric uncle's will. He has placed a huge sum of money in trust to be dispensed in the following way: you are to give $100 to every bald person whose path you run across in the course of the ordinary business of your life, and to no one else. You are, then, under a promissory obligation to give $100 from the fund to every bald person that you encounter, and not to dispense monies from the fund to any non-bald person. The obvious difficulty with acting on this principle is that the term 'bald' is vague. It is not as if by tremendous study and assiduous application of your observational powers you will reach a conclusion on what the dividing line is between persons who are bald and persons who are not bald, so that you can dispense $100 bills with confidence that you are giving $100 to the bald and not to the non-bald. 'Bald' is resistant to further inquiry in this way. The practical problem remains. You have to decide, with respect to persons that you encounter, whether to give them $100 from the trust, whether your promise gives you reason to hand over the money or to refrain from doing so.

How should you deal with this practical problem? Consider two possible solutions. On the one hand, you could simply decide, on each occasion in which you encounter a person about whom it is unclear whether that person counts as bald or non-bald, what you wish to count as bald on that occasion, and make the decision to hand over $100 on the basis of that particular decision. On the other hand, you could adopt a standing rule about how to understand 'bald,' a more determinate rule about the amount of hair on a person's head that must be missing for the person to count as bald. In accepting this standing rule, you need not accept it on the basis of the false view that there is some fact of the matter in these borderline cases about who is bald. Rather, to adopt the rule about baldness is to allow this stipulation to function as a premise in your practical reasoning, so that you can conclude from the fact of your promise to give $100 to all and only the bald and the fact that this person has one-third a head of hair that you ought (or ought not) to give the $100 to this person. The acceptance of a determination is the acceptance of a premise that makes more determinate one's practical reasoning in the relevant class of cases.

There are at least two very strong reasons for preferring the solution on which one accepts a determination rather than that on which one decides in a case-by-case way. The first concerns the demands of consistency. Suppose that you were to follow the former, decide-on-every-occasion method of satisfying the principle. It may be true that on each occasion of choice it may be impossible to show that you acted contrary to your promissory obligation in handing over or failing to hand over the money. But it may very well be true that the pattern of your choices exhibits an objectionable inconsistency. There may be no reason for saying that your refusal to give the $100 to one with one-third of a head of hair would count as flouting the principle, for it is unclear whether a person with one-third of a head of hair is bald. But if you were to give the $100 to one person with one-third of a head of hair and to withhold the $100 from another person with one-third of a head of hair, then you would be clearly under suspicion of having acted in an inconsistent way with respect to the satisfaction of your obligation.

The second reason concerns the requirements of principled conduct. In undertaking the solemn promise to manage the uncle's trust, you have taken the uncle's will as a principle for your conduct. But as it stands, the uncle's will is not sufficient to serve as such a guide. In order for you to take the will as a principle for your conduct, you must supply what is missing in it. When we are under a demand to take some norm as a principle of our conduct, yet that norm lacks the determinacy that is required for it to serve as a principle for our conduct, we have reason to render determinations of that norm that will enable it to guide our actions in a principled way.

We are now in a position to give a general answer to the problem posed at the beginning of this section. Let A and B be minimally acceptable, incompatible determinations of a requirement P: suppose 'give $100 to all and only those persons with no more than one-third of a head of hair' and 'give $100 to all and only those persons with no more than one-half of a head of hair' are minimally acceptable, incompatible determinations of the requirement to give $100 from the trust to every (and only) those bald persons that one encounters. Suppose that you decide on the former determination, but then give $100 to someone with more than one-third but less than one-half of a head of hair. How could you have failed with respect to your promissory obligation, as you performed an action picked out by a minimally acceptable determination of that obligation? The answer is that you failed with respect to that principle by acting on it in an *unprincipled* way – by going contrary to your reasonable decision about the appropriate way to go about acting on the principle.

The central point here is that there is more than one way to fail with respect to a principle. One is by performing an act that is ruled out by the content of the principle. Another is by inadequately taking the principle as a guide to one's conduct. It is this latter way of failing with respect to a principle that occurs when one does not act on one's own determination of a general practical principle.

Before we turn to consider the sort of determinations that must be eligible if this consent account of the law's authority is to succeed, I want to register a clarification of the claim that one is acting unreasonably with respect to some principle P if one fails to act on one's determination of P. I do not mean this claim to imply that once one has rendered a determination of some principle P, one is forever stuck with that determination, and acts wrongly if one ever acts contrary to the content of that determination. The claim is, rather, that *so long as one accepts a certain determination of P*, one ought to act on it; it is not that there can never be adequate reason to revise or reject a determination of P that one has already rendered.

What needs to be made clear, I think, are the different sorts of required rationales (1) for accepting a determination of a principle, (2) for altering the determination of a principle that one has previously rendered, and (3) for acting in accordance with the determination one has rendered. With respect to (1): the reason to accept a determination of a general practical principle is just so that one's action can be guided by it in particular circumstances where the principle is undoubtedly relevant yet in which it is unclear precisely what the principle requires of one. So, the reason that I have to specify the requirement to give $100 from the trust to each bald person is just that the requirement is undoubtedly relevant in all cases in which I have the opportunity to give someone $100, yet it is not clear whether the person should count as bald.

With respect to (2): the reason to preserve the determination that one has rendered does not, strictly speaking, result from the character of the requirement specified, but from the rational unseemliness of changing one's mind without adequate reason for doing so. In rational agents, decisions stand until some inadequacy in the deliberation leading to the decision is detected: some fact was overlooked, some circumstance upon which one has relied changes, some value was under- or over-appreciated. Less strictly speaking, one that constantly alters one's determinations of a practical principle has a basis to suspect himself or herself of not truly acting on the principle, but rather of letting his or her particular commitment to that principle be swayed by extraneous factors. If, upon encountering a number of attractive people with just about half a head of hair – persons I would like to have an excuse to strike up a conversation with – I have a desire to change the determination that I have settled upon from 'one-third of a head of hair or less' to 'one-half a head of hair or less,' I have reason to suspect that my determination of that requirement is being governed by considerations that are irrelevant, even if the determination newly settled upon is at least minimally acceptable. (There may be further reasons to preserve one's determinations in addition to the avoidance of irrational flightiness, but these reasons will be specific to the principles at issue; see 5.4 for one such example.)

With respect to (3): the reason for acting on the determination of the principle, as I said, is just that by specifying a principle in a certain way one has decided that this is the way that one will act on this principle, and so if one does not act in this way, then one is not adequately allowing that principle to serve as a guide to one's conduct.

5.4 Open-Ended Determinations

It can be reasonable to form and accept determinations that are *open-ended* – that is, whose content is not fixed at the time of the settling on the determination but will be fixed by the time that action is required. One might decide that as trustee for the uncle's estate, one should take pains that the bald person bonus be available in perpetuity, if possible. One might then settle upon a determination of the requirement to give $100 to each bald person that is determined each year by how much the balance in the trust fund is likely to appreciate and by the number of bald people one is likely to meet that year. The particular facts about the rate of appreciation of the trust and the number of encounters with the bald may be unavailable at the time of making the determination, but may be available to be 'filled in' before the time at which action is required. So long as the relevant facts are available before action is required, it can be reasonable to form determinations that are open-ended in this way.

But if one might form determinations whose content is open-ended, then one might form open-ended determinations whose content must be filled in by another party's say-so. Suppose, for example, that I take myself to be bound by a rule not to drink to the point of intoxication. Now, 'intoxication' is vague, and requires determination in order to be an adequate guide to action. My determination of it might involve just setting limits to my drinking that are easily ascertainable: 'no more than a drink an hour,' perhaps. But it may be the case that such a crude rule is not a very subtle guide: I might overdrink on some occasions, when the drinks are strong, or I might underdrink[1] on some occasions, when I am under fewer obligations, and thus the reasons for scrupulously avoiding even mild intoxication are correspondingly weaker. I may recognize, though, that when I am in drinking situations I am not such a good judge of these matters. It might be a good idea to rely on someone else – my spouse, perhaps – to fill in my determinations on those occasions. I might thus adopt a determination that includes in it 'do not drink past the point at which my wife tells me to stop.' This determination is open-ended, and it is to be filled in by my wife's say-so.

There are several reasons why one might adopt determinations of this sort, open-ended, to be filled in by some other party's say-so. The general form of argument in favor of such determinations is that there are some cases in which one has reason to leave determinations open-ended, has reason to allow them to filled in by another party's say-so, and has reason not to allow them to be filled in by facts other than some other party's say-so. First: while the major need for determination arises not from ignorance but from indeterminacy, it could well be that the border between what is fixed by natural reason and what is a matter of free choice is on the move, and one might not be in the best position to make that assessment for oneself. This may be the case with the intoxication principle just mentioned: someone other than the drinker himself or herself may be a better judge of the border between the rationally required and the rationally discretionary in such cases, and thus the drinker may have reason to adopt a determination that defers to another's decision in some range of cases. Second: it might be that allowing someone else to fill in one's determinations is a good for that other party, or is an expression of goodwill toward that party. So, even if I am not a bad judge of how much to drink, if my wife is thoroughly and not unreasonably worried about the tendencies to alcoholism in my family, there

---

[1] I suppose some might doubt the possibility of underdrinking. But it does seem that some people have the vice of deficiency to which the corresponding mean is temperance (*Nicomachean Ethics*, 1119a7).

may be a good in allowing my wife to complete my determinations concerning alcohol consumption. Third: it may be important for persons to have determinations that are coordinated in some way. There may seem to be little need for us to have coordinated determinations about what counts as intoxication. But suppose that you and I have differing determinations; you consume alcohol to a point that you do not deem 'intoxication' but that I deem 'intoxication'; you proceed to smash your car into mine. I claim that, as a matter of justice, you owe me compensation for driving while intoxicated; you deny this. It would be a very good thing if you and I were to share a common notion of intoxication, so that we could share a common conception of what is owed to others with respect to sobriety in driving. If you and I were to allow our determinations regarding intoxication to be filled in by some third party, this would provide a basis for such a common conception. (See also Murphy 2002a, pp. 165–166.)

Accepting open-ended determinations whose content is to be filled in by other persons, or by some other decision procedure not under one's own control, can place those other persons or that decision procedure in a position of authority. If, for example, I have a decisive reason not to drive while intoxicated, and I have accepted a determination by which some set of rules determines what counts as intoxication, then those rules have authority over me, at least in that limited domain: their say-so fixes my obligations with respect to drunk driving. Thus acceptance of such open-ended determinations can play a role similar to that which consent in the occurrence sense plays in standard consent theories. I will thus say that when one accepts such open-ended determinations, then one consents 'in the acceptance sense.'

5.5 The Natural Law/Consent Account of Political Authority

The pieces are now in place for the defense of the non-standard consent account of the authority of law. The common good principle binds agents to do their share with respect to the common good of their political community. But both 'the common good' and 'one's share' are in need of determination. Agents have good reason to form determinations that will provide a clearer guide to acting with respect to the common good. If an agent forms a determination of the common good principle that includes 'acting as the law dictates' – that is, consents to law in the acceptance sense – then one would be acting unreasonably by acting contrary to that determination. Thus, for all those who have accepted a determination of the common good principle that includes acting in accordance with the demands of law, the law is authoritative.

We require some account of why it is reasonable to form a determination of the common good principle that includes acting on the demands of the law. Looking back to the earlier discussion of reasons to adopt open-ended determinations that are filled in by others' say-so (5.4), we can see several reasons that strongly militate in favor of adopting such a determination, at least under reasonably just legal systems. First, there is the epistemic component: with respect to the demands of a good as complex and multifaceted as the common good, how it should be determined is a complicated matter. The boundary between what is required in reason for the common good and what is a matter of discretion is ever shifting. Given the opportunities for common deliberation that are characteristic of just legal systems, the epistemic credentials of the law in pursuit of the common good are characteristically superior to each individual's own epistemic credentials.

Now, one might respond that the generally superior epistemic reliability of the law in rendering determinations of the common good principle importantly fails in some cases, and in those cases the parties involved will have reason not to accept a determination of the common good principle that includes adherence to the law's say-so on that matter. Raz imagines a situation in which the law contains regulations for the use of certain dangerous tools (Raz 1984b, pp. 146–148), and argues that an expert in the use of those tools has little reason to defer to the law's authority about how they are to be used. But it seems to me that Raz is mistaken on this. The law's determination on the matter of how these tools are to be used is not to be understood, on this account, as a theoretical judgment of what sorts of uses are dangerous and what sorts are not. Rather, it is to be understood as a determination of what citizens owe with respect to one another in the use of such dangerous tools. The fact that some parties are better able to use these tools safely will, presumably, have been taken into account in the issuing of a standard for their use; and it may well be that there are good reasons to have a determination that does not distinguish between experts and non-experts in the use of these tools in the determination of what is owed by each person with respect to the common good. Taken as a piece of mere advice for use of those tools, the law's dictate on the matter might rightly be ignored by the expert. But taken as a rule that sets an appropriate common standard in light of the demands of the common good principle, there is reason even for the expert to accept that rule.[2]

Second, there is a good that can be realized through the sort of acceptance that is involved in consenting to the law as determiner of the common good and one's role with respect to it. Raz has emphasized a stance toward the law that he refers to as "respect for law," developing his account on analogy with the relationship of friendship and the reasons for action that can arise from it (Raz 1979a, pp. 250–260). Consent can have a sort of expressive value, tying one to law and signifying one's allegiance to the values that it embodies and

---

[2] It is possible that such a law might be so burdensome to the expert, with so little justification for doing so, that it would not count as a reasonable specification of what that expert owes with respect to the common good of the political community. If so, the law might fail to be backed by sufficient reasons for compliance, and would thus be defective precisely as law.

promotes. Now, Raz is insistent that respect for law, like friendship, is optional (Raz 1979a, pp. 256–257). But even while allowing that respect for law, like friendship, is optional, there are strong reasons that press one toward such a stance toward good law.

Third, and most importantly, there are reasons for coordinating our determinations, reasons to which the salient coordinator account (4.6) draws to our attention. We have reasons to form a common determination of our places in promoting the common good. One reason is that of *mere* coordination: it is nice to have a conveniently salient coordinator for our action, with the power to impose a normatively binding solution rather than to rely entirely on causal adjustment of the environment to promote effective coordination. The second reason, emphasized by Finnis, is the need for a coordinator that is practically reasonable, one that is able to recognize the boundaries between what is rationally fixed or evaluable and what is a matter of free discretion, and that has proper procedures for deciding on both aspects in the face of continually shifting, highly complex circumstances of action. A third reason is that, at times, the coordination itself must be defined in normative terms. By this I mean that we need to come to a common mind on what sorts of demands we should recognize on ourselves and what sorts of claims we can make on one another with respect to the promotion of the common good. Recall again the rule that forbids operating motor vehicles while intoxicated. The need for coordination here cannot be adequately expressed without stating the coordination problem itself in normative terms, of coming to agreement on what is owed to one another in terms of care in the operation of dangerous machines. Part of our need for coordination here involves the just demands we can make on one another: whether you can rightly demand that I refrain from driving when my blood alcohol level is above .08, or whether you can rightly demand compensation from me when, as a result of my driving with a blood alcohol level of .09, I injure you or damage your property.

All of the reasons that can support the adoption of open-ended determinations to be filled in by others' say-so can be brought to bear in showing that there is very strong reason to adopt determinations of the common good principle that include acting in accordance with the law's dictates. This is important for two reasons. First, if it does turn out that in some jurisdiction, consent in the acceptance sense is general, and thus that the law is generally authoritative in that jurisdiction, it need not be the case that law has authority only through mistakes or confusion of the citizenry. Second, as I noted earlier (5.3), one is bound to adhere to a determination only so long as one adopts it; one is able to reject it, and thus free oneself from its binding force. The fact that there is strong rational pressure to adhere to such a determination shows that the rejection of a determination displays not merely an irrational flightiness but also an unreasonable response to the demands of the practical principle that one is to act upon (see also 4.7).

5.6 The Unique Appropriateness of Consent in the Acceptance Sense

Is there any reason to suppose that consent in the acceptance sense is in any way *special*, a peculiarly appropriate way of making the law authoritative?

What makes consent in the acceptance sense a peculiarly appropriate way to make the law authoritative is, first, that, unlike other ways of making the law authoritative, the practical principle at work is the common good principle itself, and not some other. And this, to me, seems like an immediate point in its favor: the goodness of political authority resides in its capacity to direct citizens to the common good, and an account of its authority that links it most directly to the normative force of the common good seems preferable to one that does not.

A second point in favor of consent in the acceptance sense is that it does better than other accounts with respect to the avoidance of practical conflict. Suppose we make the comparison more particular, and ask: why go the route of consent in the acceptance sense, rather than, say, that of promise? The defender of promise as the best way, or an equally good way, to generate political authority might agree that political authority is needed and that the law should serve this role, and might suggest that something like a promise is a practically reasonable way to institute the law as authoritative. Well, what would the relevant promise be? The promise might be: to do what the law says to do, within the limits set by the common good principle. This would ensure that no requirement that one finds oneself under as a result of this promise goes afoul of the common good principle; whatever one is bound to do is assured to be congruent with some minimally acceptable determination of the common good principle. But it does not seem clear to me that a promise of this form would be a reasonable way to establish the law as authoritative.

Here is why. In putting into place a practical authority, we should also be concerned about the possibility of practical dilemmas: we should aim to avoid placing ourselves in situations in which we will find ourselves under conflicting practical requirements. If we make such a promise and then go on rendering our own determinations of the common good principle, we may find ourselves in just such cases of practical conflict: for we may be bound both to honor the promise and to act in accordance with our determination of the common good principle. Since there is a plurality of reasonable determinations of the common good principle, it would be sheer coincidence for the determinations rendered by the citizen and by the law to coincide. One is therefore nearly certain to end up in practical dilemmas: bound to adhere to his or her own determination, and bound to adhere to the law's.

This does not show, of course, that promising is inferior to consent in the acceptance sense as a way to make the law authoritative. Perhaps we have focused on the wrong content for the relevant promise. Instead of promising merely to *act on* the law's dictates, perhaps the promise that should be made is a promise to *accept* determinations of the common good principle that include the law's dictates. The practical conflicts resultant upon rendering one's own determinations while being bound to act on those rendered by another would be ruled out, at least for those that adhere to their promise. But what now needs to be asked is whether the inclusion of the acceptance of certain determinations within the content of the promise hasn't made the act of promising nugatory. For the promise is a reason to accept a determination, and once the determination is accepted, one is bound to act on it because it is one's own minimally acceptable determination of a correct practical principle. But we already have reasons to accept determinations – that is, that each person ought to do his or her just share in putting into place an authority that can guide agents toward the common good. And once the determination is accepted, the reason to act on it is that which is put forward in the account based on consent in the acceptance sense.

While these arguments are aimed at two particular alternatives to consent in the acceptance sense, they point to a dilemma for any attempt to put forward a mode of establishing authority alternative to consent in the acceptance sense: it will either be more prone to generating practical conflicts or it will be redundant. No doubt certain methods of generating content-independent obligations may be useful in addition to consent in the acceptance sense, but nothing can take the place of that form of consent.

Third: consent in the acceptance sense is more closely connected to what makes for law in the first place. It thus exhibits an intrinsic connection between what makes non-defective law exist and what makes that law authoritative.

Here is what I mean. It was one of the contributions of Hart's *The Concept of Law* that it firmly established that what makes a legal system present depends not merely on outward observables but on the reflective attitudes, judgments, dispositions of the officials of that system, and perhaps of the citizenry more generally. Hart claims, in particular, that a legal system is present only when (at least) the officials of that system take the internal point of view with respect to its rules, treating them as reasons for action, as a basis for compliance, as grounds for criticism. Now it seems plausible, given the argument made in Chapter 2, that 'A legal system is such that its citizens take the internal point of view with respect to it' is a necessary truth: not that every system that we would call 'legal' is such that every citizen takes the internal point of view with respect to it, but rather such that those systems in which there is not such general acceptance are defective as legal systems. And if this is so, then it seems an important point in favor of this consent account that consent in the acceptance sense bears such a close resemblance to what Hart labels the internal point of view. It is not as if we must simply define what a legal system is and then go and look elsewhere for the additional elements that would show that it is authoritative. Rather, the very description of a non-defective legal system explains why such an institution would be authoritative.

5.7 How Far Does this Consent View Establish the Law's Authority?

I have argued thus far that the law could be authoritative as a result of citizens' consenting to it in the acceptance sense, so that they adopt open-ended determinations of the common good principle that are to be filled in by the law. As we saw earlier (4.2), consent theories of political authority proceed by providing both a model of how the law might be authoritative and reasons to think that this model applies to the law in present political communities, at least in those that are reasonably just. Does this consent account provide a possible model of the law's authority? And if it does provide such a model, to what extent is this possibility actual?

One might wonder whether this is even a consent account at all. This is the lawyer's criticism. There is in law a highly specific meaning of consent, which description is not satisfied by consent in the acceptance sense. But, as Simmons implicitly acknowledges through recognizing the attitudinal sense of consent, there are other notions of consent besides the lawyer's. The root notion of consent is that of the coincidence of wills, and more particularly, of one will's falling into line with another. Consent in the acceptance sense involves taking another's will on some matter into one's own will on that matter. This strikes me as close enough to the root notion of consent for the label to be accurate.

Whether this account is a consent account is ultimately of no more than terminological interest. More substantively, one can ask whether the model really could provide an account of the law's authority. Grant for a moment that one's determinations can bind, so long as one continues to accept them. But as I conceded earlier (5.3), one can free oneself from the binding force of one's determinations simply by rejecting them. So even if a person accepts a determination of the common good principle that includes acting as the law requires, and so is bound to act as the law requires, he or she may free himself or herself from obligation simply by rejecting that determination. Consider in this regard a contrast between the requirements of reason arising from standard consent accounts and those requirements arising from consent in the present account. On the standard view, to consent to one's political authorities is to enter into a permanent – or permanent save for a few important qualifications – obligation to adhere to the dictates issued by those authorities. As such, the standard consent account can explain the *endurance* of the law's authority, the fact that one remains bound by the law, like it or not, over extended periods of time. The present consent account cannot.

How strong an objection is this to the consent theory defended here? We can assess the strength of this objection only if we begin by asking why it is that an account of political authority would have to show that the status of political institutions as authoritative is independent of one's continuing acceptance of authority. Perhaps the concern is this: unless authority is independent of one's continuing acceptance, one could too easily remove oneself from the ranks of those subject to authority. One could simply decide not to accept particular decisions whenever one is dissatisfied with them, or one might decide for some trivial reason to cease to consent to any authority. It might even be claimed that authority that depends in this way on one's continuing acceptance is no authority at all, thus bringing into question whether the refurbished consent theory could succeed in explaining any practical authority, let alone the authority of law.

I deny that this is a serious objection to this account. For, first, the fact that the reason-giving status of a determination, and thus the reason-giving status of the dictates of a party relied upon in a determination, is contingent on the agent's continuing to adopt that determination does not in the least call into question the status of that party as an authority. Whether one is an authority over another is an issue that is distinct from the issue of the conditions under which one will continue to be authoritative over that other. Often an employer is authoritative over his or her employee in some matters. That this is so is entirely distinct from the question of the terms of the employee's employment: whether the employee may leave the position at will, or whether he or she is bound to some fixed term of employment by contract. It is thus clear that the objection cannot be that the way that the law's reason-giving status can be shaken off by rejecting a determination that relies upon the law to fix the content of the common good principle ensures that the law lacks authority.

Second: it is not as if there are not other views of political authority according to which the subject's being under the law's authority is conditional on the subject's remaining in some set of circumstances, circumstances that the subject might choose to exit. The standard argument from fair play relies on voluntary acceptance of benefits: if one ceases voluntarily to accept benefits, then one ceases to be obligated (see, for example, Hart 1955 and Rawls 1964). Arguments from tacit consent, such as those that rely on residence as a sign of consent, often hold that the conditions that constitute consent hold contingently and might be exited at will. When Locke holds that it is present enjoyment of goods under some political authority that makes for consent to the rule of that authority, he also allows that should one no longer make use of these goods (for example, through emigration), obligation ceases as well (*Second Treatise*, §§119, 121). But it has not been treated as an independent argument against these fair play and tacit consent accounts of political obligation that the conditions under which one is obligated to obedience hold only contingently.

Perhaps the difference between the tacit consent/fair play accounts that I just mentioned and the argument from consent in the acceptance sense is that on the tacit consent and fair play accounts, the conditions under which one is bound to obey the law are supposed to match up with the conditions under which the subject is taken to be under the law's jurisdiction. The law claims authority over the subject when the subject is within the borders of the state, and while the subject's being under the law's authority is contingent, it is not contingent that the conditions for the law's being genuinely authoritative are met if and only if the law claims to be authoritative over the subject. But the present consent account does have a response: I can concede that if this consent view held that it is a matter of rational indifference whether one consents to law in the acceptance sense or not, and that it is a matter of rational indifference whether one continues to consent to law in the acceptance sense, then there would be a basis from which to criticize that position. But I have denied this rational indifference. Putting to the side for now the competing ends that might challenge the place of the common good in the concerns of the reasonable agent (we will return to the question in Chapter 7), it is clear that the powerful reasons in favor of furthering the common good makes the common good not merely an optional end (3.2), and so the common good principle (3.6) is not merely an optional rule of conduct. Given the considerations put forward in 5.6, then, there is decisive reason to consent to the authority of law in a political community in which that law is reasonably just and effective. So while it is possible to remain or become free of the law's authority by refusing to allow it a role in fixing the content of the common good principle, one can remain or become free of the law's authority only through unreasonableness. And it does not seem to me to be an untoward result that one can remain free of the law's authority, but only by acting wrongly.

Let us return, then, to the Humean criticisms (4.3–4.4) in order to see to what extent the difficulties that he poses for standard consent theory apply to the modified view. Recall the first of the two Humean criticisms meant to establish the *ab initio* implausibility of consent views, the *self-image* objection. According to this objection, the notion that the authority of the law is grounded in the consent of those subject to it fits poorly with the self-image both of the rulers and of the ruled. The rulers see themselves as having authority over all in their jurisdictions, regardless of their consent; the ruled see themselves as being born to authority, rather than having accepted it through their own voluntary actions. Consent theory thus has the burden of showing that the self-images of the key political actors are in error.

Consider, first, the self-image of the ruler. It seems to me that, regardless of the views of particular princes and presidents, the central issue is the self-image of the law, for it is the law that is supposed to bear authority. But if the argument of Chapter 2 was right, then it is not true that we can ascribe to the law the view that it is authoritative over citizens regardless of their consent. We have a basis to say only the following: that for whatever set of dictates some system of law lays down, the law presupposes that those dictates are backed by decisive reasons for action. (We have to be careful about scope issues here: my claim is that, for whatever dictates the law lays down, the law presupposes that there are decisive reasons to comply with them; my claim is *not* that the law presupposes that, for whatever dictates the law lays down, there are decisive reasons to comply with them.) It does not presume that it is authoritative irrespective of consent; it presumes that there is some source or sources for the reasons that back its dictates. Law need have no official view on whether this source is consent. So there is little reason to doubt this or any other consent account by appeal to the self-image of the law.

What, then, should we say about the self-image of the ruled? It may be true that citizens do not typically see themselves as bound to obedience through their consent, whether in the occurrence or in the acceptance sense. But what I want to say about this fact is that the requirements of reason resulting from consent in the acceptance sense are requirements of the sort that are most likely to be unnoticed in day-to-day life. For the requirement in question is based on a condition of one's will, something like a decision, and for the most part, people keep to their decisions without having to reflect on requirements to adhere to their decisions. For decisions are causally as well as normatively effective, and while they are normatively effective, they are not the sort of reasons that tend to come up when called upon to justify one's actions.

Here is a clearer example of the phenomenon that I have in mind. It is often held that there is a requirement to act in accordance with one's conscience, where one's conscience is one's all-things-considered judgment about what one is to do in a particular case that confronts one (Murphy 2001a, pp. 241–246). So if I confront a particular case in which my conscience tells me that, all-things-considered, I ought to tell a lie, then I ought to act in accordance with that judgment and tell the lie. In the vast run of cases in which one acts in accordance with the conscience principle, one has no particular need to call that principle to mind, and it would be strange for one to do so. One naturally acts on the basis of one's particular practical judgment; that particular judgment is causally effective in producing action, and in the vast run of cases the agent will act in accordance with it. What's more, if one were called upon to justify the action, it would be strange for one to appeal to the conscience principle: one would be more likely to justify the action by the same factors that justified the judgment – the goods to be brought about by the action, the inferiority of the other options, and so forth. The conscience principle remains invisible, brought out only in special circumstances.

Similarly, consent in the acceptance sense has its binding force through a principle that includes in its conditions of application a state of will of the agent: his or her *adopting* a determination with a certain content. And if one adopts a determination with a certain content, then one will characteristically act on it without need to ask the question: what binds me to act in accordance with this determination? For it is causally effective, helping to bring about the requisite actions; and it is normatively obscured, for one is likely to think of one's action as adequately justified by the goods to be brought about (etc.) rather than the principle itself. So, for example, return to the case of the requirement to pay $100 to each bald person out of the trust fund. One who has decided to count all those with less than one-half of a head of hair as bald has rendered a determination of that principle, and that decision will normally be causally effective in bringing about the action of paying $100 to each person with less than one-half of a head of hair. And this trustee will likely see his or her action justified just by the eligibility of the determination and the requirement to pay out the money: once a decision is made, the occasions on which there is need to reflect on why this decision is binding should be rare.

If persons generally consented to law in the acceptance sense, then it would be likely that there would be little reason to reflect on the source of the requirement to act on content of the determination rendered by the law. It would be simply the natural thing to do to rely on the dictates of law in one's ordinary practical reasoning. And this is, it seems to me, the way that most persons act on the requirements of law.

So my response to this Humean criticism is that there are some normative principles that are 'obscured': their conditions of application are such that there is rarely need to call attention to them. Obscured normative principles are such as to be very unlikely to enter into the self-image of persons as the source of their important obligations. And the requirement to act in accordance with one's determinations of general practical principles is an obscured normative principle. Thus the fact that this consent view is not part of the self-image of the ruled is not a strike against it.

Consider now Hume's *knowledge* objection. On the standard consent view, the relevant obligation results from the performance of a speech-act, the sort of act that one tends to remember if one has performed it; and what's more, the content of the consent is so momentous that it would seem improbable in the extreme that one might have performed the action yet have forgotten about it. But this objection depends on the character of the speech-act of consent as a public, datable act. Consent in the acceptance sense is, by contrast, not a public act, and is not necessarily a datable act. One's adopting a particular determination may be a drawn-out process, obvious to no one, not even to the agent. The determination that one has adopted may be clear to the agent only as a result of hard reflection on one's commitments.

Still, none of this shows that this consent account of authority explains the authority possessed by the law; all that it shows is that this theory avoids some of the more important criticisms pressed against standard consent views. How general is such consent, after all? It is obvious that this consent view does not provide a good argument for what Green takes to be *the* political obligation thesis: that all citizens are bound to all of the laws of their political community (Green 1990, pp. 225, 228–229 and Green 1996, p. 8). It seems to me that while the consent view I have defended has resources to provide an account of actual political obligation that goes beyond rival consent accounts, it surely does not approach the universality needed to satisfy the political obligation thesis. But it seems to me that even without establishing the political obligation thesis, the consent view I have defended would justify a very powerful normative conclusion: that either a citizen is bound to obey the law of his or her political community, *or* that citizen is acting unreasonably, *or* the legal system of that political community is an unreasonable one. Let me conclude this chapter, then, by discussing the scope of actual political authority on this consent view and by considering this modified version of the political obligation thesis.

We may say, first, that consent in the acceptance sense is at least not on a par with consent in the speech-act sense, in that the absence of consent in the speech-act sense does seem to be a brute, easily empirically verifiable fact. More positively, it seems to me that there is an argument that can be made that consent in the acceptance sense to the law as determiner of the common good principle is fairly widespread. Whether consent in the acceptance sense is a widespread phenomenon or not depends on the state of citizens' deliberative dispositions, on how citizens are disposed to reason practically, for consent in the acceptance sense is a disposition to accept a particular determination for the sake of practical reasoning and decision-making. The main reason to suppose that consent in the acceptance sense is a fairly widespread phenomenon is that the law *does* figure so centrally in citizens' deliberations. People do tend to treat the law's determinations on matters of public interest as authoritative. Witness, for example, drunk-driving laws, and the seriousness with which people take the particular determination of the blood alcohol level that counts as determining legal intoxication.

Now, those worried about the theory of political obligation have seemed to think: either we can provide some argument from a recognizably correct moral principle to the conclusion that the law is authoritative and thus that this particular drunk-driving law is to be obeyed, or this acceptance of the law as the determiner of what constitutes a violation of the prohibition against endangering the common good through drunk-driving is groundless. But the account that I have offered shows this dilemma to be a false one. There are good reasons to accept the law's determination in drunk driving matters: for driving while intoxicated is a matter that bears on the common good, and part of doing our share in promoting the common good is to refrain from driving while impaired by alcohol. But we do not need an argument from the law's prior authority to show that a stance of deliberative acceptance of the law's standard is reasonable: what makes the acceptance reasonable is that there is need for such a standard and that the law is the salient provider of such a standard. Those that accept the law's standard, then – and I think that there are many – may be bound to adhere to the standard in virtue of their acceptance of the law's standard as the way to act with respect to this issue bearing on the common good.

There might be an objection to my view on the plausibility of widespread acceptance of law's authority that there are some areas of law – in particular, traffic law – with which there is such widespread non-compliance that it seems wrong to suppose that there is much acceptance of law's authority in these areas. But to object to my view on these grounds would be a mistake. It is no part of my view that acceptance of a determination entails that one must act on that determination. Even those agents who consent to law in the acceptance sense are subject to all of the failures to which agents generally are subject: inattentiveness, momentary indifference, weakness of will, selfishness, and so forth. Think about it this way: I would say that most people accept the norm *lies ought not to be told (unless there is some particularly pressing overriding reason to the contrary)*. Yet people lie all the time – nine out of ten of us do so regularly, if the social scientists are to be believed (Patterson and Kim 1991, p. 45). Why should we continue to say that (most of) these people who lie so often nevertheless accept the norm against lying? First, because they say so; second, if they are caught and scolded, they treat their scolding as justified rather than as an affront. In the face of both the verbal and behavioral confirmation, we are more likely to interpret their behavior as that of flouting (for various reasons) a norm that they nevertheless accept rather than simply to deny that they accept the norm in question. I would say that the same is true for most drivers: most speeders, I think, would affirm the law's authority over the roads in such matters and would not treat attempts to enforce those standards as outside of that authority.

What is more difficult than showing the *prima facie* plausibility of widespread acceptance of the law's authority is showing that citizen acceptance of the law's determinations in these matters is acceptance *of the right sort*. If the common good principle is to provide the basis for the law's authority, it must be that as a result of the acceptance of the law, one flouts the common good principle by flouting the law. But this will be the case only if one accepts the law *qua* specifier of the common good principle. Not mindlessly. Not simply and only to be like one's neighbor. Not as a rule of thumb to avoid jail. It may seem naive to hold that people accept the law in some way as determiner of the common good principle. But I think not. As Tom Tyler's study (1990) suggests, there is a good deal of evidence that willingness to go along with the law has a great deal to do with whether the law appears to be even-handed and just, and willingness to comply correlates more closely with perceived fairness than with favorable personal outcomes. It does not seem to me at all naive, then, to think that citizens' acceptance of the law is in part acceptance of the law as marking out fair solutions to the problem of how the common good is to be promoted through unified action.

This consent account explains, I claim, to a non-negligible extent the authority of law over citizens. But one might suppose that since it falls short of establishing the political obligation thesis, it is still of little interest. There is, however, more to this natural law account than an account of how far citizens are obligated to obey the law, and in what way. The natural law view incorporates an account of the requirement to do one's share with respect to the common good and an account of why citizens ought to do their share in putting into place a practical authority that can govern action toward the common good. If there exists a legal system that is at least minimally reasonable in its procedures for generating determinations of the common good principle, then those who heed the requirements of that principle will consent to its authority, and thus make it authoritative over the way that they act for the sake of the common good. This is an important result, especially in the face of the charge that the consent account is a failure if it fails to establish the political obligation thesis. If consent in the acceptance sense is not a widespread phenomenon, it could be the case that there are very few citizens that are tied by bonds of political obligation. For those citizens, disobedience to law is not as such practically unreasonable. But this consent theory would have more to say than this: it would also offer information – although not totally unambiguous – about the citizens of a political community in which political obligation is almost wholly absent, or about the nature of the legal system within that community. With respect to the character of the citizenry: law's failure to attain to authority could mean that one's community is full of unreasonableness, that it is a community in which citizens fail to submit themselves to authority for the sake of the common good. On the other hand, the absence of political obligation might testify not to the unreasonableness of the citizenry but rather to the serious inadequacy of the legal institutions there, that they are merely ineffective at promoting the common good or that they do not embody the discernment or resolution to render a reasonable determination of that good – in other words, these institutions do not merit the consent of the citizenry, either in a wholesale way or with respect to some aspect of the common good, because those legal institutions are *defective*. It is possible, then, for the defender of this natural law/consent view to agree in substance with those philosophical anarchists (Simmons 1979; Raz 1979a; Smith 1973; Green 1990) who hold that most of us are not in fact required to obey the laws of our political communities – but to add, in order to complete the account, 'so much the worse for us.'

6

The Authority of Law and Legal Punishment

6.1 The Place of Punishment within a Natural Law Account of Politics

There is no doubt that a great deal of ordinary thought about law involves thought about punishment. But one might think, for more than one reason, that the place of a theory of punishment is bound to be at the periphery of a natural law account of political matters.

First, recall that the central thesis of a natural law political theory is that the authority of law derives from its privileged place with respect to the common good (0.1). Natural law political philosophy is concerned with law's authority. Punishment, by contrast, is concerned with law not as *authoritative* but with law as *coercive*: punishment involves the wielding of force against the unwilling to bring about certain desirable actions or outcomes. But *bearing authority* and *having the right to coerce* are two fundamentally different conditions, and neither entails the other. Needing the direction of a personal trainer, I might promise to follow your directions with respect to my exercise regimen. While that promise establishes you as an authority over me – at least in this limited domain – it does not of itself give you a right to coerce me if I fail to comply. Nor does a right to coerce entail authority. Needing help in stopping smoking, I might grant you a right to knock a cigarette from my hand if you ever see me lighting up. But my granting you the right to use force against me in this context does not make you an authority over me (Murphy 1999, p. 77). Since legal punishment is fundamentally a matter of the coercive use of state power, and the natural law view is fundamentally concerned with the nature and explanation of legal authority, the fact that the connections between authority and justified coercion are contingent and tenuous suggests that the question of legal punishment is not of central concern for the natural law view. If punishment is simply one form of the coercive activity that legal institutions carry out, then the natural law view's focus on authority rather than coercion entails that the natural law view will not take punishment to be of central theoretical concern.[1]

Here is a second way one might challenge the inclusion of a treatment of punishment within the natural law view. Again, recall that the central thesis of a natural law political theory is that the authority of law derives from its privileged place with respect to the common good. One might think that, given this central thesis, the nature and justification of legal punishment are philosophical problems that are peripheral to the problem of law's authority: punishment is needed only because of the way that people might flout authoritative legal dictates, and how we ought to respond to those that flout authoritative legal dictates is a question distinct from that of determining from what source the authority of law derives and precisely how it derives from that source. And so a theory of punishment is not an account of what belongs to legal institutions strictly, of their essence, but an account of what legal institutions happen to be in light of contingent facts about individual decision-making, prudential political judgments about how to deal institutionally with some of those less desirable decisions, tradition, custom, habit, and so forth.

There is something to these arguments. What they have in their favor is the simple point that legal punishment presupposes a departure from the standards imposed by law, and whether those under law depart from those standards is a contingent matter. But the simple point is the only thing that these arguments have in their favor. For these arguments falsely assume that punishment is essentially a matter of coercion and only contingently connected to legal authority. This has things precisely backward. The punishing activity of legal institutions is – given the existence of actual or potential lawbreakers – first and foremost, and essentially, an aspect of the law's imposition of authoritative dictates for conduct rather than an aspect of legal institutions' coercive activity. Punishment is only *accidentally* coercive;[2] it is *essentially* a matter of authoritative direction.

It seems clear that there can be punishment without coercion. Suppose that my daughter Ryan is bound by a set of rules for conduct within our household. She breaks the rules, and I impose a punishment on her: she is grounded for a week. To tell her that she is grounded for a week is, I take it, to direct her authoritatively to refrain from performing some action – that is, leaving the grounds of our home. Nothing of this yet suggests coercion. Indeed, I might

---

[1] It is a standard thesis in natural law theories of politics that legal institutions are not necessarily coercive. That thesis has a vivid theological context in Aquinas's work: there it is put forward as part of the answer to the question, "Would there have been political authority in the state of innocence?" – that is, in the condition that would have persisted had Adam not sinned (*Summa Theologiae* Ia 96, 3).

[2] For a distinct argument for the non-coercive character of law – one that rests more heavily on providing an adequate understanding of what is essential to coercion rather than on what is essential to law – see Edmundson 1998, pp. 73–124.

offer the following (sincere!) addendum: "If you choose to leave the grounds of our home, I am not going to stop you. I refuse to use force against you, or even to threaten it. I simply tell you that, because you have violated the rules of our house, you must now stay in the house for the next week." It is obvious that I have imposed a punishment on her. But it is also obvious that I have not coerced her. One might question the effectiveness of punishment of this sort, and suggest that punishment without force or threat of force is bound to be ineffective. So, while punishment is not necessarily coercive, *rationally imposed* punishment is. But this is, again, a contingent matter. My daughter might be very lax about her willingness to obey the general house rules, but very conscientious about adhering to my punishment-impositions. I might have no reason to back the punishment with force or threat of force, and indeed might have strong reasons to disclaim any intention to use force if she fails to comply.

We think of legal punishment as consisting both of the imposition of the sentence and the official action that contributes to the sentence being carried out. So punishment begins with the judge's laying down the sentence and continues with the action of other officials – bailiffs, wardens, prison guards, executioners, and so on – who fulfill some role in assuring that the sentence be completed. Now, the imposition of the sentence is obviously an exercise of legal authority. The official action that contributes to the sentence's being carried out – the construction and upkeep of prisons, the deployment of guards, and so on – is not an exercise of practical authority, but a provision of means by which the deprivation essential to punishing can take place. *But these provisions of means need not be coercive.* Legal officials might punish simply by telling those to be imprisoned to segregate themselves in houses without bars and by providing hemlock to those to be executed. Indeed, such institutions might leave the satisfaction of the sentences entirely to the punished: those punished might be sentenced to self-confinement in their homes, to self-funded and self-planned exile, or to execution by their own hands. What is crucial to legal punishment is its imposition by the law, and that is a matter of the state's exercise of authority, not of its use of force.

What these considerations suggest is that what is essential to legal institutions' punishing activity can be more illuminatingly understood in terms of their character as practically authoritative rather than as capable of wielding force. And if the punishing activity of legal institutions is to be understood first in terms of the laying down of authoritative dictates, then it is clear that the natural law view should have something to say about punishment. For the central natural law thesis is that the law's authority is to be understood with reference to the common good of the political community (0.1, 3.6). And so what is essential to legal punishment will thus have to be understood in terms of the authority of law in directing action for the common good.

On the account that we have developed thus far, the law's imposition of authoritative dictates is to be explained in terms of the common good principle: that one is to do one's share with respect to the common good of the political community (3.6). An imposed punishment – 'you are to undergo such-and-such sanction' – should then be understood in terms of this principle. To undergo a punishment is, on this view, to do one's share with respect to the common good of the political community. How can this be the case? For to undergo a punishment is to be deprived of some good, and to be deprived of a good is – given the aggregative conception of the common good defended in Chapter 3 (3.2) – to set back, rather than to further, the common good. On what basis, then, is the natural law theorist to defend legal punishment?

6.2 The Quasi-Utilitarian Natural Law Account of Punishment Rejected

There is a simple solution to the question available. Suppose that one holds that the exercise of political authority, which includes the imposition of punishment, is for the sake of the common good. What is initially problematic about punishment is that it seems to involve aiming at setting back the common good: so long as the goods of citizens are in some way constitutive of the common good, successful punishment seems to set the common good back in some measure. But it may be the case that the practice of punishment tends, over the long haul, to promote the common good. There is a bleak way of connecting punishment and the common good: those who do not fear God (enough) or care about the common good (enough) can be motivated by the prospect of punishment to avoid committing criminal offenses, thus safeguarding the common good through deterrence (*Summa Theologiae* IaIIae 87, 8 ad 2; IIaIIae 33, 6). There is a less bleak way of connecting them: those who do not yet care adequately about doing their share for the common good will have a motive for doing so supplied by punishment; if all goes well, they will become habituated to good civic acts and come eventually to see the point of and perhaps even love being law-abiding (*Summa Theologiae* IaIIae 92, 1). And just as the justification of legal punishment is this causal connection between punishment and the promotion of the common good, the scope of actions that falls within the range of criminalization and the severity of punishment that ought to be imposed is determined by effectiveness in promoting the common good.

This simple solution is the utilitarian solution. The utilitarian takes the goal of all reasonable action, individual or collective, to be promotion of overall happiness, where happiness is characteristically understood as pleasure or desire-satisfaction. Punishment is *prima facie* suspect, because it involves pain and frustration, but it can be justified as part of a practice that generates compensating good results. While the natural law view rejects the subjectivism of the utilitarian's conception of the public good (0.2), the simple solution accepts the structure of the utilitarian's punishment theory.

Some remarks of Aquinas's suggest that he would affirm some version of the simple view. In a series of articles midway through the Secunda Secundae of the *Summa Theologiae*, Aquinas has occasion to consider the extent to which the killing, maiming, striking, and imprisoning of other human beings are contrary to justice. And while, unsurprisingly, he holds that these actions constitute attacks on fundamental human goods and thus are characteristically evil, he allows that they may be performed on "sinners" – that is, against those who have been officially judged to have violated a reasonable, duly promulgated, authoritative norm. The reason that he gives for the licitness of killing sinners is as follows:

> It is lawful to kill dumb animals, in so far as they are naturally directed to man's use, as the imperfect is directed to the perfect. Now every part is directed to the whole, as imperfect to perfect, wherefore every part is naturally for the sake of the whole. For this reason we observe that if the health of the whole body demands the excision of a member, through being decayed or infectious to the other members, it will be both praiseworthy and advantageous to have it cut away. Now every individual person is compared to the whole community, as part to the whole. Therefore if a man be dangerous and infectious to the community, on account of some sin, it is praiseworthy and advantageous that he be killed in order to safeguard the common good.   (*Summa Theologiae* IIaIIae 64, 2)

The point is that through certain sorts of grievous violations of the common good, one shows oneself to be a threat to that good, and thus to promote the common good it is reasonable to destroy that threat. In some cases maiming – Aquinas has in mind the removal of an offender's limb – will be sufficient to generate the requisite restraint and to deter would-be offenders. And in some cases, blows or imprisonment will do the trick. All of this is for the sake of protecting the common good: punishing yields special deterrence against damaging the common good (*Summa Theologiae* IaIIae 87, 8 ad 2; IIaIIae 33, 6; IIaIIae 108, 1), general deterrence against damaging that good (*Summa Theologiae* IaIIae 87, 8 ad 2; IIaIIae 33, 6), and reformation of citizens who might otherwise be inclined to damage the common good (*Summa Theologiae* IaIIae 92, 1).

One common criticism of the utilitarian punishment theory is that, insofar as it appeals simply to the causal consequences of the practice of punishment, it really has no basis to refuse to endorse punishment of the innocent in cases in which it would promote the overall good to do so. We can also imagine scenarios in which, say, punishment of those who are kin to the criminal might be a happiness-promoting practice. There seems no reason why the natural law view that adopted the simple solution would not have these problems as well. (Aquinas denies the justice of punishing the innocent: he says that because the innocent do not pose the threat to the common good that the guilty pose, it cannot be licit to punish them; see *Summa Theologiae* IIaIIae 64, 6.) But I will not press them, as I am not sure as to whether a sophisticated utilitarian position (perhaps along the lines of Rawls 1955) or natural law view could avoid these problems.

What I will press against the utilitarian and simple natural law view is the plain point that such views are committed to inflicting damage on some people for the sake of others' good. These are not cases relevantly similar to warfare and self-defense, where one's aims to protect the innocent might be fully satisfied even if the attacker does not suffer. The aims of legal punishment are not successfully achieved unless the punished is made worse-off.

Usually the political authorities would not be justified in intentionally doing damage to a subject for the sake of the common good. So the idea must be that by committing a criminal act one makes this justified, one frees up political authorities to do their damage for the sake of the overall good. I have never heard a persuasive account of how this waiving of the immunity from such instrumentalization takes place. Aquinas considers the objection that killing of sinners cannot be licit, because "it is not lawful, for any good end whatever, to do that which is evil in itself" (*Summa Theologiae* IIaIIae 65, 2 obj. 3); Aquinas replies:

> By sinning man departs from the order of reason, and consequently falls away from the dignity of his manhood, insofar as he is naturally free, and exists for himself, and he falls into the slavish state of beasts, by being disposed of according as he is useful to others.   (*Summa Theologiae* IIaIIae 65, 2 ad 3)

Aquinas seems to be suggesting here that though, and insofar as, one has departed from the "order of reason" in acting, one becomes fit to be used as an instrument, in the same way that lower animals are fit to be instruments. The argument is not Aquinas at his most convincing. One who helps a convicted criminal escape punishment may be acting wrongly, but surely that is not the same unreasonableness that would be displayed if one were to try to save a chicken from being killed to feed hungry members of the political community. But these would be the same sorts of unreasonableness if Aquinas's argument were sound: one would be preventing what is rightfully used as an instrument from being rightfully used as an instrument.

My rejection of the quasi-utilitarian solution as a natural law account of the justification of legal punishment is premised on the rejection of intentional destruction of some persons' good for the sake of other persons' good. This rejection is in part based on the importance of the intended/foreseen distinction (see Murphy 2005b) and in part on the incommensurability of the goods of the persons at stake in such a choice (0.2; Murphy 2001a, pp. 205–206). It is relatively rare for philosophers now to affirm such a strong version of the immunity thesis, and it is relatively easy to conjure up cases in which we are sorely tempted to violate persons' goods for the sake of others' goods. But keep in mind that to endorse this as the natural law approach, it is not sufficient simply to note that it can, on *some* occasions, be permissible to attack one person's good for the sake of realizing some other person's good. It has to be claimed that in *all* cases of justifiable legal punishment, it is permissible to do so. One cannot simply conjure up fat men plugging the only exit from a cave rapidly filling with water, and note that in these peculiar cases one may treat the destruction of another's good as a mere means to others'; one has to say that in an enormously broad class of cases it is permissible to aim at the destruction of a person's well-being for the sake of some other person's well-being, and that this is the standard way to justify such instrumentalization.

One might think that by rejecting the view that one who does wrong loses his or her immunity from instrumentalization, one thereby gives up any hope of defending legal punishment, since successful legal punishment involves a lessening of the well-being of the punished. But we need to keep in mind that the claim that by engaging in criminal actions, one's claim to a certain level of well-being is lessened is distinct from, and does not entail, the claim that, by engaging in criminal actions, one's immunity from being used as a mere means for the promotion of others' good is lessened. Defenders of legal punishment can affirm the former claim while rejecting the latter. It is the rejection of the latter that makes the quasi-utilitarian solution unavailable to the natural law theorist. It is the affirmation of the former that makes alternative solutions to the problem possible.

6.3 The Equality Natural Law Account of Punishment Rejected

While there is no denying the presence of the quasi-utilitarian strand of Aquinas's defense of legal punishment, there is either an alternative or supplementary account to which he also appeals. On this account, the point of punishment is the restoration of a certain sort of equality that is violated in criminal acts.

The act of sin makes man deserving of punishment, insofar as he transgresses the order of divine justice, to which he cannot return except he pay some sort of penal compensation, which restores him to the equality of justice; so that, according to the order of divine justice, he who has been too indulgent to his will, by transgressing God's commandments, suffers, either willingly or unwillingly, something contrary to what he would wish. This restoration of equality of justice by penal compensation is also to be observed in injuries done to one's fellow men.   (*Summa Theologiae* IaIIae 87, 6)

This view has its contemporary defenders. Herbert Morris offers perhaps the most prominent defense of it; he writes:

A person who violates the rules has something others have – the benefits of the system – but by renouncing what others have assumed, the burdens of self-restraint, he has acquired an unfair advantage. Matters are not even until this advantage is in some

way erased.... Justice – that is, punishing such individuals – restores the equilibrium of
benefits and burdens.   (Morris 1976b, p. 34)

Sher follows Morris, and makes explicit that the extra benefit gained by the
criminal is the freedom from restraint ill-gotten by the criminal (Sher 1987,
p. 80). And Finnis, who emphasizes the presence of the equality account in
Aquinas's work (Finnis 1998a, p. 211), also defends it within his own natural
law view. He writes: "Sanctions are punishment because they are required in
reason to avoid injustice, to maintain a rational order of proportionate equality,
or fairness, as between all members of the society" (Finnis 1980, p. 262). Finnis
holds that the criminal, through the violation of the law, receives an advantage
that the law-abiding does not receive, and it is through punishment that the
equality between the criminal and the law-abiding is restored.

When someone, who really could have chosen otherwise, manifests in action a
preference... for his own interests, his own freedom of choice and action, as against
the common interests and the legally defined common way-of-action, then in and by
that very action he gains a certain sort of advantage over those who have restrained
themselves, restricted their pursuit of their own interests, in order to abide by the law.
For is not the exercise of freedom of choice in itself a great human good?
                                                (Finnis 1980, pp. 262–263)

There are at least two difficulties with the equality account. The first is that
it is far from clear that this view delivers the result that punishments should be
proportionate to the moral seriousness of the offense. Consider, for example,
the datum that a vicious murder is deserving of a more severe punishment
than is a minor tax evasion. A vicious murder might benefit no one, yet be
deeply deserving of punishment, far more so than an obviously beneficial act
of income tax evasion. Now, the defender of the equality view holds that it is
not the benefits that are contingently associated with a crime that determine
one's worthiness to receive punishment, but the benefits that are essential to the
act: in particular, the freedom that one takes for oneself in the violation of the
criminal prohibition. But it is far from clear that one who takes for himself or
herself the freedom to murder is taking a greater benefit than one who takes for
himself or herself the freedom to evade income taxes.

Sher handles the objection by equating the degree of freedom arrogated with
the degree of moral seriousness of the rule violated.

By... equating a wrongdoer's degree of benefit with his act's degree of wrongness, we
nicely resolve the problem of proportionality. But in so doing we may appear to stray from
the original intent of the benefits-and-burdens account. For how, exactly, is a wrongdoer
made better off merely by evading a moral prohibition?... To answer this question, we
must recall the earlier suggestion that wrongdoers gain extra liberty.... A person who
acts wrongly does gain a significant measure of extra liberty: what he gains is freedom
from the demands of the prohibition he violates. Because others take that prohibition
seriously, they lack a similar liberty. And as the strength of the prohibition increases,

so too does the freedom from it which its violation entails. Thus, [the murderer's and the tax evader's] gains in freedom are far from equal. Because the murderer evades a prohibition of far greater force – because he thus "gets away with more" – his net gain in freedom remains greater. (Sher 1987, pp. 81–82)

But this is clearly unsatisfactory. As Shafer-Landau notes, it is hard to see this as anything other than helping oneself to the conclusion that the defender of the equality view is looking for (Shafer-Landau 1996, pp. 302–303). Sher's task here is to show why 'greater freedom' should closely correlate both with 'greater benefit' and with 'greater violation of moral constraints': unless he can give reasons to accept both correlations, he lacks any way of showing that the equality picture will yield the result that more serious offenses merit greater punishments. But he provides no reason to think that 'greater freedom,' in the sense of freedom in which freedom is a benefit, correlates with the moral seriousness of the rule violated. (Aquinas's view, though appealing to the willfulness exhibited by the offender rather than the benefits gained through the criminal act, suffers from an analogous problem: why would we think that the level of willfulness manifested in the act corresponds to the moral seriousness of the offense?)

Indeed, there is good reason to believe that there is a *negative* correlation here – that the value of freedom *declines* with the moral seriousness of the violated rule. There is reason to doubt the view that the criminal – especially when his or her acts involve violating laws that rule out particularly evil *mala in se* acts – takes any freedom that is worth having – that is, beneficial. If one wants to say that the rapist benefits at all from raping, it is surely in some psychological state of relief rather than in the freedom he takes in subjecting another to his will. The rapist's taking such liberty for himself makes himself as such worse off, not better (cf. Raz 1986, pp. 411–412; and George 1993, pp. 176–182).

The second concern about this account is that it places equality as such as a reason for state action, when it is unclear whether equality as such is a reason for *any* action. This is particularly troubling in the case of the natural law political view I have defended (3.2), on which it is the good of the members of the political community that are in aggregate the basic reason for political action. If legal punishment is carried out, then the result is a condition in which, quite possibly, someone is made worse-off and no one is made better-off. This is a Pareto-inferior condition, and it is hard to see why a view on which the basic reasons for action are aspects of persons' well-being – rather than particular relations that agents' well-being have with respect to each other – would be concerned about the fact of inequality as such.

We are still left with the problem. Punishment is about imposing losses on criminals; it is about making them worse-off. Since the criminal is, we are to suppose, a member of the political community, this means that punishment successfully carried out at the very least makes some additional aspect of the common good – some element of the criminal's well-being – unrealized. Given the rejection of the utilitarian-style solution, how can an exercise of political authority of this sort be justified?

I will first baldly state the principle that provides the most adequate basis for a natural law account of legal punishment (6.4). The principle is a retributivist principle, in that it takes the justification for the deprivation to be simply the past wrong done by the criminal. So it is on its face going to be subject to all of the criticisms that any retributivist account will be subject to, criticisms that have been duly catalogued (and expanded!) by Shafer-Landau in his recent work on retributivism. I will thus turn to Shafer-Landau's criticisms and show how they fail either against retributivism in general or against this version of retributivism in particular (6.5). We might wonder, though, whether the fundamental principle goes astray of the conception of the common good that I used as a basis to criticize the equality account. I will thus turn next to a defense of the natural law retributivist principle, defending its status as expressive (6.6), though distinguishing the theory of punishment based on it from other recently defended expressive theories of punishment (6.7).

6.4 Natural Law Retributivism

The view of punishment that the natural law political philosopher should affirm is this.

Natural law retributivism: Insofar as a member of the political community has committed a crime, there is reason for the law to direct authoritatively that member of the political community to set him- or herself, to some extent, outside of the common good. The point of setting this criminal to that extent outside of the common good is not to promote the common good, nor is the point to equalize the condition between the criminal and other citizens in some respect. Rather, setting the criminal outside of the common good is simply an intrinsically fitting response to the common good in light of the criminal's failure to live up to his or her responsibilities with respect to it.

The reason for an instance of legal punishment is the crime, a past failure with respect to the common good that merits now some response; the response that is merited by the crime is that the criminal lose some (or all) of his or her portion of the common good.

This view of punishment is retributivist. While retributivist accounts of punishment, long out of favor, have undergone a bit of a renaissance, there has been a predictable antiretributivist backlash (for discussion, see Ellis 1995). Examining a particularly searching critique of retributivism will help us to assess the extent to which natural law retributivism is a promising account of the justification of legal punishment.

6.5 Difficulties with Retributivist Theories

Shafer-Landau has recently provided a systematic argument to the conclusion that retributivist theories of punishment are hopeless. His strategy is to put forward a set of issues central to the problematic of punishment that a theory of punishment should be expected to handle – problems concerning the appropriate scope of criminal liability, the general justifying aim of punishment, and the amount of punishment due a particular criminal offense – and to show that the retributivist theories provide implausible solutions to all of them. Examining these criticisms and the responses available from the point of view of the natural law account will give some idea both of the prospects for retributivist views in general and the natural law view in particular.

Criminal Liability

The question of criminal liability is the question of what act-types ought to be answered by legal punishment. The retributivist, Shafer-Landau notes, connects criminal liability to moral guilt. One's moral blameworthiness in ϕ-ing is somehow supposed to be the rationale for one's being subject to criminal sanctions for ϕ-ing. But why are certain acts subject to criminalization and some not? The retributivist cannot simply say that if we rank morally wrong act-types from mere peccadilloes to the most awful outrages, the punishable offenses are those the moral wrongness of which is *more serious* while the non-punishable evils are those the wrongness of which is less so: for, after all, certain rudenesses can be morally much worse than certain minor tax evasions, but for all that, we take tax evasion to be properly punishable but rudeness not. Nor is it plausible, as Hampton has argued (Hampton 1991), that those acts that are *demeaning* are subject to criminal sanction, whereas other morally wrong acts are not: it is obvious that there are a number of properly criminal acts that do not demean anybody. Nor can we simply say, with Morris, Sher, and Finnis (see 6.3), that it is acts that are *unfair* that are properly subject to sanction: for the unfair advantage that punishment aims to rectify, on Morris's and Finnis's views, is simply freedom from constraint, where the constraint is that of the criminal law. But this assumes the existence of a criminal code rather than helping us to see how a criminal code should be constructed.

One solution that Shafer-Landau does briefly consider, but takes to be too inadequately developed to count as a solution, is that punishment is for acts that are *against the state*. It seems to me that this is the type of solution that should be embraced and developed by the natural law view, at least so long as 'the state' is construed not as the hierarchical apparatus of governmental authority but rather as the body of citizens considered collectively. For the natural law view holds that acts that are subject to punishment are those that are contrary to the common good, where the common good is understood (3.2) as the state of affairs in which every citizen achieves his or her good. Now one might think this obviously far too broad, for it would seem to follow that any act in any way resulting in damage to someone's well-being – including the minor rudenesses that are obviously not fit for criminalization – is subject to legal punishment. But this seeming implication can be resisted. For this natural law view also holds that for the sake of common action, the law offers both a determination of the common good and of what counts as one's share in acting for that good (3.6). So the claim that the natural law retributivist should make is that any act that is a failure to do one's share for the common good is subject to punishment, but that what counts as doing one's share for the common good is fixed by the law. Insofar as the law is non-defective,[3] its determinations concerning the content of the common good and one's share in acting for it are binding on those living under the law. We have, then, an account that satisfies the retributivist constraint that one is punished only for doing something morally wrong, and satisfies the constraint that the class of acts deemed punishable is adequately in line with common sense.[4]

General Justifying Aim

I will turn to the fully fledged account of the rationale for punishing in accordance with the natural law retributivist principle in 6.6. I will consider at this point only Shafer-Landau's criticism of retributivist theories of punishment on the general justifying aim issue. He writes:

> The retributivist must [say] that the citizenry should be first and foremost concerned with giving legal violators their just deserts, where doing this requires forcing offenders to do more than pay compensation or restitution. The focus must be on making offenders worse off than they were status quo ante, rather than restoring a victim to previous levels. Doing this would not be costless. Because criminal sanctions are typically more severe than civil ones, procedural safeguards would have to be heightened. A broader policing network will be required. Penal institutions must be erected, and the judiciary augmented. Taxes must greatly increase to pay for these expenditures. And the inevitable miscarriages of justice will be injurious and less reparable. These costs must be incurred no matter the justification for a criminal law. But is it reasonable to incur them for the sole aim of ensuring that wrongdoers suffer commensurately to their misdeeds?

---

[3] Law will be defective if there is less than adequate consent to it, and thus it is less than fully authoritative. The complications that this generates will be considered later; see 6.8.

[4] Shafer-Landau offers as a potential criticism against this sort of view that it fails to acknowledge that "private law can and does proscribe and remedy such harms" (Shafer-Landau 1996, p. 291). But it seems to me that this is not so much a concern about getting the contours of criminal liability right as about the general justifying aim of punishment. The question to be answered is: given that the common good is built up out of the good of members of the political community, why do we not respond to wrongs against the common good simply by offering those harmed mechanisms to exact compensation from wrongdoers? I'll consider this later in 6.6.

If the answer is "No," then retributivism cannot be the proper rationale for a system of punishment. And there is good reason to think that a negative response is the appropriate one. Imagine a society that incurred these extra costs, improved its ability to mete out just deserts, and (improbably) saw their crime rate increase. It seems unlikely that morality could be so demanding as to require the additional costs when doing so diminished the security of those who had to bear them.   (Shafer-Landau 1996, p. 295)

Shafer-Landau's criticism is that it is conceivable that the maintenance of a system of punishment incurs tremendous costs to the citizenry while resulting in a net loss with respect to their security rather than a net gain. Under such circumstances, Shafer-Landau notes, we would tend to think that legal punishment would not be required, and so retributivism must be a false account of the general justifying aim of punishment.

The argument is defective. First: it saddles retributivism with extra assumptions that a still-contentious version of the view would happily reject. Let us distinguish between *weak, strong,* and *extra-strong* retributivism. Weak retributivism places a constraint on justified punishment: it is a necessary condition for the moral justification of legal punishment that the party punished in fact committed a crime. Strong retributivism claims that the point of punishment is to respond to the crime by punishing. Extra-strong retributivism claims that this response is a mandatory one. Now, natural law retributivism is not just weak retributivism. But to go beyond weak retributivism is not to commit oneself to extra-strong retributivism. One can be a strong retributivist, and say such sensible things as:

Punishment is a worthwhile thing to do in response to crimes. But there are other worthwhile things to do besides punishing. We can respond to crimes by taking steps to prevent future crimes – by education, by increased police presence, by reduction of poverty. These are all costly measures, and compete with the worthwhile goal of punishing. Sometimes the costs will be sufficient that we will have to cut back on punishment activity. Indeed, it is even conceivable that we would have to eliminate punishment altogether.

Since this reply is a sensible one, one can continue to affirm retributivism while holding that in Shafer-Landau's imagined scenario, it is permissible to cease the practice of legal punishment.

Now, one might respond on Shafer-Landau's behalf that the result of the retributivist's making this concession is really to give up retributivism. Strong retributivism was supposed to be the view that the general justifying aim of punishment was to respond fittingly to a past act, a crime. But once one allows that engaging in punishing activity can be justified only if engaging in that punishing activity promotes certain social goods, then it turns out that the justifying aim of punishing is at best hybrid: *to respond fittingly to a past act and to promote social goods.* This would be a bad argument, though. It fails to distinguish between the point of one's action and certain *sine qua non* conditions thereof. Consider two people who work in the day-care industry. One does so because children need to be cared for; he could not accept the job unless it paid enough for him to pay the bills, though. The other does so to get money to pay the bills; she could not accept the job, though, unless it satisfied some social need. The justifying point of each of these people's activity is different, though both in fact are employed because children need care and the job pays well enough to get the bills paid. It is obvious that their rationales for working in the day care industry are different because different counterfactuals are true of them. If the former suddenly received an inheritance, this would be no reason for him to stop working; if the latter received an inheritance, she would no longer have reason to work there. The same distinction holds in the case of punishment. The strong retributivist treats the opportunity costs of punishing as relevant to the *sine qua non* conditions for justified legal punishment, but not to its justifying point.

So the first concern with Shafer-Landau's argument is that it conflates *sine qua non* conditions for justified punishment with punishment's general justifying aim. The second concern addresses the intuition that we are supposed to have concerning the case in which a scheme for legal punishment is put into place yet (improbably, as Shafer-Landau notes) crime rises. It strikes me that a great deal turns on both how great the rise in crime is that results from the scheme of punishment being put into place and on what other goods or evils also accompany the institution of legal punishment. With respect to the former: suppose that the increase in crime is very slight, though statistically significant, and it is concentrated in white-collar crimes. (We might suppose that the rise in crime is the result of embezzlement from the public funds used to put into place the institutions of legal punishment; attempted bribery of judicial officials; and so forth.) It is not obvious to me that in this case we would treat the institutions of legal punishment as obviously pointless. With respect to the latter: suppose that, while an increase in crime has occurred, other goods have been realized in the wake of instituting a system of legal punishment: somehow, awareness of legal standards is on the rise, there is an increase in public-spiritedness, unemployment has decreased. Again, it is not obvious to me that in this case we would treat the institutions of legal punishment as obviously pointless.

Lurking behind Shafer-Landau's appeal to intuition is a general principle about reasonable state action – that is, that it must always be justified by reference to the well-being of the members of that political community. The retributivist, Shafer-Landau is arguing, fails to honor this principle. But the natural law retributivist *does* honor this principle: legal punishment is to be justified by reference to the demands of the common good, which consists of the well-being of all of the members of the political community, and legal punishment ought to be carried out only when it does not create unacceptable losses of well-being to members of the political community. Now, one could try to make Shafer-Landau's principle more precise: state action is reasonable only when – perhaps constrained by the rights of the members of that political community – it *best* promotes the well-being of the members of that political community. The natural law retributivist does *not* honor the principle thus formulated: he or she rejects the sense of maximizing the well-being of the members of the political community (0.2). But this is a far more contentious conception of reasonable state action – it amounts to either utilitarianism or utilitarianism-constrained-by-rights – and it is of course unpersuasive to argue that the fault with retributivist conceptions of punishment is that they are incompatible with utilitarian conceptions of reasonable state action.

While Shafer-Landau's criticism of the retributivist view in terms of its connection to the welfare of the citizenry fails, we still need to provide the positive account of the general justifying aim of the retributive principle: I turn to this task in 6.6.

Amount

The difficulties that Shafer-Landau poses for retributivist proposals in the amount (and kind) of punishment to be imposed for a given offense are two. First, the retributivist has no way of dealing with those cases in which common sense holds that a certain punishment is justifiable but in which that punishment is out of line with the retributivist view that punishment should be proportioned to the wrongness of the act. Second, the retributivist has no way to offer concrete recommendations with respect to punishments for particular offenses: while the retributivist can hold that there is something unreasonable about *sets* of crime-punishment matches, the retributivist cannot say that any *particular* crime-punishment match is unreasonable.

Shafer-Landau claims that retributivists cannot adequately account for cases in which, for the same offense, recidivists receive more severe punishments than first-time offenders; and, on his view, neither can retributivists adequately account for cases in which, for the same offense, one offender receives mercy and the other does not. For in both cases, there must be at least one offender whose punishment is disproportionate to his or her offense. The retributivist must condemn what we are otherwise inclined to accept.

Begin with the problem about recidivism. It is not at all obvious that the retributivist must lack the resources to explain why increased punishments are due for repeat offenses. For the retributivist aims to proportion punishment to the wrongness of the deed, and while in one sense the offense of the first-time offender and that of the recidivist may well be the same, in another sense they are importantly different. For there is a difference in circumstance between the recidivist and the first-time offender that is plausibly relevant and makes the deed of the recidivist worse than the deed of the first-time offender.

Here is what I have in mind. Suppose that one day my daughter, who has shown a great deal of kindness and restraint with respect to her unusually active younger brother, strikes him in anger. The boy cries and reports this event, which occasions quasi-criminal proceedings: interrogation, admission of guilt, conviction, and punishment. The next day, in otherwise similar circumstances, events of the same sort occur: her little brother makes her angry, and she strikes him in anger. It seems to me that in such cases we have good reason to say that her past action and her 'conviction' for this past action is a relevant circumstance in determining the wrongness of her action. All of us experience temptations to wrong action, and we have ways of guarding against these temptations; to do so we need knowledge of our psychological tendencies and ways to combat those that make us tend to act wrongly. My daughter on the second day had something available to her that my daughter on the first day did not – that is, ungainsayable, official notice that she is tempted to strike her brother in response to his frenetic activity. Thus her second-day assault was an action for which she was somewhat more culpable than her first-day assault was.

So I say that the retributivist can answer the charge that his or her view cannot handle our adoption of increased punishments for recidivists. The answer consists in the following claims: first, that the circumstances in which an agent acts can be relevant for determining his or her culpability in performing an act of a certain type; second, that a relevant circumstance in determining an agent's culpability is the extent to which he or she knows (or should know) his or her own psychological tendencies and has (or should have) effective means to deal with them in the face of tendencies toward wrongdoing; and third, that the recidivist characteristically has (or should have) greater knowledge of his or her own psychological tendencies toward wrongdoing and has (or should have) developed more effective means of dealing with them. If these claims are true, then there is no tension between the retributivist view that punishment should be proportioned to offense and the practice of increasing the severity of punishments for recidivists.

What, then, shall the retributivist say about mercy? As I see it, there are three relevant kinds of cases in which we might say that mercy was shown to a criminal in sentencing, but none of them calls into question the retributivist claim about proportioning punishment to offenses. First, we might say that in a particular case, the punishment of this person to the proper proportion would involve a loss of social goods to an unacceptable extent.[5] So, in sentencing, mercy is shown to the convicted criminal so that those goods will not be lost. Second, we might say that in a particular case, the punishment of a criminal in proportion to the crime would be inhumane (for example, imprisonment

---

[5] This does not strike me as paradigmatic mercy. In a paradigmatic case of mercy, the lessening of the imposed evil is done *for the sake of* the person to be punished; it is not simply the case that there is reason of whatever kind to lessen the evil imposed on the punished. But it does seem to me that we do sometimes speak of mercy being shown even when the burden is lessened, but not for the sake of the punished.

of someone very ill, or frail from age). So, in sentencing, mercy is shown in order not to act inhumanely toward the criminal. Third, we might say that in a particular case, the legal rules designating the punishment fail to adequately capture the culpability of the criminal in acting, so that the rule treats him or her as more culpable than he or she really is. So, in sentencing, mercy is shown in order to avoid punishing the criminal more severely than he or she merits.

The third of these cases is of course very different from the first two. In the third case, the sentencing judge or jury exercises discretion in order that the retributivist principle might be better satisfied. While there may be difficult questions about when such discretion is properly exercised, such cases surely make no problems for retributivist theories of punishment. While the first two are distinct from this easy case, neither do they make trouble for the retributivist. For recall that we have distinguished the strong retributivist from the extra strong retributivist: the latter holds that punishing the criminal to the proportionate severity is mandatory; the former holds only that it is worthwhile, and thus allows that worthwhile punishment can be limited by other worthwhile aims or moral constraints. The first two cases of mercy meet the description of "worthwhile aims or moral constraints": punishment is limited for the sake of preventing unacceptable loss of social goods or for the sake of avoiding treating a criminal inhumanely. Thus there is no tension between affirming retributivism and acknowledging a role for mercy in sentencing.

If there is anything the retributivist should object to, it is *capricious* mercy: mercy exhibited for no reason at all. Punishing is a worthwhile activity, and when there are legal institutions established to carry it out, departure from norms prescribing appropriate punishment for offenses requires justification. So mercy on a whim is objectionable from the strong retributivist's point of view. But this is not the sort of mercy that we commonsensically want to endorse, and it is thus not a problem for the strong retributivist that he or she refuses to do so.

In offering retributivist responses to the problems of recidivism and mercy, I have taken for granted that the retributivist can offer a schedule of punishments that are properly matched with the various offenses. But this assumption is Shafer-Landau's other target. On his view, no retributivist has ever offered a plausible account of how this standard is to be set. The standard of *lex talionis* simply ignores the fact that punishment is not imposed for harm but for wrong, leaving untouched the task of determining how the size of the offense is to be commensurated with the size of the deprivation imposed in punishment. Defenders of the equality view, which hold that punishments reestablish the equality disturbed by the crime, have never adequately explained why those crimes that are worse are always those crimes that involve a greater arrogation of freedom; nor have they adequately shown that the freedoms arrogated by criminals are invariably worth having (see 6.3).

Shafer-Landau is willing to allow for the sake of argument that one can provide a defensible scale of punishments, ranked from more severe to less severe. And he is willing to allow that one can provide a defensible scale of offenses, ranked from more severe to less severe. Such rankings do allow the retributivist a basis for assessing some sets of crime-punishment matches as unjustifiable: if crime A is ranked less severe than crime B, and punishment C is ranked less severe than punishment D, then it is unreasonable to match D with A while matching C with B. It cannot be justifiable to treat a more serious crime as meriting a lesser punishment response than a less serious crime. But we lack any basis for choosing any *particular* punishment as a response to any *particular* offense. We know that if we select a particular punishment as a response to some particular offense, then more severe offenses than that one merit more severe punishments than that one, and less severe offenses less severe punishments. But in setting a particular match – does armed robbery merit a small fine, a large fine, a short prison sentence, a long prison sentence, execution? – the retributivist view must set punishments "more or less arbitrarily" because the retributivist criterion "offers us *no* concrete guidance about where to set punishments" (Shafer-Landau 1996, p. 309).

I am inclined to agree with Shafer-Landau that we can state no rule that is very helpful in matching an offense of a particular level of moral severity with a punishment of a particular level of intensity that suits it. But I am inclined to disagree with his view that this means that the retributivist is resourceless in setting a scale of punishments for offenses, with the result that the scale of punishments set by the retributivist must be objectionably arbitrary.

The first reason for this is that Shafer-Landau understates the help that can be provided by the independent orderings of crimes and punishments. Suppose, as I shall argue in 6.6, that retributive justifications for punishment are best understood in terms of punishment as *expressive* action. In order for punishment to be expressive, there must be an adequate distinction between punishments – the range of punishments given for offenses must not cluster around a relatively small set of intensities but rather be spread sufficiently to mark the expressive distinctions we aim to make in punishing. (The main problem with grade inflation is that it causes the clustering of grades in a smaller span, making it more and more difficult to distinguish between the various levels of excellence that student work can attain.) So there is reason to set the punishment for our least severe crimes relatively low in the scale of available punishment-intensities, and to set the punishment for our most severe crimes relatively high.

The need for adequate distinction between punishments to mark the importance of the distinctions among crimes is I think the most important reference point internal to retributivism that the retributivist has in fixing a scale of punishment. There are, of course, reference points external to retributivism that the retributivist should honor: there can be limits of justice concerning the amount of suffering persons should be directed to undergo, and there can be limits of humanity concerning the sorts of punishments that are so severe as to be dehumanizing or degrading to either the person punished or the person or persons executing the punishment.

All these provide reference points in fixing a scale. Shafer-Landau could rightly remark that these leave a great deal undetermined by principles. But to this I respond, first, that it is no objection to an account of punishment that the legal rules for realizing it are determinations (3.6) of general principles that must be made more concrete for the sake of action. We should allow a significant level of discretionary fixing of punishment levels, treating it not as a mark of the failure of retributivism but as a mark of retributivism's consistency with the commonsense intuition that characteristically a criminal might receive a somewhat more or somewhat less severe punishment for a given crime without anyone's thereby being wronged.

Second, we should also note that the absence of principles that show that a particular punishment suits a particular crime does not show that reasonable agents are unable to judge correctly that certain punishments would be too severe or too mild for a given crime. Aristotle cautions us against expecting too much precision out of an ethical science (*Nicomachean Ethics*, 1094b23–26), but he also clearly allows that the person of practical wisdom is able to hit the mark in reaching practical judgments (*Nicomachean Ethics*, 1142b13–35). While I allow that it is an evasion simply to rely on practical wisdom when the going gets tough in an argument, it seems to me that we must be willing on pain of arbitrariness to allow that practical wisdom can play some role here, even if we cannot offer an informative general principle matching punishment to crime. For, after all, almost all of us believe in either the principle or the virtue of *gratitude*, which calls for us to respond properly to those who have done good for us. The response of gratitude should be proportioned to the size of the good turn, where the 'size' of the good turn depends not only on the benefit conferred but on the intentions of the benefactor, the sacrifice he or she had to make, the other reasons the benefactor had for doing the good deed, and so forth. What basis is there on which one can say that a particular gratitude-requiting act was too generous or too niggardly? The agent might not be able to afford a certain response, or it might be in some way inconsistent with his or her assumed scale of gratitude-inducing acts and gratitude-requiting responses. But might we not also say that in some cases, a certain response is *just too much* (or *just too little*)? If you hold open an elevator door open for me when I am in a rush, I might well be grateful; if I give you $1000, that is just too much, even if I can afford it and even if I am fully prepared to give to those who do even better turns for me $1,000-plus and those who do even more minor good deeds for me $1,000-minus. The principle of proportion in gratitude does seem to guide action to some extent, then. If we accept Shafer-Landau's argument that the retributive principle cannot guide action, then we must also accept an argument that the gratitude principle cannot guide action. But it seems that the practically wise can see that some gratitude-responses are just out of proportion to the benefiting deed; and so some of the practically wise might well see that some retributive responses are just out of proportion to the criminal act.[6]

In the course of responding to Shafer-Landau's attack on retributivist conceptions of punishment, I issued two promissory notes. In dealing with Shafer-Landau's worries about retributivist views of the general justifying aim of punishment, I responded only to his negative point – that retributivism seems inadequately to handle the fact that the justification of punishment seems tied to its actual consequences on human well-being – and not to the challenge to provide an account of what the positive aim of punishing is. And in dealing with Shafer-Landau's challenge to show what resources there are internal to retributivism to offer guidance in fixing punishments to crimes, I noted that an argument for spreading the range of punishments assigned to crimes would go through if part of the point of punishment were expressive. I turn now to the positive justification of the natural law retributivist principle in terms of its directing a certain sort of expressive action.

6.6 Acting in Light of the Good: Promotion and Expression

Suppose that one has a very good friend. To stand in a relationship of friendship to another is, in part, for the friend's good to provide one with reasons for action – reasons for action above and beyond those one might have with respect to other persons generally. And so one might protect one's friend from harm, or go out of one's way to do good for him or her. That an action would help or harm that friend would always be an important consideration in determining the merits of that action in deliberation.

Now, suppose that the friend becomes very ill. One would of course have reason to help to cure the illness and to ease the friend's symptoms in the interim. The friend's good is threatened by the illness, and the ways in which the illness threatens that good one has reason to block. But imagine, though, that one's efforts, and the efforts of others, are in vain: the friend dies. The friend's good can no longer be helped or harmed;[7] one is now powerless to protect and promote one's friend's good. Does the friend's good cease, then, to provide reasons for one's action? It might seem so: what one had reason to do was to promote the friend's good; the friend's good is now outside the range of promotion; thus the friend's good no longer provides reasons for action.

---

[6] It is also worth keeping in mind that concerns about setting the requisite amount of punishment for an offense plague rival theories of punishment as well. For all of utilitarianism's in-principle precision, we might reasonably ask whether a group of utilitarians would come to more agreement on the suitable punishment for a given offense than a group of retributivists would.

[7] This may not be quite right: there are questions about whether a person's life can be made better after that life has ended – by, for example, seeing to it that the person's important projects are brought to fruition. But this complication is not relevant for our purposes here.

But it seems false that the friend's good no longer provides reasons for action. Suppose that, in learning of the friend's death, one *cries*. Suppose that one ceases to carry out one's normal activities for the next several days: instead of going to the movies and to dinner with friends, one *stays at home*. *Crying* and *staying at home* are both actions the rationality of which can be evaluated, and they both seem to be rational actions in this context: it is perfectly reasonable to cry and to withdraw from one's normal activities after the death of a friend. (If a helpful person tells one, in effect, that it is stupid to cry over spilt milk – the friend is dead, you can't do anything about it, so why not get out and enjoy yourself in the usual way? – one can reasonably think that this helpful person is either callous or does not really understand what he or she is saying.) The question is how the reasonableness of these actions is to be explained. It seems plain that the reason that makes intelligible the crying and the withdrawal from normal activities is the friend's good, and the fact that it has been destroyed by the illness: this is what anyone, when asked why he or she was crying and not joining with friends after the loss of a loved one, would offer for his or her behavior.

Consider the similarities between the answers one would offer to the questions 'why are you bringing your friend medicine?' and 'why are you withdrawing from your normal activities?' Both of these would cite the friend's good and the threat to that good posed by the illness. In the former case, the threat to the friend's good is an unfulfilled one, and thus there remains the possibility that it can be blocked by appropriate interventions. In the latter case, the threat to the friend's good is fulfilled. It can no longer be blocked. If one is to respond to the friend's good, some mode of response to that good other than promotion will be necessary.

Why should we think, as I suggest that we should, that a good continues to exert normative force even after the possibility of promoting it is past? How can it be that a good that is now beyond one's power to realize nevertheless can make action with respect to it intelligible?

The first point to make here is simply a defensive one. We can distinguish between a good's possessing normative force and a good's possessing the normative force to make intelligible a certain kind of response to it–that of promoting it. For a good to possess normative force is for it to have the capacity to make eligible action performed in light of it. But the notion 'action performed in light of a good' seems to lack, of itself, any temporal orientation. This stands in contrast to the notion of promotion of the good, which possesses a present or future temporal orientation. So the first, defensive point to make is that the fact a specific mode of response to the good – that of promotion – becomes ineligible once a good is wholly past does not on its face entail the fact that the past good lacks normative force.

Second, and more positively, we can appeal to the argument, offered by George Sher, that even within the domain of promotion of the good – that is, with respect to certain actions to promote the good that require long-term, complex intentions – we must assume that goods can exert normative force even once they are beyond promoting if we are not to lapse into practical incoherence.

Sher's argument, in brief, is this. Suppose that an agent, Mary, at the time of deliberation, believes herself to have a reason to help a friend paint at t_1 and a reason to confer with a student at a later time t_2. But painting and conferring are, she believes, incompatible: if the agent paints, then she will miss the bus to campus; but she must take that bus to campus in order to confer with the student. If she helps the friend paint, then at t_2, the most worthwhile thing for her to do is to stay home and read – a worthwhile activity, but surely much less important on its own than conferring with the student. On consideration, the agent judges that she has more reason to adopt the [paint at t_1, read at t_2] sequence rather than the [ride at t_1, confer at t_2] sequence. She chooses that option, and thus intends to carry out that sequence.

But, as Sher notes, there is trouble here. If the agent believes that past reasons do not have normative force, then at the time of deliberation she will realize that at t_2 – once she has finished painting, and when she is on the verge of missing the appointment with the student – she should form the belief that she should not be missing the appointment with the student. For the reading that she is about to do cannot justify missing the appointment: she judges conferring with the student to be much more important than reading. Nor can the agent appeal to the fact that helping the friend paint is more worthwhile than conferring with the student: for helping the friend paint is a matter that is in the past, and *ex hypothesi* cannot give reasons for doing or preferring anything anymore. So the belief that reasons cannot have normative force once they are in the past generates a paradox for the deliberating agent: she will judge that a certain sequence of actions is the one that is most rational to choose, but she will judge that in the midst of carrying out that sequence, she will come to believe (correctly) that that sequence is not the sequence that there is most reason to act on. This practical incoherence can be avoided if we hold that the reason to help the friend paint continues to exert normative force even when in the past, so that in assessing the merits of the alternative actions, one can continue to count the reason that one has to help the friend. Thus we should hold that reasons that are in the past can exert normative force in the present (Sher 1983, pp. 188–197).

Arguments of the form 'agents must assume that p if their ϕ-ing is not to be practically incoherent; therefore, p' are always, of course, subject to the criticism that agents' ϕ-ing *is* practically incoherent or the criticism that the fact that an agent must assume that p in order to avoid practical incoherence does not entail that p. But the coherence of the sort of action that Sher appeals to is not very controversial. And, given the defensive point that the very idea of normative force does not seem to entail that the temporal direction of the normative force must be future- or present-rather than past-oriented, it is hard to see why one would take the required assumption to be a pragmatically required falsehood rather than a simple truth about goods and their reason-giving force.

The third point in support of the view that past goods continue to exert normative force is that we can offer a useful characterization of the sort of action that stands in contrast to promotion. We can call it 'expression,' though this way of describing these sorts of action elides certain important distinctions that we will do well to bring into relief (6.7). What is common to the case of crying over the loss of the friend and ceasing to go about one's normal activities because of the friend's death is that crying and withdrawing somehow express the value of the good lost when the friend died. Before the friend's good is out of reach, one can respond to it in the mode of *promotion*; after the good is out of reach, one cannot reasonably respond to it in the mode of promotion, but one can still act in a way that expresses its value.

Expression is a rational mode of response to the good not only when the good is in the past. Suppose that the friend is severely ill, yet one is powerless to do anything to help: one might cease to carry out one's normal activities in light of the friend's illness even when it is still possible that he or she should could be saved. One might nevertheless say: expression, even if it is not always about a past good, is about a good that it is out of one's power to promote. After all, it would be very strange for someone who is able to promote some valued good to choose instead to do something to express its value. We would not think much of someone who was able to attend to the sick friend's needs but chose instead simply to cry and withdraw to one's room. But this is a specious argument. Part of the reason that we would look askance on someone who chose to express the value of the sick friend's good through crying and withdrawing rather than helping is that helping when one is able to do so is the clearest way of expressing its value: every act of promoting a good *qua* good expresses its value. And even if one is able to do something to help the sick friend, we would recognize the further eligibility of expressing the value of the friend's threatened good in other ways besides promotion: by wearing somber rather than festive colors, for example. (If one were to wear festive colors, one could justify doing so only by the aim of helping the sick friend: cheering him or her up, making things seem not so hopeless, and so forth.)

To some extent, the range of action-types that express the goodness of something the promotion of which is no longer available is a conventional matter. This is not a surprise. But it is not as if there is nothing here but convention. That good is to be promoted rather than blocked or thwarted is not conventional, and there are certain types of action that are intrinsically more apt to express the good than others. Consider the independent reflections on these points by Sher and Perry. Sher writes:

If a general disposition to respond to past acts is explained and justified by the general requirements of coherence in intending, then dispositions to respond in particular ways to past acts may be explained and justified by the requirements of coherence in holding particular sorts of intention. Because this is so, [one] may well be able to explain and justify our actual backward-looking practices by showing that certain sorts of intention are standard or unavoidable. . . . If our backward-looking practices can be explained and justified in these and related ways, then such backward-looking attitudes . . . may be understood simply as ineffective impulses to perform the appropriate acts.

(Sher 1983, p. 198)

There is a deflationary way to take Sher's point – that is, that there is something pathetic about backward-looking acts, because they involve one's mimicking the actions of promotion of the good when the possibility of promoting it is past. (Note Sher's description of such acts as "ineffective impulses.") But there is a less negative way to understand the point: even if such backward-looking acts cannot aim at *effectiveness* – that is, at fulfilling what one has basic reason to do or promote – they can aim at something other than effectiveness that is nevertheless modeled on and derivative from what there is basic reason to do or promote. I will call this fairly abstract thought "Sher's Principle": given an intrinsically appropriate primary response to the good (promoting it, respecting it, doing one's share with respect to it) and the present impossibility of adopting any such primary response, one has reason to carry out a secondary response, and this response is intelligibly related to the primary response.

Stephen Perry's reflections on the suitability of requiring those at fault in tort to pay compensation for damages to the victim appeal to something like Sher's Principle.

In cases of harm-producing actions involving wrongful intent it is appropriate that we regard the action with agent-regret, which in such a case means wishing that we had acted otherwise so as to not have produced the wrongful outcome. But we cannot change the past, so agent-regret properly takes on a normative aspect that may affect our present and future reasons for action vis-à-vis the outcome in question.   (Perry 1993, p. 42)

Suppose that one has a responsibility to show due care for a good, and fails to do so, and the good is damaged as a result. This failure is over and done with: no time machine is going to allow one to undo it. Given the impossibility of carrying out the primary response, the second-best is a secondary response, one that is intelligibly related to the primary response. Since one's duty was to look after some good, the secondary response is to try to restore matters with respect to that good to what they would have been if the failure of duty had not occurred. Some failures of responsibility may be less complete, and the backward-looking reasons different – "the agent may have reasons only to obtain assistance, express regret, or make . . . symbolic recompense" (Perry 1993, p. 44). But in any of these cases, the secondary response looks back to the primary response as its model.

Again: consider the case that I employed earlier – that of taking oneself out of circulation after a friend's death. The idea here is that one's good is supposed to be tied to one's friend's good: the friend, as Aristotle puts it, is a second self. Yet the friend has undergone the drastic reversal. Usually the way to handle reversals in friends' lives is to commiserate, to enter into the badness of the situation, either really or virtually. Here there is no chance of that, but one can deprive oneself of certain goods out of solidarity with one's friend.

Expression, then, is a response to the good that does not exhibit an intrinsic temporal orientation: expression is a way of responding to past, present, and future goods. Since the notion that goods have normative force does not require a specific temporal orientation, and neither does expression as a mode of response, it seems that nothing should bar us from holding that goods in the past can genuinely make eligible present or future action. And we can go some way toward showing why certain actions express the good properly while others do not.

Now, the natural law account of political authority holds that the exercise of political authority is to be understood with reference to the common good of the political community. Punishment is first and foremost an exercise of authority. If we were convinced that the only reasonable response to the good is that of promotion, then we would have to hold that what justifies punishment – an authoritative dictate the following of which by some agent is meant to bring about a deprivation to that agent – is that it somehow promotes the common good. This would be a utilitarian, or (to take into account the differences between a utilitarian and a natural law conception of the common good) quasi-utilitarian, theory of punishment. But I have argued that there is a mode of response to the good other than promotion – that of expression. So we have an open possibility that punishment as an exercise of political authority is to be justified in terms of its role in expressing rather than promoting the common good.

We can make the argument in two steps. The first is that the common good is a genuine good, and its aspects are the goods of the people who are members of the political community. Because it is good, it is worth promoting. But sometimes agents act in ways that are contrary to what is minimally due from them with respect to the common good, and as a result some aspect of the common good *necessarily* is disregarded or devalued and *characteristically* destroyed or damaged. But even if that aspect of the common good is destroyed, and the world is now such that it cannot be promoted, it does not follow that that aspect of the common good ceases to exert normative force. It still calls for a response, even if the possibility of promoting it is past. *Ex ante*, one can comply with the authoritative legal norm and thus respond properly to the common good. If one fails to comply, this opportunity is lost forever. But *ex post*, one can respond to the common good in some alternative way, a way that expresses the value of the aspect of the common good that one neglected in failing to comply with the original norm. And one such alternative way is to undergo legal punishment.

Why is punishment a peculiarly appropriate response to violations of authoritative legal norms? According to Sher's Principle, a secondary response to a good should be modeled on, and thus intelligibly related to, the primary response. So no account of punishment that appeals to its point in expressing the goodness of some aspect of the common good can succeed unless it provides an account of why punishment in particular expresses that goodness. It would be too strong to claim that nothing else can express it: what we need is some account of why punishment is one peculiarly appropriate response to wrongdoing.

Here is the second step. The common good is the good of all – it is made up of everyone's good – and it is the responsibility of all – everyone is bound to do his or her share with respect to it. The 'all' here is the 'all' of 'all members of this political community.' Those who do not belong to the political community do not enjoy (except accidentally) the achievement of its common good, nor do they bear (except accidentally) the responsibility to realize it. Suppose that one sees what one's responsibility is with respect to the common good, and does not care for it one bit. One does not aim to do his or her share with respect to its realization. So long as one does not aim to do his or her share, one ought to place oneself outside that political community's membership. For the responsibility to do one's share is tied to one's membership, and the rejection of responsibility should be tied to the rejection of membership.

Suppose, though, that one has failed to do one's share with respect to the common good and has failed to withdraw himself or herself from membership in the political community. Think now about how Sher's Principle suggests that we think of action oriented by a past reason: the action should in some relevant way mimic the action that should have been undertaken in light of a present or future reason. I say that appeal to Sher's Principle explains the eligibility of legal punishment as a response to violations of the common good principle. For just as setting oneself outside of the political community is an appropriate *ex ante* action in light of a future intention not to live up to the responsibilities of the common good principle, setting oneself outside of the political community and the goods of living in it is an appropriate *ex post* response to one's actually not living up to it.

Legal punishment directs one authoritatively to set oneself outside, either in whole or in part, permanently or temporarily, of the good available within the political community. It does so in order to express the goodness of that to which the criminal inadequately responded when he or she failed to adhere to the authoritative specification of the common good principle. Thus legal punishment, like all exercises of the law's practical authority, is justified by reference to the law's privileged role in setting the conditions for appropriate response to the common good.

I have claimed that the choiceworthiness of legal punishment as an author-itative response to failures of responsibility with respect to the common good is explicable in terms of the expressive features of punishment. Even if one were to grant the choiceworthiness of punishing as a response to such fail-ures of responsibility, one might ask why punishing is to be chosen instead of, say, compensation as a response. The boring but correct answer is that there is no competition between these two responses. The punishment response is violator-centered; it responds to the failure in action of the criminal. The compensation response is victim-centered; it responds to the person whose good, no more and no less than any other person's, constitutes the common good and thus merits that share in the common good of which he or she was deprived. These two are distinct responses. Even in a tort system in which violators of duties are held liable to pay damages to those harmed by their breaches of care, there is a clear distinction: for, characteristically, the defendant who is held liable is responsible only for making sure that the victim receives compensation; the defendant is not required to pay that compensation out of his or her own funds. (One's friendly aunt can pay a judgment against one; one's friendly aunt cannot do one's prison time.) And sometimes the failure to do one's share with respect to the common good does not result in any harm to be compensated: the attempt to do damage to another's well-being might fall short of its mark and leave its intended victim with no loss to be compensated. Victim-oriented and violator-oriented responses to violations of authoritative standards are not essential competitors.

6.7 Difficulties with Expressive Views of Punishment

I defend natural law retributivism by appeal to the expressive features of legal punishment. A number of writers have recently advocated 'expressive theories of punishment,' and these theories of punishment have been thoroughly criticized. But it is worth keeping in mind the enormous variety of expressive theories that there are, and that the difficulties for one form of expressive theory might have no relevance for another.

There is one sense of 'expressive theory' in which the expressive elements of punishment are noted simply in order to highlight an important element of what distinguishes punishment from other forms of hard treatment. These are *definitional* expressive theories. All that the definitional expressive theorist wants to say is that it is essential to a practice of punishment that punishment express something – characteristically, condemnation of the criminal. We might, according to these views, have a practice of authoritatively imposing harsh treatment on people for their misdeeds, but unless this practice expresses condemnation of the criminal, it is not a practice of punishment (cf. Feinberg 1970b; Hampton 1984, p. 212). No stance need be taken by the defender of the definitional expressive theorist as such on whether this expressive element enters into the justification of the practice of punishment. While the notion that punishment is by definition expressive seems right, we are interested here in the justification, rather than the definition, of punishment. Indeed, if it turned out to be wrong that punishment were essentially expressive, that would not show up those theories of the justification of punishment that rely entirely on expression as false: all that would show is that practices of punishment that are not expressive are unjustified.

So we are interested in those expressive theories that take the expressive element of punishment to be in part or in whole the justification of the practice of punishment. These are defenders of *normative* rather than definitional expressive theories of punishment. Consider first the *causal-normative* theorist. The causal-normative theorist holds that the expressive element of punishment is instrumentally important for promoting valuable ends. There are various valuable ends here that one might affirm. One might claim that deterrence is a crucial aspect of any system of criminal law, and hold that the fact that punishment condemns the criminal makes it a more effective deterrent than other sorts of response to crime. Or one might claim that it is valuable for societies to be able to 'blow off steam' with respect to crimes against the public good, and a particularly effective way to blow off steam is to perform actions that dramatically condemn wrongdoers. Or one might claim that it is valuable for societies to educate criminals to the wrongness of their deeds, and the fact that punishment expresses widespread condemnation of the deed (or the agent *qua* doer of the deed) is helpful in educating the criminal. All of these would be instances of the causal-normative expressive theory of punishment.

These causal-normative theories are subject to two broad lines of criticism: first, that the alleged connections between the expressions of condemnation present in punishment and the realization of these beneficial results are insufficiently defended; and, second, that even if there were such a connection, it is unclear whether the benefits yielded justify (or could justify) the costs involved in punishing. The causal-normative expressive theories are just utilitarian (or quasi-utilitarian) theories (cf. Moore 1997, pp. 84–85), and are thus subject to the same sorts of worry to which utilitarian (or quasi-utilitarian) theories are subject.

The natural law view that I have defended is not a causal-normative view, for it does not take the point of punishment to be the promotion of some further end beyond the expression that occurs in the punishment. Rather, the idea is that the point of punishment is the expression itself. Call such views *constitutive-normative* accounts.

The constitutive-normative expressive theory that I am offering on behalf of the natural law view is not to be identified with the view that punishment is an act of *communication* by the punishing agent to the party punished. Nozick makes much of the fact that we want the party being punished to recognize that he or she is being punished, and this is readily explicable if we conceive punishment as an attempt to communicate something to the party punished (Nozick 1981, pp. 370–374). To this view I reply, first, that the fact that we want the punished party to recognize that he or she is being punished is explicable other than in terms of punishment being a communicative act. Part of legal punishment is an authoritative branding of someone as criminal, and this is bad because of its depriving persons of the good of community with their fellow citizens: this is accomplished more fully to the extent that the punished party is aware of it. Second, if we were to make the expression in question essentially a communication, it is likely that this will lead to a rejection of a constitutive-normative expressive theory in favor of a causal-normative theory. For characteristically communications have a point beyond themselves. (An exception, perhaps, is casual conversation. Punishment isn't like *that*.) On similar grounds, I want to distance the view I am defending from any view on which the point of punishment is to communicate to society the wrongness of the act, or to assert society's commitment to the wrongness of acts of that sort, and so forth. While, on my view, punishment is an expressive act, it is not essentially a communicative act.

The expressive theory I defend is not a communicative theory of punishment. But neither is it a 'natural manifestation' view. I call a 'natural manifestation' view a theory of punishment according to which certain attitudes are normatively justified, and punishing is a 'natural manifestation' of those attitudes. This is, to follow Skillen's suggestive language, the "nothing more natural" view (Skillen 1980). In some circumstances, it is proper to be sad, and when sad, there is *nothing more natural* than crying. Similarly, it is right to resent criminals, and when one is resentful, there is *nothing more natural* than subjecting them to punishment. As Skillen notes, one problem with the natural manifestation view is that it is hard to see that there is any emotion for which punishment is really the natural expression other than the uninformative and neologizing emotion of *punitiveness*. But there is a more severe difficulty at hand. It is hard to see why the act of punishing would be justifiable simply because it is a natural expression of an emotion that is justified. It is far from clear that justification is *inherited* in this way from dispositional states to the actions flowing from those dispositions. (For similar worries about inferring, from the rationality or rightness of a disposition, the rationality or rightness of an action flowing from a disposition, see Parfit 1984, pp. 39–40.) But the fact that the natural manifestation view provides no justification for legal punishment does not make difficulties for my view, for my view is not a natural manifestation view.

Expression can mean 'natural manifestation' and it can mean 'communication.' I have distanced this theory of punishment from both of these. It is best to describe the view I am defending as expression as *symbolic marking*. Think again of the person who gives up his or her normal activities after the death of a friend. There is no intended audience for the action; one is not trying to communicate to anyone. (If there is an intended audience, then one is not properly grieving for one's friend; one is making a pretense of grieving.) Nor need the giving up of one's activities take its justification from its being a natural manifestation of one's emotional state. For one thing, one may feel strangely cold to the friend's death – perhaps the reality of it has not fully set in – while seeing that the giving up of one's normal activities is *the*, or *a*, thing to do.

(One might ascribe the emotion to the person consequentially (cf. Nagel 1970, pp. 29–30) – that is, holding that one who carries out the relevant acts for the relevant reasons by that very fact counts as having the mournful emotions. But that would not suffice for the natural manifestation picture, which requires the emotions to be prior to the acts, for the emotions are held to be causally relevant to the production of the acts.) But such a person might see that the friend's death calls for a response, and withdrawal from normal activities is a sensible way of symbolically marking that loss.

To defend some sort of action as symbolic marking, one needs to show that there is something worth symbolically marking, that the action in fact properly symbolically marks it, and that the costs of that action are worth it. The arguments for the ultimate political importance of the common good (3.2) suffice to show that it is worth taking notice of, and the argument of 6.6 aims to show why punishment is an appropriate response to failures to live up to the demands of the common good. One might continue to wonder, though, whether punishment is worth it: whether it does someone – either the criminals that are directed to it, or the society that bears the associated costs of it – injustice. The question of injustice is one that arises for *any* costly symbolic action. The building of the Washington Monument was extremely risky to the workers involved, and cost (and continues to cost) the taxpayers funds that could have been used elsewhere. Whether its building (and continued upkeep) is justifiable depends on whether the bearing of those costs can be endorsed from the relevant impartial standpoint (3.5). And in answering that question, we would keep in mind the associated benefits of the symbolic action, even if it is not the general justifying point of it: the Washington Monument has some aesthetic features, and it serves as a landmark for those lost in the vicinity, and it enables visitors to get a breathtaking view of the Washington area.

Punishment is a symbolic activity, but this does not mean – as I have heard it suggested – that in justifying punishment, we must ask simply whether the enormous costs of the criminal justice system could possibly justify symbolically marking failures with respect to the common good. While I think that the objector is likely to understate the importance of symbolic marking, the main point to make is that in assessing the justice of such a system, we would have to take into account the associated effects that are (or can be) realized through it, such as lowering of crime. The general justifying aim of punishment is to respond in a fitting way to failures to be responsible for that good. Whether that general justifying aim can be justly carried out must embrace far more than the question of whether punishment is fitting for crime.

6.8 Authority, Coercion, and Punishment

I have defended as the most plausible natural law account of punishment a view on which law's punishing activity is first and foremost an exercise of legal authority (6.1): in punishing, legal institutions direct subjects to undergo certain deprivations on account of their failure to do their share with respect to the common good (6.5). Their undergoing such deprivations is for the common good because it expresses the value of the common good in the face of the wrongdoer's past devaluing or damaging it.

We will conclude our consideration of the natural law account of punishment by returning to the question of the relationship between punishment and coercion. I took pains at the beginning of this chapter (6.1) to emphasize that the links between authority and coercion are tenuous and contingent and that punishment is not a matter of coercion but authoritative guidance. But nevertheless there are important questions that might be raised about the fact that the authoritative guidance that is essential to punishment is, as a matter of fact, accompanied by a willingness to use coercive measures to bring about compliance. Given the fact that the status of some party as authoritative does not entail that that party has the right to coerce compliance with its dictates (6.1), and given the fact that the authoritative dictates that constitute punishment-norms bring about harm, sometimes grave harm, to the subject punished, it is worth asking how the natural law view would justify the law's willingness to coerce compliance with its dictates regarding punishment.

The characteristic sort of case in which legal coercion is justified is that in which the subject is threatened by legally authorized parties in order that he or she will carry out some course of action, which course of action (1) is (even independent of the threat of coercion) a reasonable action for the subject to perform, and (2) is such that the subject's failure to perform it would place an unjust burden on other members of the political community. In typical cases of justified coercion, that is, what the law is forcing the subject to do is what he or she had adequate reason to do anyway, and if the subject fails to do it, the negative consequences of that failure fall on other members of the political community. Both conditions are important. The former condition deprives the coerced of a basis for complaint on the basis of the nature of the required act; the latter condition deprives the coerced of a basis for complaint on the basis of the fact that a threat is being imposed on him or her. Note also the qualifications. The claim is not that these conditions are sufficient for legal coercion to be justified: there may be cases in which the side-effects of coercing compliance impose an even greater burden on the law-abiding, and thus it would not be just or prudent to coerce compliance. Nor is the claim that these conditions are even necessary for compliance: there may well be extraordinary cases in which subjects may be justifiably coerced to perform actions that they otherwise would not have adequate reason to perform; and there may be cases in which paternalistic coercion, whose rationale is not based on injustice to others, is fully justifiable.

Given this account of characteristically justified legal coercion, then, the argument for the justification of coercion for the sake of generating compliance with non-defective law is straightforward. What makes law non-defective is, in part, its being an authoritative norm for dividing up the collective responsibility of acting for the common good. Suppose, to adopt my preferred natural law account, that all consent to law in the acceptance sense (5.5), and that the law is at least a minimally acceptable determination (5.2) of how the responsibilities to act for the common good are to be apportioned. In such a condition, subjects have adequate reason to adhere to the law's demands – law is authoritative in its fixing the content of the common good principle, and that principle is one with which subjects have decisive reasons to comply – and subjects' failure to adhere to the law's demands means that the burdens of promoting the common good have been shifted from some subjects to others. Thus the coercion of non-compliers is at least presumptively justified: legal coercion may be applied to motivate a potential lawbreaker to do what he or she already has sufficient (normative) reason to do, and what, if he or she fails to do, will constitute an injustice to his or her fellow subjects.

Equally straightforward is the application of this account in the case of punishment. If we think of punishments as authoritatively imposed deprivations that are, nevertheless, ways of acting for the common good, then those convicts who are unwilling to submit to their punishments are failing to do their share with respect to the common good. The violation of a (non-defective) criminal law constitutes an initial failure to do one's share with respect to the common good; the refusal to comply with a (non-defective) legal order sentencing one to punishment constitutes a subsequent failure to do one's share with respect to the common good. In both cases the rationale for legal coercion is the same: the subject has adequate reason to adhere to the norm, and the failure to adhere to the norm counts as an injustice with respect to one's fellow subjects.

It follows that on the view defended here, the connection between coercion and legal orders sentencing subjects to punishment is no closer than the connection between coercion and any other duty-imposing laws. If officials have a basis for thinking that subjects have become dangerously lax in their compliance with authoritative traffic laws, they may take measures that are coercive: they may undertake a campaign against speeding, increasing police presence on the roads, and making widely known threats that those who are caught speeding will be subject to stiff fines. If segregationists announce their intention to defy a court order and block the entrance to a high school that has begun to integrate its student body, officials may announce that there will be deputies present to arrest those who defy the court order. In both cases we have coercion for the sake of generating compliance with authoritative legal norms, norms (1) with which subjects have reason to comply independent of the coercive threat, and (2) the failure to comply with which is unjust to fellow subjects. I say that there is no important difference here between these cases of justified legal coercion and the coercion that is employed in legal punishment. That there is a standing policy to coerce those who fail to comply with the terms of their authoritatively rendered punishments does not mark any essential difference between the case of punishment and the case of the speeders and the case of the segregationists. In all of these cases, what is primary is the authoritative legal norm that is justified in terms of the common good; what is secondary is the coercion that may justifiably be used in order to ensure compliance with the authoritative norm.

Now, one might concede that all of this is a plausible account of the justification of coercion for the sake of legal punishment in a political community in which the law is fully authoritative. But in Chapter 5, I conceded (5.7) that on the consent account of legal authority that I think is most promising for exhibiting the possibility of non-defective law, the law's authority is in fact far from complete. There may be large swaths in which acceptance of the law's authority is patchy. Given the existence of less-than-complete authority in these areas, does it not follow that the characteristic way of justifying legal coercion will be unavailable in explaining why these non-consentors can be justifiably coerced into complying with duty-imposing norms to which they do not consent? And, given the existence of less-than-complete authority in these areas, does it not follow that the characteristic way of justifying legal coercion will be unavailable in explaining why these non-consentors can be justifiably coerced into submitting to legal punishment for violating those norms?

These putative consequences do not follow. To see why they do not follow, consider the following case, which is of course a variation on the case considered at length in Chapter 5 (5.3). Again the story begins with your wealthy bald uncle who wants to distribute windfalls to the bald. But the case is somewhat different. Instead of distributing the mere $100 to each bald person, your uncle aims to distribute $100,000 to all and only those bald persons born in his hometown. Before his death, the uncle holds a public meeting with all of the native-born townspeople – all the bald and potentially bald – and tells them of his plan. He turns to you and asks whether you, in consideration of some substantial sum, will promise him and the townspeople to distribute his estate to all those townspeople who go bald, at $100,000 a head, until the uncle's estate is depleted. You make this solemn promise to him and to them. Five years later, your uncle dies and you are bound to implement his wishes. A claimant who has lost one-third of his hair appears at your door and asks for the $100,000. He has made plans for the money, knowing that he is likely to lose his hair: he can send his children to college, perhaps aid his poor parents. Your view, though, is that you want to count only those who have lost at least half their head of hair as bald. You refuse to hand over the $100,000. This is a serious practical conflict between the two of you. He accuses you of withholding the promised money: you, after all, made a promise to every member of the town to pay him or her $100,000 if he or she were to go bald. You accuse him of trying unjustly to take advantage of your uncle's generosity and your fidelity to your promise by counting that relatively hairy head as bald.

On the one hand: would it be wrong for the claimant, or some third party acting on the claimant's behalf, to try to coerce you into handing over the $100,000? On his view, after all, you are violating your promise, to his severe detriment. Any argument that he is acting unjustly will have to rely on the claim that you are not breaking your promise; and the claim that you are not breaking your promise will have to rely on the claim that the claimant is not bald. But it is far from obvious that he is not bald. Given his particular way of determining the notion of 'baldness' – a way that is not clearly in error, and due to the vagueness of 'bald' cannot be shown to be in error – he is making no mistake if he is willing to coerce your compliance.

On the other hand: would it be wrong for you to resist and resent the coercion that the claimant attempts to use against you? On your view, after all, you promised your uncle not to distribute the money to the non-bald, and the claimant wishes to coerce you into breaking this promise. Any argument that you are wrong to resist or resent the coercion will have to rely on the claim that you are breaking your promise to pay the bald townspeople, and the claim that you are breaking your promise to pay the bald townspeople will have to rely on the claim that the claimant is bald. But it is far from obvious that he is bald. Given your particular way of determining the notion of 'baldness' – a way that is not clearly in error, and due to the vagueness of 'bald' cannot be shown to be in error – you are making no mistake by resisting or resenting those coercive efforts.

We should think about legal coercion in a condition of less-than-full legal authority in the way that I have suggested that we think about coercion in the money-for-baldness case just described. When the law determines the common good principle in a certain way, then by the law's lights, subjects must adhere to that way if they are to do their share for the common good rather than foist their burdens on others. If the law coerces a non-consentor to adhere to the law's determinations of the common good principle, the situation is precisely analogous to the vaguely bald person who coerces you for the sake of getting you to hand over the $100,000. Because 'doing one's share for the common good' is, like 'bald,' rife with indeterminacy, it involves no mistake on the law's part to be willing to coerce a non-consentor's compliance, and it involves no mistake on the non-consentor's part to resent and even resist that coercion.[8] This implication also holds in the case of legal punishment. The law makes no mistake in using coercion to ensure the punishment of non-consentors, because from its point of view, undergoing legal punishment is part of the lawbreaker's

---

[8] My claim here is not that the non-consentor has made no errors. Indeed, if the legal system that holds sway is minimally just, effective, and so on, then the practically reasonably choice would be to consent to that *de facto* authority and thus make it *de jure* authoritative over him or her (4.7). My claim is, rather, that so long as the non-consentor remains a nonconsentor, he or she makes no *further* error in resenting or resisting the coercion that the law imposes on him or her.

responsibility to the common good; non-consenting criminals make no mistake in resisting that coercion, because from their point of view, they have violated no binding standard and thus there is no reason for them to set themselves outside of the common good.

The moral to draw with respect to the non-consentor is not, then, that because law is not authoritative in these cases it may not justifiably coerce compliance. Rather, it is that because the law is not authoritative in these cases, it is *indeterminate* whether its coercion is justifiable. How should this indeterminacy be dealt with? We have been through this problem before (4.6). What we have before us is a case of practical conflict the reasonable solution to which is the institution of authority. (Is it not clear that this is the reasonable way to deal with the money-for-baldness case – to put into place an arbitrator, or some other procedure, whose outcome authoritatively resolves the practical conflict between you and the claimant, and indeed between you and all such potential claimants?) So the fact that there are large areas in which there is not consent does not show that legal institutions act wrongly by coercing non-consentors; rather, it makes the case for consent to a *common* standard all the more pressing.

7

Beneath and Beyond the Common Good

7.1 Two Challenges to the Common Good Principle

Recall that natural law political philosophy takes as its central normative concept that of the common good (0.1). It is the common good, that is, that ultimately provides the normative force for law, rendering it (under suitable conditions) authoritative. And so the common good must be something that there are very strong reasons to promote and protect, and the common good principle (that is, the requirement to do one's share with respect to the common good of one's political community) must be a principle that there are decisive reasons to honor (3.6). For the demands of the common good principle are supposed to explain the normative demands of the law; consent, though necessary (4.7), is relevant only because we must appeal to consent to explain why to flout the law is to flout the common good principle (5.5).

It was in light of this normative role that the natural law view I have defended selects the aggregative conception of the common good: for what this natural law view needs is a conception of the common good that carries sufficient normative weight that it can underwrite the decisive force of the common good principle, and the aggregative view both makes a plausible case on its own account (3.2) and clearly fills this role better than the alternative natural law conceptions on offer (3.3, 3.4). The complex state of affairs that is the good of a person does seem to be a reason for action for each member of the political community, and when the goods of each and every person within a political community are aggregated, the resulting state of affairs is one that there is enormous reason to promote and protect. But even if we grant the enormous force of this reason, it must be acknowledged (as it was in 3.6) that the enormous force of this reason does not show that the common good principle is a decisive guide to conduct, one that it is never reasonable to flout. But the common good principle must have that level of normative force, that of *decisiveness*, if it is to do the job set for natural law political philosophy by natural law jurisprudence – that is, showing how it is possible for there to be non-defective law (3.1). For law is defective if it is not backed by decisive reasons for action (2.3, 2.4).

The case for acting in accordance with the common good principle is sufficiently strong that the failure to honor it requires justification. The strength of the reason to act in accordance with that principle is sufficiently great that we cannot plausibly think of the principle as optional in the absence of a showing that there are *competitors* to that principle, where a competitor to the common good principle is a reason or set of reasons for action that point one toward courses of action distinct from those to which the common good principle points one and which are not simply outweighed by (or otherwise excluded by) the common good principle. The most serious remaining difficulty for the defender of the natural law account of politics is that there *do* seem to be competitors to the common good principle: a *subpolitical* competitor and a *superpolitical* competitor.

Here is the challenge from the subpolitical. "The common good on the aggregative view consists in the aggregation of the goods of all of the various members of the political community. Within this aggregate, each counts for one, and only for one. And this makes sense: from the point of view of the common good, which is impartial within its limited domain, there is no basis to privilege some persons' goods over others'. But the point of view of the common good is not the uniquely reasonable point of view. There is a point of view in which it is simply not the case that everyone counts alike: from this point of view, friends and family count for more, simply in virtue of the special relationships that hold between the agent and these others. Now, the courses of action toward which these subpolitical reasons point one are not always the same as the courses of action toward which political reasons point one. Sartre imagines someone having to decide whether to stay with his ailing mother or join the Resistance: this is a clear case in which subpolitical concerns seem at odds with political concerns. But the conflicts of this sort seem to be legion: whether to devote one's scarce resources of money, time, and energy to doing one's share for the common good or to one's more particular relationships is a real choice between distinct options, not a case in which all of the distinct reasons point in a single direction. What's more, it is not clear that the political reasons outweigh, or otherwise exclude, these subpolitical reasons: this is why, in the Sartre case, one should rightly sense that there is a real openness to the decision, and this is why, when Forster expresses the hope that if given a choice between betraying his friend and his country, he has the courage to betray his country, we can see the sense of this wish, even if we do not share it. Thus subpolitical reasons are genuine competitors to the reasons of the common good, and thus the common good principle cannot claim to be a decisive principle of action."

Here is the challenge from the superpolitical. "The common good on the aggregative view consists in the aggregation of the goods of all of the various members of the political community. Each counts for one, and only for one.

And this makes sense: from the political point of view, which is impartial within its limited domain, there is no basis to privilege some persons' good over others. But this political point of view is not the uniquely reasonable point of view. For it is not a requirement of reason to stick to this limited domain, with impartiality reigning within that domain: instead, one might take a more cosmopolitan perspective. The superpolitical perspective, by contrast, takes the good of persons to be fundamentally and non-derivatively the object of practical concern, refusing to accept any principled difference between the goods of members of one's political community and the goods of non-members. What one must do from this perspective may clash with what one must do from the more limited political perspective: resources might well need to be diverted from those within the political community to those outside it. And it is hard to see why the political perspective necessarily trumps the superpolitical: to give such an argument requires an explanation as to why we must disregard or devalue some persons' goods, when the only difference between them and us is that they happen not to be members of our own communities."

The subpolitical and superpolitical challenges are the most serious threats to the normative authority of the common good principle, and so it is a fitting way to conclude our treatment of the natural law account of political authority to ask to what extent the natural law theorist can offer convincing responses to them. Before I turn to an explanation of why these challenges are bound to be extremely difficult to meet (7.2), and to an account of how the natural law view tries to meet them (7.3), it is worthwhile to pause to note that these challenges do not provide any evidence that we made a wrong turn in preferring the aggregative to the instrumentalist (3.3) or distinctive good (3.4) conceptions of the common good. For the pressing questions about the subpolitical and superpolitical points of view can be raised with equal force against both the instrumentalist and distinctive good conceptions. We can ask the defender of the instrumentalist conception, "What is the relationship between the reasons for me to promote the conditions that can help to make all in my community well-off and the reasons for me to promote the conditions that can help me and my friends to be well-off?" and "Why should I not aim at the conditions that all persons, not just those in my community, can draw on to further their own reasonable ends?" We can ask the defender of the distinctive good conception, "What is the relationship between the reasons for me to promote the distinctive good of my political community and the reasons for me to promote my own individual good (or the distinctive good of my family)?" and "Why should I not aim at the realization of the distinctive goods of all political communities, not just my own?" The questions raised from the subpolitical and superpolitical points of view against the decisive force of the aggregative common good can be just as easily raised against these rival conceptions, and thus *prima facie* provide no basis for thinking that the acceptance of the aggregative conception was a misstep.

Nor does the pressing of these embarrassing questions give any basis *prima facie* for holding that natural law political philosophy has taken a wrong turn in appealing to the common good to provide the basis for political authority. As we noted earlier (2.6), appealing to a partial end like the common good is crucial to meeting the particularity requirement that accounts of political authority must satisfy.[1] And so *any* view, whether of the natural law variety or not, will have to handle questions like these, even if not in precisely the form that they arise in the natural law view.

7.2 Why the Challenges Are Especially Difficult to Meet

The particularly vexing problem for the defender of the natural law view is that the subpolitical and superpolitical challenges are not independent. The natural law defender cannot devote his or her attention to the subpolitical challenge, offer a response, and then turn to the distinct line of objection raised by the superpolitical challenge. For the subpolitical and superpolitical challenges are, rather, simultaneous assaults from different directions. And as is the case when one must defend against attacks on two fronts, devoting resources to resisting an attack on one front results in having fewer resources to resist the attack on the other front. When the natural law political philosopher attempts to answer one challenge, he or she commits himself or herself to positions that make the natural law view even more vulnerable to the other.

For, after all, what is the most natural response to the subpolitical challenge? The most natural response to the appeal to more limited perspectives is, while affirming the goods of special relationships, noting both the equal reality of the goods of others' special relationships and the fact that these goods can come into conflict with one another. The wider political common good is a more impartial point of view from which we can assess these conflicts and decide how to deal with them, and thus we should assign judgments and decisions made from the point of view of the political common good priority over those made from the point of view of more particular relationships. But it seems that if the natural law political philosopher takes this sort of stand, it will be even harder to ward off the challenge from the superpolitical. For the advocate of the superpolitical challenge might well note how the various partial *political* concerns can come into conflict, and we need a more impartial point of view for the making of such decisions. And once we adopt this more impartial point of view, it is unclear whether the common good principle can serve as a decisive principle of conduct.

---

[1] The particularity requirement – recall (3.6) – is that a theory of the authority of law must explain why a subject is bound in a special way to the norms issued by his or her own legal system; for discussion, see Simmons 1979, pp. 30–35 and Green 1990, pp. 227–228.

By contrast: what is the most natural response to the superpolitical challenge? It is to note that there is a reason for focusing on the fellow members of one's political community: one is in a special relationship with these people that one does not have with respect to others, and thus one should give the political priority over the superpolitical. But once we have accepted the importance of special relationships in determining the priority of one's concerns, why should one not think of these other special relationships (friendship, kinship) as coming into conflict with, and sometimes even defeating, the claims of the political common good?

The trouble is that the political common good is *hybrid* – it affirms impartial concern for the human good, but only within a limited range.[2] When it tries to answer questions about why one's concern should not be more limited, it cannot *simply* appeal to the value of impartiality: because there is a more impartial point of view that one might adopt than the political point of view, and this superpolitical point of view threatens the political point of view. When it tries to answer questions about why one's concern should not be more impartial, it cannot *simply* appeal to the value of limited concern: because there are relationships of even more limited concern than political relationships, and these special relationships threaten the decisiveness of the claims of the political.

7.3 The Aristotelian Reply to the Challenges to the Common Good Principle

The most promising natural law response to the subpolitical and superpolitical challenges to the common good principle follows Aristotle. The Aristotelian reply draws on three theses that are central to Aristotle's defense of a particular sort of political community as ideal: first, that *prima facie* the more inclusive a community, the more authoritative is the good of that community; second, that there is an upper limit on the size that a political community can have; and, third, that living in political community is a very important human good. The first of these theses suggests the proper response to the subpolitical challenge; the second and third suggest the proper response to the superpolitical challenge.

The political common good is privileged with respect to more particular goods because it is fully inclusive of them. As Aristotle's *Politics* begins:

We see that every city-state is a community of some sort, and that every community is established for the sake of some good (for everyone performs every action for the sake of what he takes to be good). Clearly, then, while every community aims at some good, the community that has the most authority of all and encompasses all the others aims highest, that is to say, at the good that has the most authority of all. This community is the one called a city-state, the community that is political.   (1252a1–7)

---

[2] For a discussion of the weaknesses introduced into theories by their hybrid character, see Parfit 1984, pp. 140, 192.

The common good of the political community takes in all of these other, more partial goods. This is obviously the case on the aggregative conception. For it includes the good of each and every member, in all of its completeness, and so every fulfilling partial relationship in which one finds oneself is included within that ideal. So the sense in which the aggregative common good is superior to any of these more partial goods is straightforward: the aggregative common good includes each of these more particular goods, and more as well. Thus there is a clear basis for holding that the common good is superior to any of the more partial goods realized in special relationships within the political community.

This response has a bit of sleight-of-hand about it. But it is true that, *as an ideal*, the aggregative common good involves a higher aspiration than the ideal of any more particular, subpolitical relationship. What makes for tension between the subpolitical and the political is the actuality of one's particular subpolitical relationships and the *determination* of the aggregative common good, and of one's share with respect to it, reached within one's political community.[3] Even if one allows that the ideal of the aggregative common good has more to commend it than the ideal of one particular special relationship, the specific *truncations* of the aggregative common good that are settled upon and the specific *precisifications* of one's responsibilities with respect to the common good may generate conflict between the demands of the political common good and the demands of one's more particular relationships. And so the subpolitical challenger might seize on this tension as a way to reestablish the objection.

But the defender of the political common good has a response. "The only reason that tension has been created," he or she might say, "is that the goods of these special relationships are not all co-realizable, or are incompatible with other goods, or would require the performance of actions that are outside the realm of the reasonable. Determination of the common good, insofar as it involves paring away at the ideal, is never done without reason. Because each person within the political community counts for one, and only for one, each person's good is adequately taken into account in specifying the common good for the sake of common action. And think of the alternative: if the goods of these special relationships were not encroached upon by our common determination, that would mean that someone else's good would be disproportionately encroached upon. Since the alternative is injustice, you really have no basis for complaining against this determination of the common good principle."

The best answer to the subpolitical challenge is the appeal to the wider inclusiveness of the aggregative common good, along with a defense of the justice of any determinations of that aggregative common good that encroach on more particular relationships. Needless to say, this best answer will not succeed if

---

[3] Recall that a 'determination' of some objective O (or principle P) is some objective O* (or principle P*) that stands to O (or P) either as a realizable approximation to an unrealizable ideal or as a more precise specification of a vague objective (3.6).

the determinations of the aggregative common good are not reasonable or are reached unreasonably; if that is the case, then the defender of the subpolitical will have an obvious basis for objection – that is, that his or her special relationships were not adequately taken into account. The important point, though, is that reasonable political decision-making should allow any determinations of the aggregative common good to inherit the authority over any more particular special relationships that the ideal of the aggregative common good enjoys.

What, then, is the Aristotelian response to the superpolitical challenge? In the context of Aristotle's political theory, the question arises as one of scope: given the general principle, enunciated at the beginning of the *Politics*, that the more inclusive the common good at which a community aims, the more authoritative that common good, why should not the city-state expand indefinitely, thus becoming more inclusive and more authoritative? Aside from Aristotle's concerns about the quality of the people that one might find out there to include, there is an in-principle basis for restricting this expansion: given the centrality in the life of the best kind of polis of assessing and rewarding virtuous conduct, the polis cannot become so large that portions of the citizenry must be unfamiliar to each other. So what puts the brakes on the expansion of the city-state, and thus on the practical concern that citizens must have for their fellow citizens, is that the political good can be realized only if the size of the city-state, and thus the scope of citizen concern, is kept in check.

What the natural law view draws upon here is not the notion that politics is centered on assessing and rewarding virtue – while virtue is among the human goods, it is only one aspect of the aggregative common good, and I have offered no basis for thinking that the best determinations of the aggregative common good would make direct appeals to the virtue of the citizenry in determining benefits and burdens – but is instead the more general claim that an important human good can be realized only by limiting citizens' practical concerns in some way. While granting the *prima facie* rationality of adopting a cosmopolitan pattern of concern and action, the natural law theorist can hold that this pattern of concern and action must be displaced by a more partial pattern of concern – that of concern for the political common good, if the important human good of political community is to be realized. For community is the human good that consists of pursuing a common end with others in a coordinated way (Murphy 2001a, pp. 126–131). While one can take a cosmopolitan practical stance, community is not possible with the world-at-large, for there is no basis for unified common action with all of the objects of one's practical concern. But where there is an effective authority in place, there is the possibility of coordinated action for a common end, and thus for the good of community to be realized. Thus, in political communities where there is an effective authority in place, citizens have reason to adopt the more limited pattern of practical concern exhibited in the common good principle to the exclusion of the more cosmopolitan pattern of concern suggested by the superpolitical challenge.

7.4 Doubts About the Aristotelian Reply

The Aristotelian reply to the subpolitical and superpolitical challenges is not entirely convincing. There is some merit to the response to the subpolitical challenge: anyone who wants to claim that his or her special relationships deserve consideration, even from the more impartial political point of view, will be hard pressed to explain why the argument from greater inclusiveness does not show that the aggregative common good is authoritative over any more particular relationships within a political community.[4] But the defender of the subpolitical point of view who holds his or her ground and simply says that these special relationships provide a distinct point of view from which practical matters are decided will be able to resist the Aristotelian reply. "What I am denying," the advocate of the subpolitical challenge might say, "is that we should accept absorption of these special, more partial points of view into a more impartial point of view. Perhaps each of us, on his or her own account, should try to reach some sort of *modus vivendi* between our more partial and more impartial points of view. But that does not mean that we should accept that the point of view of the aggregative common good is supreme and authoritative, properly capturing within it all that is of importance about my special relationships."

Again: there is some merit to the Aristotelian reply to the superpolitical challenge. If community is good, and the conditions for community are available at a political level but not a more expansive level, then we can see some basis for restricting one's practical focus on the political common good, making these goods of community possible for oneself and for one's fellow citizens. But it is hard to see whether this single point can bear the weight that it must bear for the superpolitical challenge to be fended off. For, first, in conditions of fairly severe scarcity of goods globally considered, it is hard to justify the massive privileging of the common good of one's own political community. If the material conditions across political communities were fairly equal, one could see a justification here: everyone could tend his or her own garden, realizing the goods of political community made possible through coordinated common action. But present conditions are not like this. So departure from privileging the common good of one's own political community seems to be at least a rational option, and perhaps even a requirement of practical reasonableness. And, second, the unprecedented expansion in technologies of communication and opportunities for cross-boundary cooperation call into question the view that the most extensive opportunities for community must be centered on the political common good. As Finnis, in a very striking passage, remarks:

There is no reason to deny the good of international community ... in the order of reciprocal interactions, mutual commitments, collaboration, friendship, competition, rivalry ... If it now appears that the good of individuals can only be fully secured and

---

[4] Cf. Sidgwick's limited arguments against the egoist: see *Methods*, pp. 379–382.

realized in the context of international community, we must conclude that the claim of the national state to be a complete community is unwarranted.   (Finnis 1980, p. 150)

Finnis does not hesitate to draw the further conclusion that, given this unanswered challenge from the superpolitical order, "The postulate of the national legal order, that it is supreme and comprehensive and the exclusive source of legal obligation, is increasingly what lawyers would call a 'legal fiction'" (Finnis 1980, p. 150).

The natural law theorist's best hope to respond to the subpolitical and superpolitical challenges seemed to be in the Aristotelian solution. But the Aristotelian solution itself seems to be as yet unconvincing, with the result that the natural law political philosopher's account of the authority of law at present falls short of the mark. The present lacuna in the natural law account of course provides no basis for doubting our earlier jurisprudential conclusion that law is backed by decisive reasons for action, in the sense that law that fails to be backed by decisive reasons is as such defective (2.3, 2.4, 2.6). What it provides is a basis for thinking that the natural law political philosopher's attempt to carry out the task set by natural law jurisprudence – to exhibit the possibility of fully non-defective law – is at present still a failure.

Works Cited

Works are cited in my text by the author's last name and the year the work was published. Exceptions include classic works by Aristotle, Aquinas, Hobbes, Locke, Rousseau, Hume, Bentham, Austin, Mill, and Sidgwick: all of these texts are cited by (sometimes abbreviated) title. References are given by page number in the cited edition unless otherwise indicated in the bibliographical entry.

Alexy, Robert. 1998. "Law and Correctness." In Freeman 1998, pp. 205–222.
Alexy, Robert. 1999. "A Defense of Radbruch's Formula." In Dyzenhaus 1999, pp. 16–39.
Alston, William P. 1999. *Illocutionary Acts and Sentence Meaning*. Cornell University Press.
Anderson, Elizabeth. 1993. *Value in Ethics and Economics*. Harvard University Press.
Anscombe, G. E. M. 1969. "On Promising and Its Justice, and Whether It Needs to be Respected *In Foro Interno*." *Critica* 3, pp. 61–83.
Aquinas, Thomas. 1981. *Summa Theologiae*, trans. Fathers of the English Dominican Province. Christian Classics. References given by part, question, and article number.
Aristotle. 1998. *Politics*, trans. C. D. C. Reeve. Hackett. References given by Bekker numbers.
Aristotle. 1999. *Nicomachean Ethics*, trans. Terence Irwin. Hackett. References given by Bekker numbers.
Austin, John. 1995 [first published 1832]. *Province of Jurisprudence Determined*, ed. Wilfrid Rumble. Cambridge University Press.
Ayer, A. J. 1946 [first published 1936]. *Language, Truth, and Logic*, 2nd ed. Dover.
Bedau, Mark. 1992a. "Where's the Good in Teleology?" *Philosophy and Phenomenological Research* 52, pp. 781–806.
Bedau, Mark. 1992b. "Goal-Directed Systems and the Good." *Monist* 75, pp. 34–51.
Bentham, Jeremy. 1996 [first published 1789]. *Introduction to the Principles of Morals and Legislation*. Clarendon Press.
Bix, Brian. 1993. *Law, Language, and Legal Determinacy*. Oxford University Press.
Bix, Brian. 1996. "Natural Law Theory." In Patterson 1996, pp. 223–240.
Bix, Brian. 1999. "Patrolling the Boundaries: Inclusive Legal Positivism and the Nature of Jurisprudential Debate." *Canadian Journal of Law and Jurisprudence* 12, pp. 17–33.
Bix, Brian. 2000. "On the Dividing Line Between Natural Law Theory and Legal Positivism." *Notre Dame Law Review* 75, pp. 1613–1624.

Bix, Brian. 2002. "Natural Law Theory: The Modern Tradition." In Coleman and Shapiro 2002, pp. 61–103.

Borchert, Donald, ed. Forthcoming. *The Encyclopedia of Philosophy*, 2nd. edition. Macmillan.

Chappell, Timothy. 2005. "The Polymorphy of Practical Reason." In Oderberg and Chappell 2005, pp. 102–126.

Christiano, Thomas. 1996. *The Rule of the Many: Fundamental Issues in Democratic Theory*. Westview.

Cochran, Clarke E. 1978. "Yves R. Simon and 'the Common Good': A Note on the Concept." *Ethics* 88, pp. 229–239.

Coleman, Jules, and Brian Leiter. 1996. "Legal Positivism." In Patterson 1996, pp. 241–260.

Coleman, Jules, and Scott Shapiro, eds. 2002. *Oxford Handbook of Jurisprudence and Philosophy of Law*. Oxford University Press.

Coleman, Jules. 1982. "Negative and Positive Positivism." *Journal of Legal Studies* 11, pp. 139–164.

Coleman, Jules, ed. 2001. *Hart's Postscript: Essays on the Postscript to the Concept of Law*. Oxford University Press.

Cooper-Stephenson, Ken, and Elaine Gibson, eds. 1993. *Tort Theory*. Captus Press.

Dupré, Louis. 1993. "The Common Good and the Open Society." *Review of Politics* 55, pp. 687–712.

Dworkin, Ronald. 1977a. *Taking Rights Seriously*. Harvard University Press.

Dworkin, Ronald. 1977b. "Hard Cases." In Dworkin 1977a, pp. 81–130.

Dworkin, Ronald. 1982. "'Natural' Law Revisited," *University of Florida Law Review* 34, pp. 165–210.

Dworkin, Ronald. 1986. *Law's Empire*. Harvard University Press.

Dworkin, Ronald. 2002. "Thirty Years On." *Harvard Law Review* 115, pp. 1655–1687.

Dyzenhaus, David, ed. 1999. *Recrafting the Rule of Law*. Hart Publishing.

Edmundson, William. 1998. *Three Anarchical Fallacies*. Cambridge University Press.

Edmundson, William, ed. 1999a. *The Duty to Obey the Law: Selected Philosophical Readings*. Rowman and Littlefield.

Edmundson, William. 1999b. "Introduction." In Edmundson 1999a, pp. 1–15.

Edmundson, William. 1999c. "Introduction: Some Recent Work on Political Obligation." *APA Newsletter on Law and Philosophy* 99, pp. 62–67.

Edmundson, William. 2004. "State of the Art: The Duty to Obey the Law." *Legal Theory* 10, pp. 215–259.

Edmundson, William, and Martin Golding, eds. 2004. *Blackwell Guide to the Philosophy of Law and Legal Theory*. Blackwell.

Ellis, Anthony. 1995. "Recent Work on Punishment." *Philosophical Quarterly* 45, pp. 225–233.

Feinberg, Joel. 1970a. *Doing and Deserving*. Princeton University Press.

Feinberg, Joel. 1970b. "The Expressive Function of Punishment." In Feinberg 1970a, pp. 95–118.

Finnis, John. 1980. *Natural Law and Natural Rights*. Oxford University Press.

Finnis, John. 1984. "The Authority of Law in the Predicament of Contemporary Social Theory." *Notre Dame Journal of Law, Ethics, and Public Policy* 1, pp. 114–137.

Finnis, John. 1996. "Is Natural Law Theory Compatible with Limited Government?" In George 1996b, pp. 1–26.

Finnis, John. 1998a. *Aquinas: Moral, Political, and Legal Theory*. Oxford University Press.

Finnis, John. 1998b. "Public Good: The Specifically Political Common Good in Aquinas." In George 1998, pp. 174–209.

Foot, Philippa. 2001. *Natural Goodness*. Oxford University Press.

Frankfurt, Harry. 1988a. *The Importance of What We Care About*. Cambridge University Press.

Frankfurt, Harry. 1988b. "On Bullshit." In Frankfurt 1988a, pp. 117–133.

Freeman, Michael, ed. 1998. *Current Legal Problems 1998: Legal Theory at the End of the Millennium*. Oxford University Press.

Fuller, Lon. 1964. *The Morality of Law*. Yale University Press.

Gardner, John. 2001. "Legal Positivism: $5\frac{1}{2}$ Myths." *American Journal of Jurisprudence* 46, pp. 199–227.

Gauthier, David. 1986. *Morals by Agreement*. Oxford University Press.

Geach, Peter. 1956. "Good and Evil." *Analysis* 17, pp. 33–42.

George, Robert P., ed. 1992. *Natural Law Theory: Contemporary Essays*. Oxford University Press.

George, Robert P. 1993. *Making Men Moral: Civil Liberties and Public Morality*. Oxford University Press.

George, Robert P. 1996a. *The Autonomy of Law: Essays on Legal Positivism*. Oxford University Press.

George, Robert P., ed. 1996b. *Natural Law, Liberalism, and Morality*. Oxford University Press.

George, Robert P. 1996c. "Natural Law and Positive Law." In George 1996a, pp. 321–334.

George, Robert P. 1996d. "Preface." In George 1996a, pp. vii–viii.

George, Robert P., ed. 1998. *Natural Law and Moral Inquiry: Ethics, Metaphysics, and Politics in the Work of Germain Grisez*. Georgetown University Press.

George, Robert P. 2000. "Kelsen and Aquinas on 'the Natural-Law Doctrine.'" *Notre Dame Law Review* 75, pp. 1625–1646.

Gilbert, Margaret. 1999a. "Reconsidering the 'Actual Contract' Theory of Political Obligation." *Ethics* 109, pp. 236–260.

Gilbert, Margaret. 1999b. "Social Rules: Some Problems for Hart's Account, and an Alternative Proposal." *Law and Philosophy* 18, pp. 141–171.

Goldsworthy, Jeffrey D. 1990. "The Self-Destruction of Legal Positivism." *Oxford Journal of Legal Studies* 10, pp. 449–486.

Grasso, Kenneth, Gerard Bradley, and Robert Hunt, eds. 1995. *Catholicism, Liberalism, and Communitarianism*. Rowman and Littlefield.

Green, Leslie. 1990. *The Authority of the State*. Oxford University Press.

Green, Leslie. 1996. "Who Believes in Political Obligation?" In Sanders and Narveson 1996, pp. 1–18.

Griffin, James. 1986. *Well-Being: Its Meaning, Measurement, and Moral Importance*. Oxford University Press.

Griffin, James. 1996. *Value Judgement: Improving Our Ethical Beliefs*. Oxford University Press.

Grisez, Germain. 1978. "Against Consequentialism." *American Journal of Jurisprudence* 23, pp. 21–72.

Hampton, Jean. 1984. "A Moral Education Theory of Punishment." *Philosophy & Public Affairs* 13, pp. 208–238.

Hampton, Jean. 1991. "A New Theory of Retribution." In Morris and Frey 1991, pp. 377–414.

Hart, H. L. A. 1955. "Are There Any Natural Rights?" *Philosophical Review* 64, pp. 175–191.

Hart, H. L. A. 1983a. *Essays in Jurisprudence and Philosophy*. Oxford University Press.

Hart, H. L. A. 1983b. "Introduction." In Hart 1983a, pp. 1–18.

Hart, H. L. A. 1983c [first published 1958]. "Positivism and the Separation of Law and Morals." In Hart 1983a, pp. 49–87.

Hart, H. L. A. 1994 [first published 1961]. *The Concept of Law*, 2nd ed. Oxford University Press.

Himma, Kenneth Einar. 2001. "Law's Claim to Legitimate Authority." In Coleman 2001, pp. 271–310.

Hobbes, Thomas. 1994 [first published 1651]. *Leviathan*, ed. Edwin Curley. Hackett. Cited by part, chapter, and page number of 'Head' edition.

Hook, Sidney, ed. 1964. *Law and Philosophy*. New York University Press.

Hume, David. 1948a. *Hume's Moral and Political Philosophy*, ed. Henry D. Aiken. Hafner.

Hume, David. 1948b [first published 1748]. "Of the Original Contract." In Hume 1948a, pp. 356–372. Cited as "Original Contract."

Hume, David. 1978 [first published 1730]. *Treatise of Human Nature,* ed. L. A. Selby-Bigge. Oxford University Press.

Hursthouse, Rosalind, Gavin Lawrence, and Warren Quinn, eds. 1995. *Virtues and Reasons.* Oxford University Press.

John XXIII. 1962. *Mater et Magistra*. Discoveries Press.

Kramer, Matthew. 1999. *In Defense of Legal Positivism: Law Without Trimmings*. Oxford University Press.

Kretzmann, Norman. 1988. "*Lex Iniusta Non Est Lex*: Laws on Trial in Aquinas' Court of Conscience." *American Journal of Jurisprudence* 33, pp. 99–122.

Leiter, Brian. 2003. "Beyond the Hart/Dworkin Debate: The Methodology Problem in Jurisprudence." *American Journal of Jurisprudence* 48, pp. 17–51.

Lewis, David. 1969. *Convention*. Blackwell.

Locke, John. 1988 [first published 1689]. *Second Treatise of Government*. In *Two Treatises of Government*, ed. Peter Laslett. Cambridge University Press. References given by section number.

Lyons, David. 1984. *Ethics and the Rule of Law*. Cambridge University Press.

MacCormick, Neil. 1972. "Voluntary Obligations and Normative Powers – I." *Proceedings of the Aristotelian Society* 46 (suppl.), pp. 59–78.

MacCormick, Neil. 1992. "Natural Law and the Separation of Law and Morals." In George 1992, pp. 105–133.

Marmor, Andrei. 1992. *Interpretation and Legal Theory*. Oxford University Press.

McInerny, Ralph. 1988a. *Art and Prudence: Studies in the Thought of Jacques Maritain*. University of Notre Dame Press.

McInerny, Ralph. 1988b. "The Primacy of the Common Good." In McInerny 1988a, pp. 77–91.

Merricks, Trenton. 2001. *Objects and Persons*. Oxford University Press.

Mill, John Stuart. 1979 [first published 1861]. *Utilitarianism*, ed. George Sher. Hackett.

Moore, Michael. 1987. "Authority, Law, and Razian Reasons," *Southern California Law Review* 62, pp. 827–893.

Moore, Michael. 1992. "Law as a Functional Kind." In George 1992, pp. 188–242.

Moore, Michael. 1997. *Placing Blame: A General Theory of Criminal Law*. Oxford University Press.

Moore, Michael. 2001. "Law as Justice." *Social Philosophy and Policy* 18, pp. 115–145.

Morris, Christopher S., and Raymond Frey, eds. 1991. *Liability and Responsibility*. Cambridge University Press.

Morris, Herbert. 1976a. *On Guilt and Innocence*. University of California Press.

Morris, Herbert. 1976b. "Persons and Punishment." In Morris 1976a, pp. 31–58.

Murphy, Mark C. 1994. "Acceptance of Authority and the Requirement to Comply with Just Institutions: A Comment on Waldron." *Philosophy & Public Affairs* 23, pp. 271–277.

Murphy, Mark C. 1995. "Was Hobbes a Legal Positivist?" *Ethics* 105, pp. 846–873.

Murphy, Mark C. 1997a. "Consent, Custom, and the Common Good in Aquinas's Account of Political Authority." *Review of Politics* 59, pp. 323–350.

Murphy, Mark C. 1997b. "Surrender of Judgment and the Consent Theory of Political Authority." *Law and Philosophy* 16, pp. 115–143.

Murphy, Mark C. 1999. "Moral Legitimacy and Political Obligation." *APA Newsletter on Law and Philosophy* 99, pp. 77–80.

Murphy, Mark C. 2001a. *Natural Law and Practical Rationality*. Cambridge University Press.

Murphy, Mark C. 2001b. "Natural Law, Consent, and Political Obligation." *Social Philosophy and Policy* 18, pp. 70–92.

Murphy, Mark C. 2002a. *An Essay on Divine Authority*. Cornell University Press.

Murphy, Mark C. 2002b. "The Natural Law Tradition in Ethics." *The Stanford Encyclopedia of Philosophy*, ed. Edward N. Zalta. URL = http://plato.stanford.edu/archives/win2002/entries/natural-law-ethics/

Murphy, Mark C. 2003. "Natural Law Jurisprudence." *Legal Theory* 9, pp. 241–267.

Murphy, Mark C. 2004. "Natural Law Theory." In Edmundson and Golding 2004, pp. 15–28.

Murphy, Mark C. 2005a. "The Common Good." *Review of Metaphysics* 59, pp. 143–177.

Murphy, Mark C. 2005b. "Intention, Foresight, and Success." In Oderberg and Chappell 2005, pp. 252–268.

Murphy, Mark C. Forthcoming. "Authority." In Borchert, forthcoming.

Nagel, Thomas. 1970. *The Possibility of Altruism*. Princeton University Press.

Nozick, Robert. 1981. *Philosophical Explanations*. Harvard University Press.

Oderberg, David, and Timothy Chappell, eds. 2005. *Human Values: New Essays on Ethics and Natural Law*. Palgrave Macmillan.

Parfit, Derek. 1984. *Reasons and Persons*. Oxford University Press.

Patterson, Dennis, ed. 1996. *A Companion to Philosophy of Law and Legal Theory*. Blackwell.

Patterson, James, and Peter Kim. 1991. *The Day America Told the Truth*. Prentice Hall.

Perry, Stephen. 1993. "Loss, Agency, and Responsibility for Outcomes: Three Conceptions of Corrective Justice." In Cooper-Stephenson and Gibson 1993, pp. 24–47.

Pius XI. 1931. *Quadragesimo Anno*. Barry Vail.

Plamenatz, J. P. 1968. *Consent, Freedom, and Political Obligation*. Oxford University Press.

Rawls, John. 1955. "Two Concepts of Rules." *Philosophical Review* 64, pp. 3–32.

Rawls, John. 1964. "Legal Obligation and the Duty of Fair Play." In Hook 1964, pp. 3–18.

Rawls, John. 1971. *A Theory of Justice*. Belknap Press of Harvard University Press.

Raz, Joseph. 1972. "Voluntary Obligations and Normative Powers – II." *Proceedings of the Aristotelian Society* 46 (suppl.), pp. 79–102.

Raz, Joseph. 1979a. *The Authority of Law*. Oxford University Press.

Raz, Joseph. 1979b. "The Claims of Law." In Raz 1979a, pp. 28–33.

Raz, Joseph. 1981. "Authority and Consent." *Virginia Law Review* 67, pp. 103–131.

Raz, Joseph. 1984a. "Hart on Moral Rights and Legal Duties." *Oxford Journal of Legal Studies* 4, pp. 123–131.

Raz, Joseph. 1984b. "The Obligation to Obey: Revision and Tradition." *Notre Dame Journal of Law, Ethics, and Public Policy* 1, pp. 139–155.

Raz, Joseph. 1985. "Authority, Law, and Morality." *Monist* 68, pp. 295–324.

Raz, Joseph. 1986. *The Morality of Freedom*. Oxford University Press.

Richardson, Henry S. 1990. "Specifying Norms as a Way to Resolve Concrete Ethical Problems." *Philosophy & Public Affairs* 19, pp. 279–310.

Richardson, Henry S. 2000. "Specifying, Balancing, and Interpreting Bioethical Principles." *Journal of Medicine and Philosophy* 25, pp. 285–307.

Richardson, Henry S. 2002. *Democratic Autonomy: Public Reasoning about the Ends of Policy*. Oxford University Press.

Rousseau, Jean-Jacques. 1968 [first published 1762]. *The Social Contract*, trans. Maurice Cranston. Penguin.

Russell, J. S. 2000. "Trial by Slogan: Natural Law and *Lex Iniusta Non Est Lex*." *Law and Philosophy* 19, pp. 433–449.

Sanders, John T., and Jan Narveson, eds. 1996. *For and Against the State*. Rowman and Littlefield.

Scanlon, T. M. 1998. *What We Owe to Each Other*. Harvard University Press.

Searle, John R. and Daniel Vanderveken. 1985. *Foundations of Illocutionary Logic*. Cambridge University Press.

Shafer-Landau, Russ. 1996. "The Failure of Retributivism." *Philosophical Studies* 82, pp. 289–316.

Shapiro, Scott. 1998. "On Hart's Way Out." *Legal Theory* 4, pp. 469–507.

Sher, George. 1983. "Why the Past Matters." *Philosophical Studies* 43, pp. 183–200.

Sher, George. 1987. *Desert*. Princeton University Press.

Sidgwick, Henry. 1907. *Methods of Ethics*, 7th ed. Hackett.

Simmons, A. John. 1979. *Moral Principles and Political Obligations*. Princeton University Press.

Simon, Yves. 1962. *A General Theory of Authority*. University of Notre Dame Press.

Skillen, Anthony. 1980. "How to Say Things With Walls." *Philosophy* 55, pp. 509–523.

Smith, M. B. E. 1973. "Is There a Prima Facie Obligation to Obey the Law?" *Yale Law Journal* 82, pp. 950–976.

Smith, Michael. 1994. *The Moral Problem*. Blackwell.

Soper, Philip. 1983. "Legal Theory and the Problem of Definition." *University of Chicago Law Review* 50, pp. 1170–1200.

Soper, Philip. 2002. *The Ethics of Deference*. Cambridge University Press.

Taylor, Charles. 1997a. *Philosophical Arguments*. Harvard University Press.

Taylor, Charles. 1997b. "Irreducibly Social Goods." In Taylor 1997a, pp. 127–145.

Thompson, Michael. 1995. "The Representation of Life." In Hursthouse, Lawrence, and Quinn 1995, pp. 247–296.

Tuckness, Alex. 1999. "The Coherence of a Mind: John Locke and the Law of Nature." *Journal of the History of Philosophy* 37, pp. 73–90.

Tuomela, Raimo. 1995. *The Importance of Us: A Philosophical Study of Basic Social Notions.* Stanford University Press.

Tyler, Tom R. 1990. *Why People Obey the Law.* Yale.

van Inwagen, Peter. 1990. *Material Beings.* Cornell University Press.

Waldron, Jeremy. 1993. "Special Ties and Natural Duties." *Philosophy & Public Affairs* 22, pp. 3–30.

Wolfe, Christopher. 1995. "Subsidiarity: The 'Other' Ground of Limited Government." In Grasso, Bradley, and Hunt 1995, pp. 81–96.

Index

Printed by Printforce, United Kingdom